BUILDING OUTDOOR PLAYTHINGS FOR KIDS
WITH PROJECT PLANS
BILL BARNES

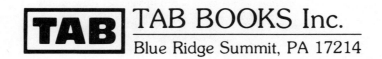

TAB BOOKS Inc.
Blue Ridge Summit, PA 17214

FIRST EDITION

FIRST PRINTING

Copyright © 1985 by TAB BOOKS Inc.

Printed in the United States of America

Library of Congress Cataloging in Publication Data

Barnes, Bill.
Building outdoor playthings for kids, with project
plans.

Includes index.
1. Playgrounds—Equipment and supplies.   2. Playgrounds
—Design and construction.   I. Title.
GV426.5.B37   1985   796'.06'8   85-1085
ISBN 0-8306-0971-7
ISBN 0-8306-1971-2 (pbk.)

Contents

Introduction

THIS BOOK DIFFERS IMPORTANTLY FROM other how-to-do-it toy-and-play-equipment books. In addition to the plans, specifications, and materials lists, this book explains how the equipment can be used to best advantage for your child's physical, social, emotional, and intellectual development. One example will suffice here. Many parents will be unaware of the connection between water play and mathematical concepts. Fewer still will know how to transfer the aspects of water play to a sandbox so that a young child's playing does more than simply keep him or her out of the way while mom and dad get on with their tasks of daily living. This book tells you how to do it. My wife, Sylvia, who has been trained as an early childhood education specialist, puts her training and experience at your disposal in several chapters.

Trained as a secondary teacher, I am also experienced at being a father and a home handyman. I have made many of the projects in this book for my four children, and I have helped neighbors with similar projects. Still other designs are modified from well-used public playground equipment. While some pieces of equipment are fantastically appealing to adults, they leave children cold. Such designs have been omitted from this book.

Some of the designs are for families who need to stretch their recreational equipment budgets to cover as much equipment as possible. If the materials that a piece of equipment calls for are available free or at low cost, that fact is mentioned in the discussion that accompanies each project. There is an advantage beyond cost saving to the use of inexpensive or free materials: they are often more attractive to children than higher-priced goods. Some of you will have experienced the frustration of seeing a child be more interested in the wrapping paper or box than in the Christmas present it contained.

In addition to child appeal, the projects in this book are meant to have adult appeal in that they can be built by most adults with simple tools and no more than the average handyman's technical ability. A few of the projects are so simple that they do not even require that much skill. All the projects should give you the sense of satisfaction at providing something that is both lasting and worthwhile for your children, grandchildren, nephews, nieces, or friends.

The projects can, of course, be modified to suit your needs. Actually they should be. They should all be used and placed with your child's safety foremost in your mind. Suggestions for safety appear throughout the book.

Remember, too, that a safe piece of equipment can create a danger if placed carelessly in relation to other pieces of equipment. A low slide with a gentle slope must not deliver its user into the path of a high-flying swing, even if its seats are soft and pliable. Having the slide terminate in the sandbox would not be so bad, however, and may actually be advantageous—depending on the number and size of children using the play equipment at any one time. The placement of equipment for safety and learning and enjoyment is discussed in Chapter 2.

This book is also intended to help you wherever you are—whether in temperate, tropical, or desert climate. You will find designs and helpful suggestions to enable you to take advantage of local materials and conditions.

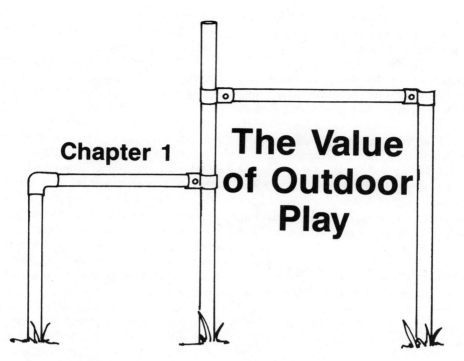

Chapter 1

The Value of Outdoor Play

NOTHING IS QUITE SO SAD AS THE SIGHT OF a playground without children. We've all seen playgrounds full of static equipment without little bodies climbing, twisting, running, hiding, or just sitting quietly. Absent are the sounds of children's whispers, shouts, giggles, laughter, and songs. We assume, perhaps, that the surrounding neighborhood has changed and that young children no longer live in the area.

Yet, at other times in other areas, we have seen children walking or riding bicycles great distances or begging mom and dad to drive them to the playground with the "long slide" or the "nifty treehouse" or "those wobbly tire things." What makes one playground more attractive than another? Do playgrounds have to provide gimmicks to be successful? No. For success, a playground merely has to be conducive to play.

When considering playground equipment for children, whether it be at a public park or a private backyard, you must first be concerned with providing an environment that will entice children to play. How is it done? You may have momentary success by providing the latest, wildest, most fantastic piece of equipment on the market, but you can be almost certain that the novelty will fade quickly if children give it much use. Success lies in the knowledge and understanding not only of what will attract children immediately but also of what will retain that attraction and interest, spark their imagination, and challenge them in every area of child development. We mean development in its broadest sense—physical, cognitive, and social-emotional.

PHYSICAL DEVELOPMENT

Most people accept the fact that children benefit from playing outdoors, but the benefit is usually seen strictly in terms of "letting off steam" rather than in terms of enhancing or extending a child's development. Some people will go a step farther and admit that their children's physical development benefits from outdoor play. The gross motor skills (those involving the use of large muscles) are fairly obvious. Children run, balance, climb, jump, crawl, and hop. We see children on swings, pumping with

1

their legs, racing to swing higher and higher. We are well aware of the muscles being used in their legs, their arms, and their backs.

When a child is sitting—scooping sand with his hands and releasing it slowly through his fingertips, watching as it falls—do we recognize he is aiding his physical development? Balanced with the gross motor skills are the fine motor skills (those involving the use of the small muscles). Picking blades of grass and splitting them, creating chains of daisies, and collecting and skipping stones across a creek not only bring children close to nature. The fine muscles that are used in many obviously school-related activities—writing, drawing, cutting, pasting—are also being exercised, used, and perfected.

COGNITIVE DEVELOPMENT

Have you ever considered that the outdoor environment you provide for your children can aid their cognitive (or intellectual) development? By carefully planning your outdoor environment, you can provide more scope for your child's cognitive development outdoors than you provide inside. The mere fact that the playspace is generally larger should help convince you. Let's examine cognitive development and draw conclusions as we proceed.

Play that aids cognitive development is often seen in terms of very concrete activities. A child dismantles and reassembles a jigsaw puzzle. He was presented with a problem and solved it. Perhaps he builds two block constructions and wants to join them. He discovers that the join can be a bridge and that the bridge can be made of a certain type and number of blocks. Again, the child was confronted with a problem, and he solved it.

Using your own imagination and experience, take these cognitive experiences and recreate them outdoors. What sorts of jigsaw puzzles are offered in an outdoor environment; what sorts of construction questions are posed? Sometimes the answers are just too obvious to see. A jigsaw outdoors might be the boxes, blankets, boards, and chairs needed for the creation of an impromptu playhouse in a given space. The child is presented with a problem that he must solve. In doing so, he uses his abilities to

measure and estimate, and his concepts of size, space, and area to fit his assorted "jigsaw pieces" into a foreign space.

Let's consider a construction question. Two children are playing in a sandbox that has had a river dug right through the center. An elaborate road system runs parallel to the river on each side. The children run their cars along the roads, making all the shrieking, squeeking, honking sound effects appropriate to this type of play. It's fun, but sooner or later the children want to take their cars to the other side of the river. How will they get them across? They could get up and walk, but that would interrupt rather than extend their play. The construction of an overpass—which might be simply sand or a combination of sand, rocks, sticks, and other material—would enhance their play. The children would experiment, construct, and solve their problem.

Cognitive development includes all areas of experimentation, testing, and discovery. Consider a child sitting at a small table with a piece of paper and a box of crayons. He may walk around the house collecting a number of items such as paper clips, bottle tops, string, and fabric scraps. Putting each item in turn underneath his paper, he may take his crayons and rub them across, creating an interesting pattern of various textures. He discovers texture variance and different sizes and shapes, and through his experimenting he makes comparisons and reaches conclusions.

An identical exercise can be done outdoors. The outdoor environment may be far more inviting and exciting for the child, and the realm of possibilities for his etchings may be greater. In nature he can collect natural items such as leaves, grasses, stones, bark, and wood. He will become aware of building materials such as brick, concrete block, metals, wires, and rough and smooth woods. His etchings will be reproductions of the outdoor environment that he knows well. Again he will discover the variety of textures, and he will make comparisons of size and shape. From his experimenting and testing, he will reach conclusions.

The acquisition of language is a very important element of cognitive development. We've all been told of the importance of providing rich language experiences for our children. We are encouraged to play games, usually indoor games, with our children to teach them such things as spatial concepts (for example, in, out, around, and through). One such game has the child sit at a small table. The adult sits across from the child and places a box in front of the child. The adult hands a toy dog to the child and instructs him to place the dog in the box, under the box, and to take the dog for a walk around the box. How much better the game would be if the child, himself, were involved! Outdoors the child can run around a table, climb to the top of a ladder, or crawl through a pipe. The spatial concepts now become a part of the child's own experience, and he is more likely to achieve an accurate understanding of the concepts.

Children and adults alike tend to feel a certain exhilaration outdoors. A sense of openness and freedom exists in the fresh air. Questions are sparked from the child. "Does the tree touch the sky? Why do you look little when I am on top of my climbing frame? Where does the water go after it rains?" These questions need answers. The more questions and the more answers, the greater the increase in your child's language acquisition and conceptual understanding.

SOCIAL DEVELOPMENT

The third area of child development is social-emotional development. Outdoor play most definitely can contribute in this area, and the importance of social play cannot be minimized. Children playing with other children learn about being human. They thrive on acceptance and friendship; they hurt when they're rejected. They relive experiences through their imaginations and come to terms with those experiences. The play is not logical because each child has a different set of experiences on which to build.

Dramatic play is a broad term; it encompasses nearly all forms of spontaneous play. Children assume roles—mother, father, dog, cat, mailman, ballerina, clown, monster, Superman, tree, and flower—and in ceasing to be themselves, they make an effort to gain understanding of those roles. By making comparisons they slowly become more aware of what they (the children themselves) really are. They compare roles, swap roles, misinterpret roles, and combine roles, but the quest for understanding is always present.

Outdoors, the child is apt to have more playspace for this questioning, testing, and conclusion making. More movement and noise are acceptable. The child is also more likely to find that little nook where he can be just himself, by himself, for a little while, to reflect, to dream, to wonder, and to consolidate his increased knowledge in order that further questioning will begin.

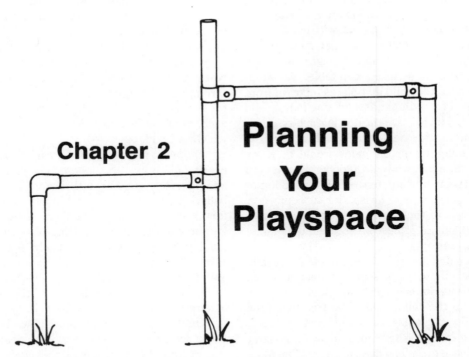

Chapter 2

Planning Your Playspace

HAVING ACCEPTED THE FACT THAT OUTDOOR play is not solely to occupy your child and to provide you with a bit of hassle-free time, consider next what equipment you feel your family wants and needs, where it should be located, and why. Each home, each family is different; therefore, each outdoor playspace should be unique. The acceptance of this uniqueness is vitally important if you are to create a successful outdoor playspace.

I have suggested several designs for houses and lots that should approximate most families' circumstances. These hypothetical plans show various positions for the points of the compass.

It is unrealistic to plan only for the children. Adults have needs for recreation, too, and I've kept those needs in mind. I haven't included detailed plans for these, for that would be outside the scope of this book. The example site plans also exclude such things as swimming pools and dog kennels, simply because I had to draw the line somewhere. For the adult need for recreation, I included areas for outdoor entertaining, such as patios and outdoor

barbeque areas; vegetable gardens, for those who like to dig, grow, harvest, or just get their fingernails dirty; tool sheds, for all kinds of tools; potting studios and shops for woodworking or other adult crafts. To be successful, these adult recreation areas must meet the same four criteria as children's play equipment: they must be attractive, they must offer challenges, they must invite manipulation, and they must provide a means of getting away from it all for a few moments of privacy.

Consider what will be attractive to your children. What will draw them into activity? For some children color might be of prime importance. For others the type of building materials might matter most. For others the overall look of the finished equipment might be the priority. Whatever your child's preference, the equipment must tempt your child to investigate it. Once drawn to the equipment, your child must feel a need to be personally involved with it. A mass-produced swing set might fulfill the child's need for attraction—they are colorful and seem to present a few options for activity. The initial involvement usually ends when the child is tired of swinging, sliding, or climbing, Involvement is limited by the equipment; the child himself is not limited.

The equipment must provide your child with challenges. In the area of physical development, for example, you must be concerned with what stage your child has reached because offering physical feats that are too easy or too difficult will only prove frustrating and limiting. What equipment provides for cognitive challenge? Are there options open to the child? For example, is there only one swing available? If so, how many different ways can a child use it? Can it be modified to provide more ways for him to use it? In considering social-emotional development, look to see if more than one child can be involved in play at the same time. For example, can two children use the swing at the same time? Is there scope for development of dramatic play?

Your child must be able to manipulate the equipment, adding and taking away adjuncts as his evolving play dictates. Hand-in-hand with the manipulation goes experimentation, a necessary element in all areas of child development. What happens if a board is added to the side of the climbing frame? Is it long enough? Will your child be able to use it as a slide? Can it become a path from one point to another?

For your playspace to be especially unique to your child, you must remember the provision of privacy. Children love their own personal space where they can hide and feel alone in order to create, to think, to plan, and to observe. One of my sons, for example, especially loved a patch of bamboo growing next to his sandbox. He would spend hours in the bamboo, sometimes completely absorbed in dramatic play; sometimes he'd drag a stool to the bamboo patch and just sit. It was his personal place; he related to it well. My elder daughter used an old packing crate as her personal space, sometimes crawling inside with a book, sometimes climbing on top, hidden in the orange tree, to view the happenings in the neighborhood. Each child felt happy and secure in his space, yet the spaces were very different.

NEW WAYS OF LOOKING AT YOUR HOUSE AND LOT

Leaving planning theory for a few minutes, take a practical look at your yard. What direction does your house face? Do you have fences? What else do you want to add to your yard besides your play equipment? Do you dream of a swimming pool? Do you grow prize roses? Is your barbeque fixed or movable? Are you a potter with a large, outdoor kiln in the making? This is where your uniqueness begins to show.

Some of the areas are firmly established—house and garage, for example—some are planned, and some may be far-fetched dreams. But, each area must be considered. For example, do you live in a duplex that has very little front yard where you plant all your garden each spring, leaving your backyard area completely free as a play area? Or, do you have a multitude of activities in a comparatively small backyard area, making it necessary to double up on space? Is your garage used to park your car, to house your tools and workbench, and as part of your outdoor entertainment area as well? Do you have a small, bare area that must grow a few vegetables and provide playspace as well?

How are you going to separate your areas, if you feel separation is necessary? Fences are common dividers; however, they are not the only ones. Your prize roses might be used to divide two areas. Shrubbery and trees naturally divide. Are you located on a hill; can terraces be used as dividers?

Your next step should be to take a long tape measure and several sheets of graph paper to make an accurate site plan of your house and lot. Draw your plans to scale so that you will know if a given space will be large enough for a piece of equipment. Mark the directions of the compass on your site plan, for providing both sunny and shady play areas is vital. If winds are strong enough to be a problem, mark in their directions as well. The minimum needs the play area should meet are these: sunny and shady areas, ground-level and elevated areas, running room, and a place for privacy.

STARTER HOUSE AND LOT

Figure 2-1 shows a typical "starter house" and lot,

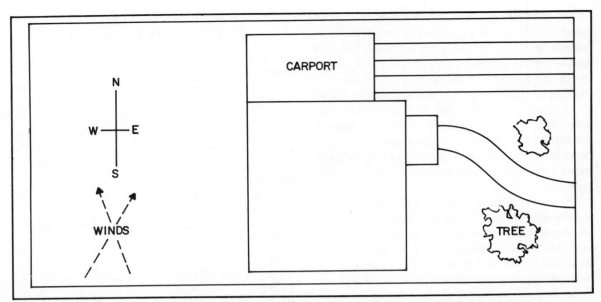

Fig. 2-1. A typical starter house. Two small trees, a driveway, and curving sidewalk in the front. Backyard is bare.

that is, one many young couples buy as their first house. The lot measures about 60 feet by 120 feet. The driveway consists of two narrow ribbons of concrete. There are two small trees in the front yard,

none in the back. Winds come from the south and southeast, but they are never too strong to prevent outdoor play.

Figure 2-2 shows how the family's recreation

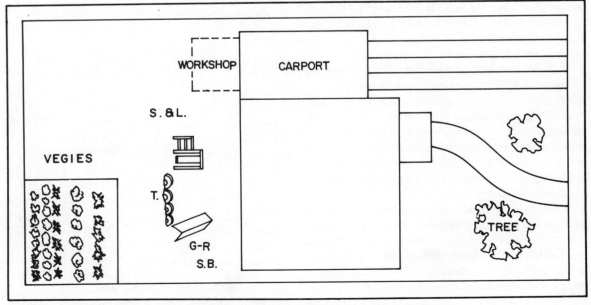

Fig. 2-2. Starter house with vegetable garden, workshop, and play equipment added.

6

needs may be met. For the adults, a workshop is sited just behind the carport. This location usually means electricity can be run to the shop at least expense. For the adults and the children, a vegetable patch has been put in one back corner of the yard. A simple divider of stakes driven into the ground at the edge of the garden, with sisal twine stretched between them, will keep the kids from trampling the cabbages. For outdoor entertaining, a portable barbeque can be set up near the carport, where card tables can be erected, with chairs brought from the house.

For the children, there is a swing and ladder combination, marked S. & L. on Fig. 2-2. Plans are shown in Chapter 4 (Fig. 4-2). The gable-roofed sandbox (Figs. 3-22 and 3-23) is marked G-R S.B. It meets several needs. It provides a slide, shelter from the sun, and an elevated perch. To create unity between these two pieces of equipment a row of tires has been half-buried in the ground. Always keep in mind that you are creating playspace, not just individual pieces of play equipment, which would be far more limiting to your child.

Let's examine the swing and ladder combination closely. Its design (Fig. 4-2) is especially practical for the family with young children. The swing, an inside-out tire, is safe for even very young toddlers, allowing them to sit securely in the swing. As the children mature, different types of swings may replace this starter swing.

The ladder construction actually is a very basic climbing frame. The child climbs, both up and down, exercising his large muscles, gaining self-confidence, and viewing his environment from a different perspective. Imagine the young child has reached the top of the ladder. He stands there for a moment, thrilled with his achievement. His gaze takes him to the tires. What ideas can the tires spark in his imagination?

Perhaps the child will use the tires to practice the climbing skills he has achieved, but they will offer a different sensation from the stable rungs of the ladder. He'll discover that the tires move and collapse and that it takes a certain amount of balancing to accomplish the stepping from one to another. He may decide the balancing is too difficult for

him and practice his jumping from one tire at a time. Later, when his skills are more developed, he may find that he is able to jump from one tire to the next.

When the child reaches the end of the tire chain, he will be confronted with the sandbox construction. This piece of equipment presents many possibilities for climbing—up to the top of the roof and back again, up the slide and down the ladder, up to the roof and down the slide. The child will crawl inside the sandbox and a new realm of possibilities will confront him.

Reversing his course, having spent some time in the sandbox, he'll see the tires differently. Perhaps he'll make them a continuation of a road construction he has begun in the sand. His sand-tire road may continue up a plank that has been hooked over one ladder rung and down another plank on the opposite side. The road may be for small cars or trucks, or it may be the child himself is the vehicle, and he'll continue up, down, over, and across his equipment until his play dictates change.

Perhaps his sandbox will become a cubbyhouse and the climbing frame will be his shop, his neighbor's house, or the fire or police station. What can he do to extend the equipment to further his play? A blanket pinned to one rung of the ladder and stretched to the ground, secured by bricks, can form another building. It can be a very private space as well. A blanket or rug placed on the ground between the sandbox and swing will further combine all the fixed elements of the playspace, encouraging the child to expand his ideas.

These are examples of equipment that is unified and can be joined or combined in a variety of ways. The child is attracted by the variety of possibilities. He is challenged within those possibilities, and he can change the environment to meet his needs. He can also find or create within the playspace a very special, private place for himself.

HOUSE AND LOT ON CUL-DE-SAC

Figure 2-3 shows a house located on a cul-de-sac lot. The lot is wedge-shaped; it may be flat or sloping. (See Figs. 2-7, 2-8, and 2-9 if your lot slopes.) There is little natural shade in this hypothetical lot.

Figure 2-4 shows the addition of the family's

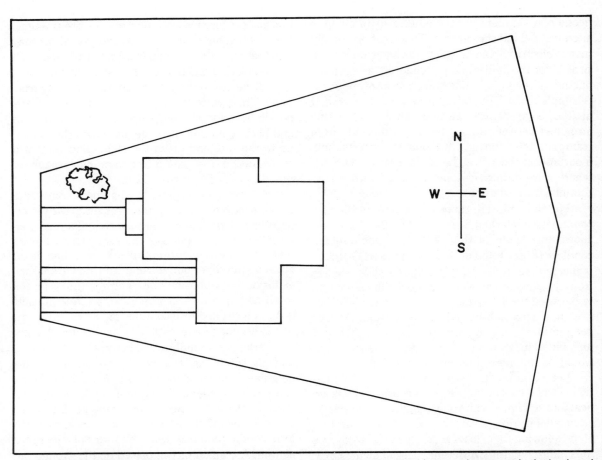

Fig. 2-3. Typical house on a cul-de-sac. The location of the house close to the street leaves a large area in the backyard for developing.

recreational needs. A potting studio has been added at the back of the garage. Fruit trees have been planted along the western boundary, and a vegetable garden has been added along the southern boundary. This leaves a large, open, though unshaded, area for playspace. A sandbox with a hinged lid (Figs. 3-20 and 3-21) is adjacent to the climbing frame. There is plenty of room for running and ball games and extension of the basic equipment.

The climbing frame (Fig. 4-4) is more complex than the previously described swing-ladder combination. Because it is cubelike, we can see the children have six sides to use, both inside and outside. The platform at the top provides a high level for play, and the area underneath the platform is low

and shaded. Different apparatus can be included on each side, enabling children to learn to move their bodies in many different ways. Simple climbing of the ladder on one side becomes more complex when a child moves to the tire ladder and most complex when a knotted rope on the third side provides the means of getting from a lower level to a higher one.

The sandbox below can be a soft landing area when children jump from the platform, or it can be used separately. A cubbyhouse is formed by the open sandbox lid. Children can crawl inside for privacy and shade. The children's play can flow freely between the parts of the equipment.

Possibilities for changing and adding to the equipment are numerous. Using planks, boards, ladders, swings, blankets, boxes, and rugs, the children can create and build what they feel is necessary to extend their play.

LARGE HOUSE SET LENGTHWISE ON ITS LOT

Figures 2-5 and 2-6 present a large house set lengthwise on its lot. The paved driveway leads into an attached garage. The house is close to the street, and the front yard is landscaped. A large covered patio is at the back of the house. It can be used for outdoor entertaining, using a portable barbeque and folding tables and chairs. It can also provide added playspace for children.

For the adults, a workshop has been added along the northern side of the house, making possible an easy and inexpensive connection of electricity. A vegetable garden has been placed along the southern side of the house, taking advantage of the best sun. A rose garden (or hedge) at the back of the vegetable garden helps discourage play from being extended into the garden.

The lot allows the use of the established trees to best advantage, making the play equipment an extension of the natural environment. The platform-tree house is built into the tree, giving height and privacy to the children's play. The single fireman's pole provides access to and from the platform, but it still allows the children to invent alternatives, such as rope ladders, planks, or using the tree itself as a ladder.

The open space between the trees can be left

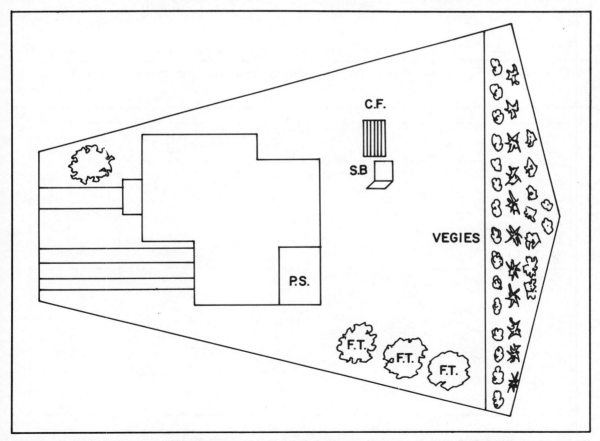

Fig. 2-4. House on a cul-de-sac with backyard developed to include play equipment, pottery studio, fruit trees, and vegetable garden.

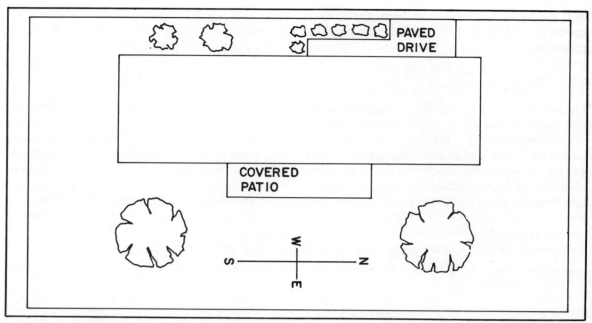

Fig. 2-5. Large house set lengthwise on its lot. Two large trees and covered patio in the back add interest and challenge to the developer.

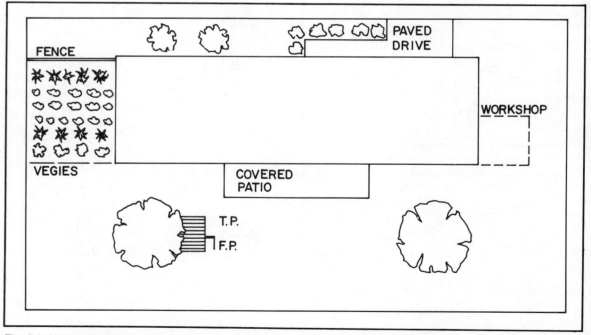

Fig. 2-6. House placed lengthwise on its lot extended to include vegetable garden, rose garden, workshop, and play equipment.

as free running space, or a pathway to the other tree can be created by including balance beams, stepping stones, or tires, either fixed or loose. The other tree forms a different sort of climbing frame, a natural climbing frame. A variety of swings can be hung from its branches to give play more scope. For instance, an inside-out tire swing can be used for a young child; a horizontally hung tire swing, suspended by three ropes or chains, will allow three older children to swing together; a vertically hung tire presents challenges to all children. How do they climb inside, on top of, or through?

There has been no special provision for a sandbox in this plan. Many types could be included, depending on your needs. One might be placed underneath the tree house-platform.

The covered patio allows the children access to a different environment—cement opposed to grass and trees—and will provide children with different challenges. The patio might become a house by adding a few old blankets, curtains, chairs, and tables. A chalkboard might inspire a schoolhouse to develop. Empty boxes usually indicate a shop in the making. On a hot day the children may want to lie quietly on the cool cement, comparing its texture to that of the hot grassy areas of the backyard.

Many of the inside-oriented activities naturally will happen on the hard-surfaced patio. Drawing and painting are easier here than in the grass. Children may gather all the "treasures" they have found in the backyard and classify them, placing the leaves and flowers in long rows. On the patio they'd be more protected and more easily compared and studied. Children can draw in chalk on the cement, creating beautiful pictures or the age-old game of hopscotch passed from one generation to the next.

HOUSE ON A SLOPING LOT

Figures 2-7, 2-8, and 2-9 show a typical house and lot on a sloping site. The highest point of the lot is at the back. The front yard contains a long, curving driveway and a sidewalk. The front yard is land-

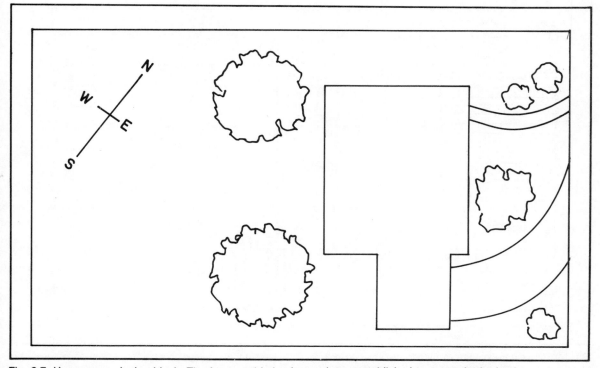

Fig. 2-7. House on a sloping block. The front yard is landscaped; two established trees are in the back.

Fig. 2-8. House on sloping block altered to include patio and barbeque area and climbing equipment.

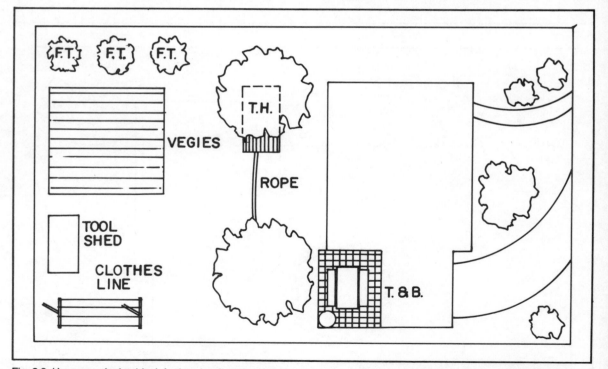

F.T.   F.T.   F.T.

VEGIES

T.H.

ROPE

TOOL
SHED

CLOTHES
LINE

T. & B.

Fig. 2-9. House on sloping block further developed to include barbeque area, patio, vegetable garden, fruit trees, clotheslines, tool shed, and play equipment.

scaped, and the garage is located on the eastern side of the house.

The family wants a permanent barbeque area. The ground behind the garage is leveled and paved to form a patio. A barbeque, tables, and benches are set up on the patio. The family also elects to use solar power to dry their laundry, so they build clotheslines at the back of the lot. Along the back boundary they build a tool shed and plant a large vegetable garden. Finally, fruit trees are planted along the western boundary.

As in the previous example, the two established trees in the yard are incorporated into the equipment design. The slope, rather than hindering the development of play, is used to advantage. For example, the slope allows for quite a long rope on the tire swing, an added challenge to older children who want the swing to go high.

A different tree house-platform is built into one of the trees. Access to the treehouse is by rope ladder on one side and a fixed ladder on the other. A rope is strung from the platform to the tree. This simple installation presents a huge challenge to children—can they, hanging by their hands from the rope, hand-step from one tree to the other? Thus, there are two ways of travelling between the trees, the upper route and the ground-level route. A sandbox has not been included, but one certainly could

be added. Because grass is not likely to be growing under the trees, either sand or tanbark can be used to cushion the ground surface.

The trees provide privacy, the slope provides challenge, there is plenty of room for social interaction, and the equipment calls to the children to change and manipulate it.

OLDER HOUSE AND LOT

Our final example in Figs. 2-10 and 2-11 is an older house and lot with large, established trees and considerable shade. This is a narrow lot, and the bulk of the family's activity will take place in the vicinity of the house. The unshaded portion of the lot at the northern boundary is used as a vegetable garden with clotheslines opposite.

The garage has been extended and a woodworking shed established. A sandbox has been suggested between the garage and the house. The opened sandbox cover can be fastened to the side of the garage for safety.

A tree house-platform has been built into one of the large trees. Using the new trees that spring up from dropped fruit, or the saplings that come up as suckers from the existing tree roots, bays have been formed (Fig. 2-12). Bays can also be formed from shrubbery and some large flowers (Fig. 2-13). The bays are unusual in that they provide children

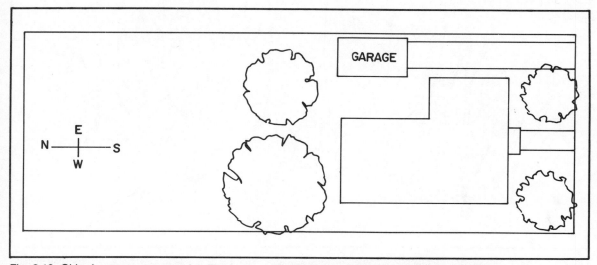

Fig. 2-10. Older house on a narrow lot. The backyard is shaded by two large, established trees.

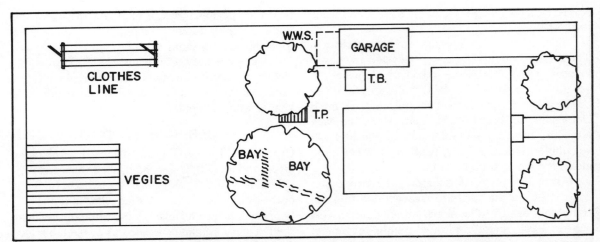

Fig. 2-11. Older house with backyard developed to include a woodworking shop, sandbox, vegetable garden, clotheslines, and play equipment built into the large trees.

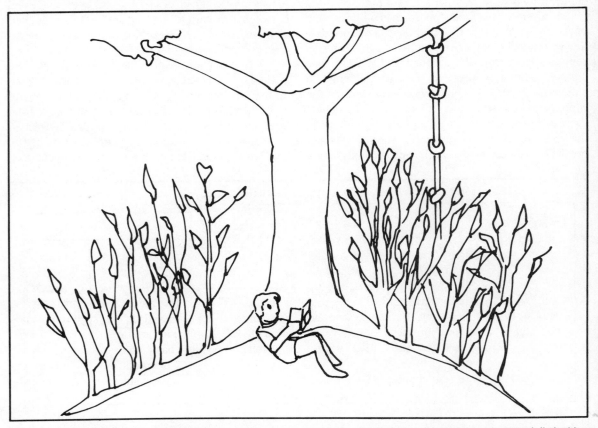

Fig. 2-12. A very special, private place in a bay made from saplings. The use of plants in playspace is especially inviting to children.

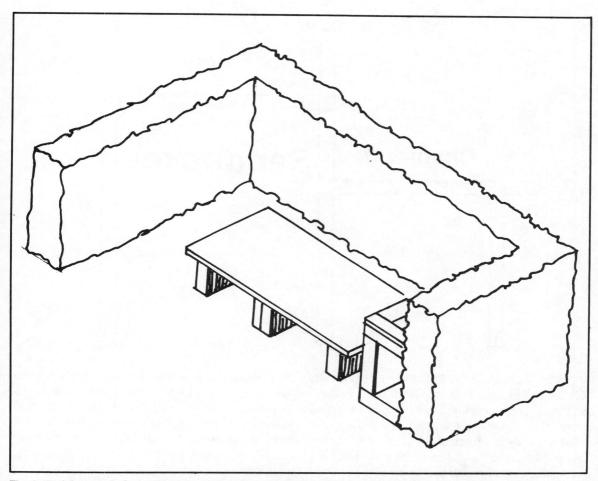

Fig. 2-13. A bay made from shrubbery. Included are examples of junk materials that can add scope to play.

with a totally different experience from tree houses and other cubbies. They are natural, giving a different textural sensation and a different emotional experience. They, therefore, encourage play development differently. We have not joined the tree house-platform with the bay, but unity can be established with a variety of the adjuncts mentioned earlier and described in detail in later chapters.

I have attempted in this chapter to define and illustrate the basic idea of playspace and to show that you don't need a great deal of equipment to establish it. I have purposely kept the number of pieces of recreational equipment to a minimum in each example, to show how much can be done by children with, seemingly, so little equipment. This is not to say only a few pieces are recommended. Far from it—I recommend that you have as much or as little as your family requires. In the chapters that follow I present basic equipment designs and show how they can be modified and extended, thereby becoming uniquely suited for your family's needs.

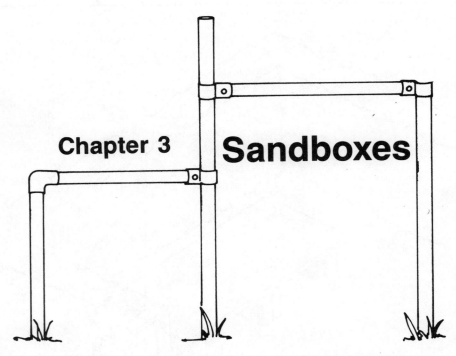

Chapter 3 Sandboxes

FEW THINGS INVITE INSTANT, DIVING-IN action as does a fresh pile of sand. Many a backyard handyman builder has come home to find a load of sand, delivered during his workday, scattered to the four corners of the yard—if not to the four winds—by joyful children who considered it a godsend. Such calamities can be avoided by covering the pile of sand with a tarpaulin, a ground cloth, a painter's drop cloth, or something similar upon delivery. If the sand is actually for the children to play in, the sandbox should be constructed before the sand is delivered. It can be dumped directly into the sandbox, or, if that is not possible, it can be transferred there with relative ease and speed by wheelbarrow or garden cart.

SITE SELECTION

The more permanent your sandbox, the more thought you must give to its site. Simple wooden boxes, tractor tires, and even constructions of heavy timber, such as railway ties, can be moved, but you almost always lose some sand in the process. If your sand is inexpensive or free, that might not be a problem, but if you must buy washed builder's sand from a building-materials yard, you will want the sand to stay where you put it for as long as possible. Other factors to consider in site selection include safety, comfort, health, and the availability of building materials.

Sandbox users start at the lower end of the age range, and some young kids have to learn the consequences of throwing sand. Consequently, if your kids are still small, try to put the sandbox where you can keep an eye on it from your usual work stations such as the office, kitchen, den, or family room. If more than one site is possible, keep your long-term plans in mind. Do not put the box where a shrub or fast-growing garden plant might obscure your view in a few months.

Sand that spills out of the box mixes with the dirt surrounding it, making an excellent medium for starting certain kinds of seeds. If you like to grow things, look carefully at the types of soil in your yard. You may find clay in one spot and a good loam in another. If all other factors are equal, choose a loamy spot for the sandbox. If your yard is built on clay, remember that clay holds water better than any other earth; therefore, the sandbox must not be located in a low spot.

If you have planted any trees, vines, or shrubs, you will know what sort of earth your yard contains. If you have not done any landscaping, take a spade or shovel and dig a few holes here and there. They need not be big, or deep; two or three spadefuls will suffice. A few inches of loam over clay won't ruin your chances of having an excellent lawn, and the digging exercise will give you valuable data to consider in placing your sandbox and in constructing it. For if you plan to dig the sandbox in, you must be sure that such a construction is possible. Large rocks close to the surface of the ground may have to be removed, broken up, or built over. Even if you can build on or around the rocks, remember that

you may want to provide some shelter for the kids using the sandbox. If that shelter is to be a tree or a vine, you might still have to move the rocks.

SAFETY

The sandbox should not be placed near a driveway or place where vehicles will create a danger. Even bicycles become a hazard if an older child whips one around in a swoop of exuberant freedom and knocks over his kid brother or sister. Motorcycles, of course, are even more hazardous. They are bigger, more powerful, heavier, and sometimes more enticing to touch. Small children like to look at brightly painted, shiny, or chromed objects. A motorcycle can therefore be a hazard if parts of it are hot, even if the cycle has been carefully walked (pushed by hand) into place. If no other site but one near a vehicular driveway or parking spot is available for

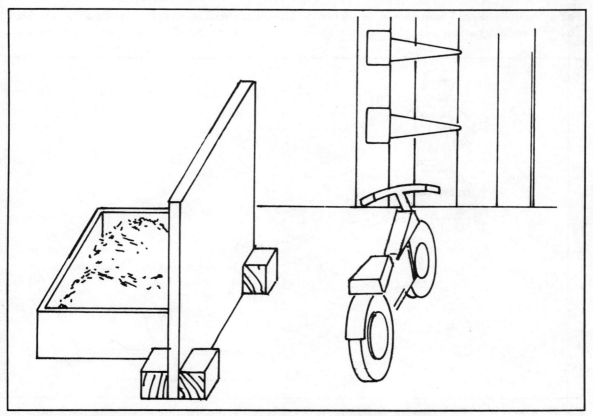

Fig. 3-1. An attractive danger, like a motorcycle, should be screened off from the sandbox.

your sandbox, put some sort of barrier between the box and the vehicles. (See Figs. 3-1, 3-14 to 3-17 for some examples.)

The sandbox must be safe from flying objects. The most common danger is a ball launched by an older sister or brother. Frisbees, arrows, or any other thing that can be thrown must be kept clear of the sandbox users. A lawn mower can also be a missile launcher. Rocks, sticks, bits of wire or metal can kill or cripple a child if flung by a mower to strike the child in a vulnerable spot. If you are driving the mower, you can avoid injuring your own kids. If your yard is on a slope, however, it is possible your neighbor will accidentally launch a few rocks your way while operating a mower on his side of the fence (Fig. 3-2). Therefore, you may need to site your sandbox on the lower side of your yard. Finally, although it usually does not fly, the door of a garage or shed should not open so that it can hit or bump a little sandbox user. There should be plenty of clearance so that you can go to and fro and so that

a sudden gust of wind will not cause the door to suddenly flatten a child in the process of constructing the world's most elaborate sand castle or system of roadways and tunnels.

Other pieces of equipment must be placed so that they create no hazard to the sandbox users. A child does not have to be absent-minded to stand up and back two steps away from a sandbox construction. He or she may simply be looking at it with an architect's or builder's critical eye. Therefore, swings, seesaws, and other pieces of equipment with moving parts must be located well away. A slide may be placed so that it deposits its passenger into the sand, if the slide is small enough so that the slider does not flatten or maul the sandbox construction worker. Some pieces of equipment can be built over or near the sandbox to provide shelter for it.

HEALTH

If you or a nearby neighbor has cats, you will need to cover your sandbox. Dogs also like to lie in sand,

Fig. 3-2. A good lawn mower can also launch missiles like rocks and sticks. Use your mower when your kids are not around. Build a tall fence between the sandbox and the neighbor's yard.

especially if it is shaded and the weather is warm. Because you cannot always prevent your pet from getting fleas or worms, you should consider ways of keeping dogs out of the sandbox. This can be done with any number of cover designs, and many of the covers can be made to do double duty. (See Figs. 3-18 to 3-22). If you use a tree for sheltering the sandbox, you might want a cover to prevent leaves, sticks and twigs, or ripe fruit from falling into the sand.

The hazards of locating the sandbox in a low spot in a yard of clay were mentioned under "Site Selection." It is also wise to make sure that the sand itself contains no clay. Clay stains kids' clothes. It cannot be brushed off clothes and shoes, so it often gets tracked into the house. And once it is wet, it stays wet because the sand helps prevent evaporation. Wet clay can ferment, causing a disagreeable odor in the sandbox.

SHELTERING THE SANDBOX

Depending on the climate, you should consider the need for providing shelter from wind, rain, sun—or all three. If the wind gusts strongly enough in your location, consider wind screens, such as baffles (Fig. 3-24), to keep the sand from being blown into the children's eyes. If you do not want a permanent screen, a tent or a canvas cloth can be rigged for windy periods.

Long rainy spells that keep kids housebound can shorten the tempers of parents and kids alike. A rain-sheltered sandbox that kids can escape to will save much nervous wear and tear. These sandbox shelters can be free-standing (Fig. 3-24) or attached to a garage or shed (Fig. 3-25). Modify those designs to suit your needs, but try to design some open space into your construction. This is desirable for several reasons. The air needs to circulate around the sandbox. Light is also necessary, and it comes through open spaces even better than through fiberglass or plastic translucent roofing or wall materials. A third reason for including open space is to create a feeling of airiness and freedom. Kids do not want to leave the house just to get claustrophobia in their sandbox.

CONSTRUCTION MATERIALS

The designs that follow show a variety of sandboxes made from many different materials. Anything that will keep the sand from spreading is a good material. If you plan a round, oval, or irregularly shaped sandbox, use bricks or some other material that can be arranged in curves. "Box" usually brings a square or rectangle, constructed with wooden planks, to mind, but don't discount concrete products. Wood has become very expensive, and if a local concrete-pipe manufacturer will let you have all the broken or chipped material you want, free, you can spend the money you save on other pieces of equipment.

If you are short of ideas for construction materials, telephone the parks and recreation director in your town or city. Tell the director your problem and ask for suggestions. Other good idea sources are teachers, YMCA and YWCA officials, and other youth organizations. Ask your friends and relatives for ideas. After consulting all these people, go to the hardware stores and building-materials yards. You will how have a much better idea about what is available and about what you should buy.

SIMPLEST SANDBOXES

Figure 3-3 shows two of the simplest sandboxes you can provide for your children. The first is an old tractor tire. You don't have to do anything to it to get it ready—just dump the sand right in. The tires are available from most tire dealers. Many dealers will happily give you all the tires you will take. Some will even deliver the tire to your house, provided you do not live too far from his depot. Disposal of used tires is a nationwide problem, which makes tires a valuable source of free playground equipment; more about tires in Chapter 7.

Because the tire from a tractor (or large truck, or grader, or big piece of earth-moving equipment) is black, it will absorb heat from the sun. In the winter, this heat will be welcome. In the summer it means you must find some means of cooling the tire or provide some shade for it. Some folks cool their tires daily by turning on the sprinkler. The kids put on their swimming suits and run through the wa-

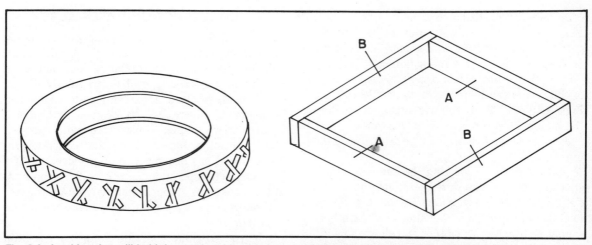

Fig. 3-3. Anything that will hold the sand and keep it from spreading all over the yard is a good sandbox. A tractor tire (left) can usually be obtained from tire dealers at no cost. The simple box on the right is easily constructed.

ter. This cools the kids, cools the tire, and provides some water for the lawn. Other folks cool their tire permanently by painting it white. Most enamels adhere well to the roughed-up rubber, by you should be sure to scrub off any dirt and grease. Any light color, of course, is suitable for the tire.

The other sandbox in Fig. 3-3 is a simple square made from 2-inch-by-6-inch planks of pine or any available lumber. Several factors should guide you in your choice of lumber. How long will the wood last? If not treated with a preservative, pine rots fairly quickly. If you live in Arizona, that may not bother you, but if Mississippi is your home, you might need another kind of lumber. Try to find out what is available free in your area. For example, a shipping company or warehouse might give you some old or damaged pallets. The heaviest pieces of pallets are often very hard and long wearing. Be sure to inspect them for nails or splinters that must be removed before they can be used as sandbox materials.

Although the sandbox in Fig. 3-3 is a square, you can design a rectangle if that shape fits your purpose. Let's work through the construction step by step, taking special note of unforeseen problems.

Site Selection

Let's assume you have a fairly small back yard,

made even smaller by a garage that comes within 5 feet of the 7-foot privacy fence between your yard and the apartment house behind you. Your children are 3 and 5 years old. You wish to retain as much of the yard as possible for running games, rolling or kicking balls, and other movement activities. The sun can be mighty hot for the youngsters, but you have noticed that your garage provides some afternoon shade for the otherwise unused space between the garage and privacy fence. Although you will not be able to see the kinds from the house, you decide that their temperament is such that you can just check on them every half-hour or so. So, the "waste" space it is for the sandbox.

Construction Method

The next step is to measure the space exactly. If necessary, squint along the wall of your garage and along the fence. Look for corrugations, dents, bulges—anything that might keep the box from fitting the space. Let's say there is exactly 5 feet of space between the fence and garage and 14 feet from one corner of the garage to the other. You decide on a 5-foot-square sandbox. That will leave some of the space for other purposes.

Having noticed that a local discount-lumber and handyman chain store is having a sale on 2 × 6 pine pieces 5 feet long, you zip down and buy four at a

20

bargain price for the sandbox. Now, the box cannot be constructed from the four pieces you come home with because the pieces marked A in Fig. 3-3 must be cut to allow for the depth of the other two pieces. You measure them exactly and find they are 1.75 inches wide. Together they total 3.5 inches to be cut off two of your pieces of lumber.

Cut your wood and take a good look at your nails. Each nail must go at least an inch into the piece of wood you will nail it to. It is a good idea to drill holes for the nails to go through, but drill only in the pieces marked B. Choose a drill bit that is slightly smaller in diameter than the nail. The drill bit may not go all the way through the wood. Don't worry, just drill as deep as you can. A hole going part way through the planks marked B will keep the nails straight so that they will go in a true path into the planks marked A. The top hole can be drilled with all the planks in place, but it is easier to drill the holes with the plank lying flat. Tap a nail into each of the holes of one plank B. If you are working on concrete, put a piece of wood under the plank where you expect the nail to come through; this precaution prevents the nail from blunting itself if you tap it a bit too far. When all the nails are started (driven until the pointed ends are just beginning to protrude through the planks marked B), put the planks into place.

The next step is easiest if you have someone to help hold the planks in place while you hammer them together. Always try to hammer into something solid, or, to put it another way, try to have the force of your blow end in something solid, not air. Imagine yourself hammering any of the four nails shown in Fig. 3-3. Imagine the force of each blow traveling through the nail, down the entire length of plank A, through the depth of the other plank b, and out. If there is nothing but air for the force of your blow to go into, you will find that the sandbox skitters across the surface you are working on, the nails will not go as far into the wood with each blow as you expect them to, and the nails will tend to go crooked instead of straight and true into plank A. However, if there is something solid, like the wall of your garage, for the force to go into after it has traversed the length of plank A and the depth

of the other B, all those problems will be lessened; the nails will go in smoother, straighter, and easier. If you can not arrange for a garage wall to absorb the force at the end of your blow, have someone sit down and brace his or her feet against the plank. If nothing else is available, load a box with bricks or concrete blocks or cans of oil—anything, as long as it is the heaviest thing you can find—and put it in position to absorb the force of your hammer blows.

If no one is available to hold the planks in place, put boxes, bricks, or concrete blocks on either side of plank A to keep it in place. Next, straddle the plank, facing in the opposite direction in which the nails will go. Bend over from the waist. Using your free hand, hold the planks in place and carefully hammer in the top nail. You should be able to hammer in the bottom nail as well, as long as the nail is not too close to the surface you are working on. Should that be the case, hammer in the top nail on the other end of your plank B; carefully turn your construction over and hammer in the other two nails, which now are on top.

Three sides of your sandbox are now assembled and complete. Now that nails partially protruding from the other plank B will not be in the way of the garage wall or the feet of the person bracing the plank to catch the force of your hammer blow, lay this plank flat and carefully start a nail in each hole. Set the plank in place and carefully nail it onto the construction.

You can start using the box immediately, but it would be a better idea to finish the surface of the wood first. You can use paint, but I prefer a stain manufactured for outdoor use. Outdoor stains come in many colors, and they can go right on the wood— no sanding is necessary. They penetrate the wood better than paint, yet the surface is just as waterproof, they do not cake up and flake off the surface eventually, so after a year or 18 months you can put on a fresh coat of stain without having to scrape off flakes and without having to do any sanding. Besides preserving and beautifying the wood, staining or painting it before use requires you to look carefully at every inch of the surface. If you missed any splinters or rough or jagged places, you can remove them now, before your kids find these hazards in the process of using the sandbox.

As soon as the paint or stain is dry, fill the box and let the kids start enjoying it. I recommend that you do not put a bottom in the box. Some people go to the expense of buying exterior plywood for the bottom of the sandbox, on the theory that grass and weeds will not grow up through the sand and spoil the kids' fun. This works all right, but the bottom of the box also keeps water in, which means the sand stays wet longer after rains (assuming you do not have a waterproof cover over the box) or after the kids have made rivers and lakes with water from a handy hose or faucet. Lining a sandbox with a sheet of plastic creates an even worse drainage problem.

SANDBOXES FROM THIN WOOD

If you can find some solid planks at least an inch thick (an inch as sold by the timber companies, measures about 7/8 inch), you can construct a sand-

box like the one described above. The difference is that you should connect the planks at the corners by a different method to avoid splitting the wood (Fig. 3-4). If you have access to plywood planks, you can use wood thinner than an inch. The sides may bulge or curve, but you can turn this feature to your advantage.

Site and Plan Selection

A rigid sandbox made from 1-inch-by-6-inch or 1-inch-by-8-inch planks can go just about anywhere, between a garage and privacy fence, on a concrete slab, or on earth. Thinner timbers ought to go on earth, however, so that stakes can be used to control the bulge as the weight of the sand makes the sides of the sandbox move outward.

Construction Method

The drawing on the left in Fig. 3-4 shows a method of connecting the corners of a sandbox constructed from solid 1 × 6 planks. If you try to put a nail

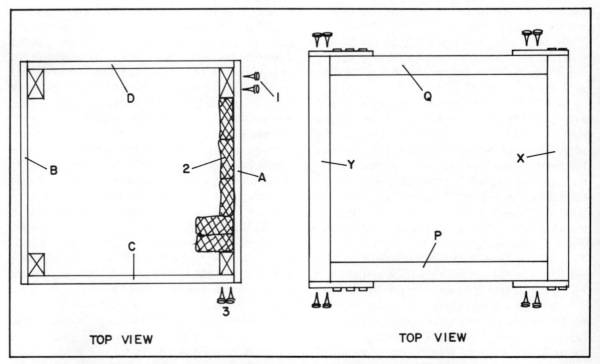

TOP VIEW   TOP VIEW

Fig. 3-4. Alternative means of fixing corners when the planks are thin (left) or very thick (right).

through the depth of one plank into the length of another, you will risk splitting the second plank. The method shown here avoids that problem by having the nails go into 2 × 4 corners.

After measuring the space for the sandbox, cut the planks to the required sizes. Cut four pieces of 2-inch-by-4-inch wood for the corners; their length should equal the width of the planks, for example 6 inches long for 6-inch wide planks, 8 inches long for 8-inch planks. The 2 × 4 pieces are marked with an X in Fig. 3-4.

Set all the pieces in place and plan your nailing sequence. First, nail through plank A into two 2 × 4 corner pieces; the corner pieces should be recessed to allow planks D and C to butt against plank A. Next, nail two corner pieces to plank B in the same way. Planks A and B are now ready to have planks C and D nailed into place, but if you try to nail through plank C into the corner piece on A, you will risk dislodging the corner piece and damaging the corner connection. To prevent the corner pieces from moving as you nail into them, put something rigid between them. Figure 3-4 shows bricks (indicated by the numeral 2) laid into place between the corner pieces that were nailed onto plank A. With the bricks in place, you can nail planks C and D into the corner pieces on A without risk of ruining the connection (numeral 3). You need not use bricks to keep the connecting 2 × 4 pieces in place, of course, for any solid objects will do—concrete blocks, a length of wood, or a combination of things.

After nailing planks A, C, and D together, transfer the bricks or other materials between the connecting 2 × 4 pieces on plank B; then nail planks C and D to B. Finish the sandbox with paint or stain, put it in place, and fill with sand.

I constructed a sandbox for my kids using this design but substituted screws for nails. This does away with the problem of inadvertently moving the 2 × 4 connecting pieces when you nail plank D to A. If you want to use screws, hold the connecting piece to plank A with a C-clamp, drill guide holes (choosing a bit that is slightly smaller in diameter than the screws), and drive the screws into place before removing the C-clamp. When you get to step 3 (attaching plank C to plank A), you may find that

your C-clamp is not big enough to hold plank C to the 2 × 4 connecting piece. You will have few problems if you do one screw at a time, putting a screw near the top or the middle before flipping the box, if necessary, and putting in a second or third screw. Screws do not have to go into the 2 × 4 connecting pieces as far as nails to get a good, firm grip, but they should go in at least 5/8 inch. A full inch is better, but if you go beyond that you are usually just making extra work for yourself unless the wood is exceptionally soft.

SANDBOXES FROM TIMBERS

The drawing on the right in Fig. 3-4 shows a means of connecting the corners of a sandbox constructed from timbers with a depth of 3 inches or more. Figure 3-5 shows a combination connection that adds a diagonal piece across the top of the planks that can serve as a seat as well as a connector.

Materials Selection or Acquisition

In Australia I constructed a sandbox using jarrah wood that had been cut for fence posts. Some of the pieces had weak spots that made them undesirable for fence posts, so the lumber company sold them at a small fraction of the regular price. The wood was exceptionally well wearing—hence its desirability for fence posts—but it would have taken a 5-inch nail to make the kind of connections shown in Fig. 3-3, hence the alternative methods.

Railway ties come immediately to mind when we think of this kind of sandbox, but, in fact, any big, thick plank is suitable. Nor does the plank have to be first quality. Well-weathered and even partially rotted planks can be used, depending on the circumstance. For example, if all other materials are very expensive, and if you will not need the sandbox for too many years, either because your kids will outgrow it or because your employment will take you to another city, you might choose to make do with some very poor quality timber. Remember, all it has to do is keep the sand from spreading; it does not have to support a wall or roof.

Construction Method

Follow the usual steps of measuring the site and cut-

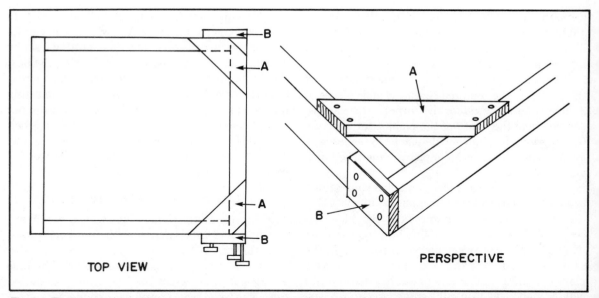

TOP VIEW   PERSPECTIVE

Fig. 3-5. The best method of fixing corners when the wood is old, loose grained, or slightly rotten. Only four nails are shown for piece A and for piece B, but enough should be used to make the corner strong. Drive nails in at an angle.

ting the planks to size. Select and cut to size four pieces (marked B in Fig. 3-5) for the corners. The width of these pieces should be as close as possible to the width of your planks; in the alternative, use two narrower pieces for each corner. The longer these pieces are, the stronger the construction will be, but even pieces as short as those drawn in Fig. 3-4 will do. Set all the pieces in place and think through the construction. Two nailing sequences are shown in Fig. 3-4. The one on the left is the better, especially if you are working alone. The sequence on the left allows you to lay planks P and Q on their sides, making it easier to nail on the connecting pieces. Planks X and Y are nailed on last. Before nailing through the connecting piece into plank Y, brace the entire construction against the wall of your garage or put something solid at the end of the plank to absorb the force of your blow. If you nail in the sequence shown on the right side, nailing the connecting pieces first onto plank X, do not try to nail through the connecting pieces into planks P and Q until you have stacked in something solid between P and Q, as the bricks were stacked or laid between the 2 × 4 pieces in the drawing on the left. If you fail to put something solid between P and Q, the

force of your hammer blows will tend to pull the nails out of the end of plank X.

Figure 3-5 shows a corner construction like that just described, but with a strengthening diagonal piece added on top. Construct the corners first, then the diagonals. When I constructed a sandbox like this I thought the diagonals (marked A in Fig. 3-5) would make good seats. They did, but not when the kids were in the sandbox. When they had their backs to the sandbox, for example, while playing cars just outside it, they sat on the seats, but when they were in the sandbox they sat on the sand itself.

This construction is especially good if your timber is of poor quality. Use several nails, not so few as we have drawn in the figures. Also, drive the nails in at an angle. In fact, all nails should be driven in at angles, but it is especially important with poor quality timbers.

IRREGULARLY SHAPED SANDBOXES

A round, oval, or kidney-shaped sandbox can be an attractive addition to your yard and furnish your kids with hours of fun. A basic rule in planning such a sandbox is to keep the material in mind. Round building materials, such as logs or concrete pipes, are best. You can use bricks if the box is to be large enough, but any three-dimensional rectangle larger than an ordinary brick is too big.

Building with Brick

The drawing at the top of Fig. 3-6 shows a simple round sandbox that can be made from bricks. The figure at the bottom shows the most obvious pitfalls of designing too small a sandbox to be made from brick; at each point labeled X, an exceptional amount of mortar, or a piece of brick that may be difficult for an amateur to cut, would be required. Therefore, if you want a kidney-shaped box, be sure it is at least 9 feet long. Do not plan to wrap it around a tree that has not already reached most of its full growth, or the roots will grow up and make your sandbox crack and break.

If the above discussion has not discouraged you, and you still want to build with brick, the best thing to do next is to call the building inspectors in your city government offices. Tell the inspector what you have in mind and ask his advice. He will be your best advisor on the type and size of foundation, although many inspectors will not recommend types of bricks and mortar. That kind of advice can usual-

ly be obtained by a friendly visit or telephone call to a builder or contractor. If you are not an experienced bricklayer, I recommend you try no short cuts. First, talk to disinterested experts; then go ahead. We have lived in places where the soil shifted so much when it rained that walls of houses would move and crack. Such conditions called for pier-and-beam construction, and you saw few brick masonry houses in that city.

Assuming that you have done all the homework necessary before proceeding, buy a trailer load of sand, half a load of aggregate, and as many sacks of cement as your contractor friend/advisor said you would need. Dig out the excavation for your foundation. Put sand in the bottom; 4 to 6 inches is usually recommended. Line the sides with lumber or with tar paper reinforced with stakes to make the forms. If you are using wood that you want to reuse, coat it with a light oil, paint it, or get a commercially prepared mixture to prevent the concrete from adhering to the wood. A common mix of ingredients for the concrete is one shovelful of cement, two of sand, and four of aggregate (gravel or small rocks), but you should double check this mix with your contractor/advisor. Mix the concrete in a mixer, which

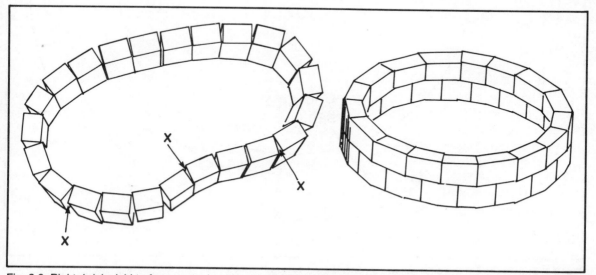

Fig. 3-6. Right: bricks laid to form an oval or circular sandbox. Mortar is not shown, and the drawing is exaggerated in the lower right to show how the brick on top fits on the bottom course. Left: the pitfall of designing with brick—it won't bend. The places marked with an X would require too much mortar to make a strong bond between bricks. The solution is to make the whole sandbox bigger or to make the curves less severe.

saves muscle power, or on a flat piece of metal at least 3 feet wide by 5 feet long. Add water sparingly at first. The concrete should be wet but not sloppy; too much water will make it weak and promote cracking. Mix it with a shovel or garden hoe. Shovel it into place and leave it at least 24 hours before removing the forms. If you can keep the concrete wet, it will cure to a harder finish. Sprinkle it with the garden hose every 8 hours and try to cover it with old sacks or sand.

The length of time you must leave the concrete foundation to cure, before putting the bricks on it,

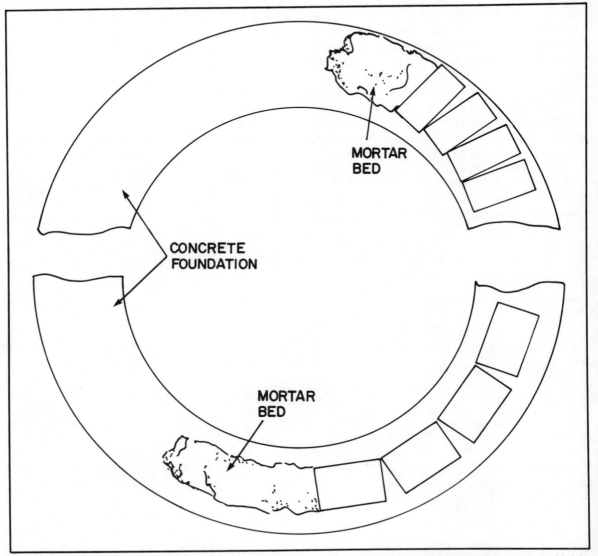

Fig. 3-7. The top half of the circle shows a concrete foundation that has been laid wide enough for a course of bricks to be laid side by side. This is called a header course. The bottom half of the circle shows a slightly narrower concrete foundation, but one wide enough for a course of bricks laid end to end, a stretcher course. The mortar bed is sufficient to take the next two bricks. It should never be prepared to take more than five bricks at a time because the mortar will dry too much. The bricks must be clean.

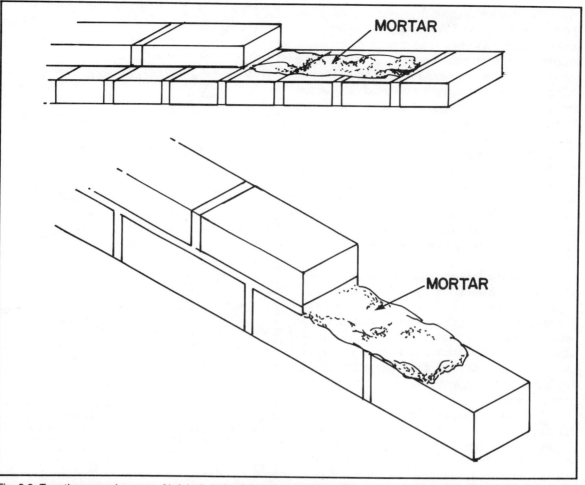

Fig. 3-8. Top: the second course of bricks is being laid as a stretcher course on top of the first course, which is a header course. Bottom: the second course, and the first course, being laid as stretcher courses. The top construction is slightly stronger than the bottom but is usually not necessary for sandboxes. All succeeding courses will be laid as stretcher courses. In hot, dry weather, dip the bricks in water before laying them. This prevents the brick from robbing the mortar of water, thus weakening the mortar and reducing the longevity of the sandbox.

depends in part on the weather and climate in your area. You will certainly make no mistakes by pouring the foundation one weekend and laying the bricks on the next weekend.

Mixing your own mortar from the individual ingredients will save you some money, but, if your project is small, you may be better off buying a ready-mixed bag of mortar. A good mix consists of 1 sack of portland cement, 6 cubic feet of damp sand, and 50 pounds of hydrated lime. Mix all this

together dry for at least 3 minutes in a strong wooden box before adding water. Mix some more. If it then sticks to the tools, add more sand. If it lacks cohesive properties and will not stick to the bricks, add more lime. If it seems too stiff and hard to work, add a little more water. Fill a tub or garbage can with clean water and keep it nearby to rinse your tools in.

When the mortar is thoroughly mixed, put two shovelfuls onto a 24-inch-by-24-inch mortarboard constructed of one-inch thick plywood nailed to two 24-inch long pieces of 2-inch-by-4-inch wood. Buy or borrow a good trowel. Hold it much as you would a tennis racket, but with your thumb on top of the handle rather than encircling it. Reach over the pile of mortar and, holding the trowel blade almost flat on the mortarboard, scoop a trowelful toward yourself. Holding the trowel directly over the pile of mortar, tilt the edge of the trowel closest to you downwards, allowing the mortar to drop off. In a similar fashion, take a few trowelfuls from each side of the pile of mortar and drop them back onto the pile. Feel its consistency. A bit more water or sand can be added if necessary. (Note: If you are right-handed, you should be scooping up the mortar with the left edge of the trowel; if left-handed, with the right edge.)

Now take a few trowelfuls of mortar and plop them on your foundation. Spread the mortar till it is about an inch thick. Press the tip of the trowel downward and draw it toward you, creating a wide, shallow furrow. The furrow should be no shallower than 1/2 inch. The strongest connection between two bricks is created by 1/4 inch of mortar. You can use 1/2-inch thick mortar bonds with a slight reduction in strength.

Using your free hand, pick up the first brick by grasping it with your thumb on one side, all four fingers on the other. Press it firmly into the furrow in the mortar. If you are right-handed, work from left to right around the foundation. Shake all the excess mortar off your trowel onto the mortarboard. Using the edge of the trowel, carefully scoop up the excess mortar that bulged out on the left side of your first brick. In other words, leave all the mortar under the brick and the excess mortar bulging out on the right side, but clean excess mortar off the foundation on the left of the first brick.

If you plan to lay the first course of bricks as shown in the top drawing in Fig. 3-7, you will need to hold the second brick by one side so that you can "butter" (Fig. 3-9) the entire other side. If you are laying the first course in the same way as you will lay the second and succeeding courses, hold the bricks as you did the first one, with thumb on one side and all four fingers on the other, and butter the

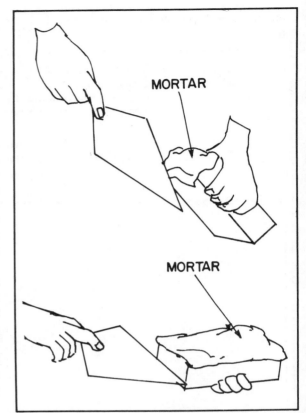

Fig. 3-9. Each brick must be buttered with mortar before it is added to a course. The top drawing shows the end of a brick being buttered for a stretcher course. The bottom of the brick need not be buttered because it will be pushed directly into the mortar bed. The lower drawing shows a brick being prepared for a header course. The side of the brick being held by the bricklayer's four fingers will go directly into the mortar bed. Bricks are buttered over the mortarboard with as much mortar as they will hold. Excess mortar falls back onto the board to avoid waste.

end of the brick that is closest to your thumb and forefinger. Butter the bricks by scooping up a bit of mortar with the tip of your trowel. Bring it to the brick. With a quick twist of the trowel, flick the mortar onto the edge of the brick. Then scrape the top surface of the trowel along and downward on the edge of the brick, thus leaving the mortar on the entire side of the brick. Butter your bricks over the pile of mortar, so if any falls off it won't be wasted. Also, butter on as much as the edge of the brick will hold. None will be wasted because you will scrape up the excess bulges and return them to the mortar board.

Place the buttered side of the second brick next to the first brick so that the mortar will go between them. Press the second brick firmly into place. Lean or stand back and look at the bricks. Holding the trowel the same way as when you carry the mortar, turn the tip skyward and use the butt end of the handle to gently tap any high corner of a brick down level. Use a spirit level frequently to check that the course of bricks stays level. Before buttering the third brick, use the edge of the trowel to clean off the excess mortar from all sides of the brick except the side the next brick will go on.

As you lay the bricks, you will find your confidence and skill increasing. The only pitfall is spreading too much mortar on the foundation and letting it dry a bit before you get the bricks pressed into it. Incidentally, spreading the mortar is called preparing the mortar bed, and a bed will be prepared on the first course, in exactly the same way, to receive the second course of bricks, once the

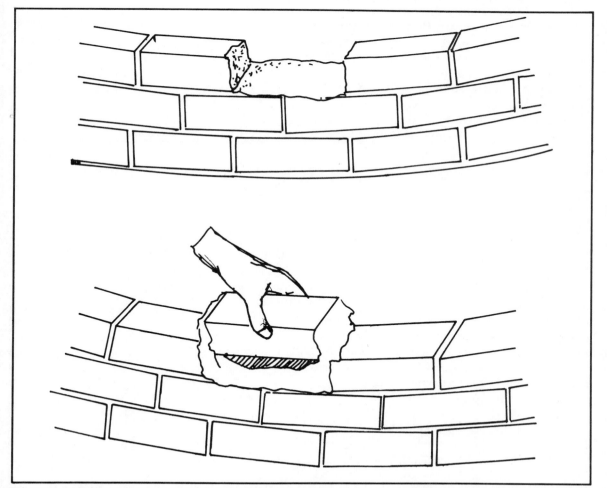

Fig. 3-10. A closure joint prepared to receive the last brick in a stretcher course. Note the mortar on the bed and on the sides of the bricks. The last brick being pushed into place (lower drawing) has both ends buttered. This ensures that more than enough mortar is set in initially, and that the brick will squeeze out all the excess, thus forming a strong bond. Too little mortar would form a weak bond, and the brick would loosen and fall out after little use of the sandbox.

first has been completed. When you get good enough to lay a bed for five bricks, do not work any farther ahead because the mortar will dry out too fast.

When you come within 10 bricks of completing the circle to form the first course, set enough bricks on the ground just inside the foundation to complete the circle. This will give you a close estimation of whether the fit will be just right or a bit tight or whether you will have to make all the remaining mortar joints a bit thicker to complete the circle. The aim is to have the joints of a nearly uniform thickness of mortar and to avoid a final joint that is 3/4 inch thick when all others have been 1/4 inch thick.

The major rule to remember when putting in the last brick is to use more than enough mortar. You will already have mortar on the bed. Butter up both sides of the bricks that the last brick will go between; then butter it as well (Figs. 3-10 and 3-11). Press the last brick firmly into place.

When the first course is in place, you can begin the second course immediately. In fact, you can go as high as eight courses, which will probably be

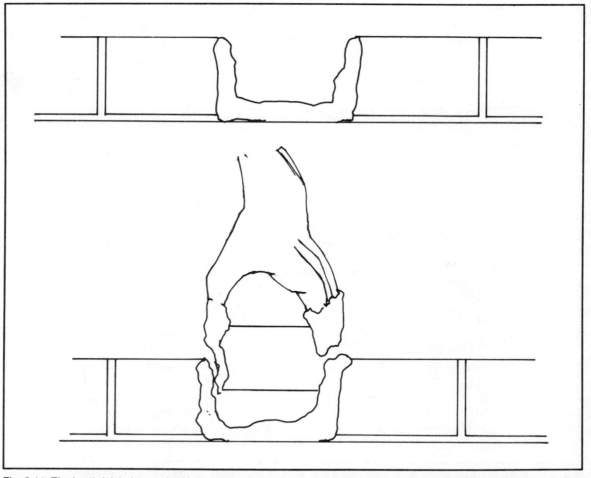

Fig. 3-11. The last brick being pushed into a closure joint (lower drawing) in a header course. Note the mortar on all three sides (top drawing) that the brick will fit into. Note also the mortar on the thumb and fingers of the brick layer. A tub of water should be kept close for rinsing tools and fingers.

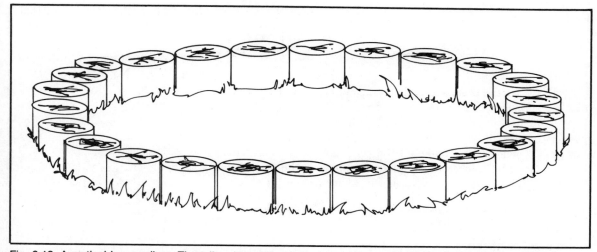

Fig. 3-12. A vertical log sandbox. The taller side of the box can serve as a retaining wall in sloping yards.

more than you need for a sandbox, without having to let the mortar on lower courses dry and harden before going higher.

You will probably have some mortar left over. This will crumble fairly easily when dry, but it should not be put into your garden or flower beds unless you have a highly acid soil that you want to change toward the neutral center of the scale.

Wash your bricks in a tub of water before laying them. This step is especially important in hot, dry weather. Not only will mortar stick better to clean bricks, it will also cure better. Like concrete, mortar does not actually dry; it hardens by a chemical reaction between the cement and water. Dry bricks can rob the mortar of water, making it weak and susceptible to cracks.

Vertical Log Sandboxes

Figure 3-12 shows an oval-shaped sandbox made from large logs. Figure 3-13 shows the method of construction, but in this case the shape of the box is less regular. The oval-shaped box is a design borrowed from a school my children used to attend. The tall side of the sandbox served a double purpose. Not only did it form one side of the sandbox; it also formed a retaining wall for a small area of the playground that otherwise would have continually been crumbling away. The sandbox was 25 feet at its widest, 15 across the middle the other way. Such a sandbox in your backyard need not be so large, of course, and using logs or other materials with a round profile will enable you to shrink the size without creating the building problems encountered when you shrink a design made for something rectangular—like brick.

Finding the Materials

At the former school the logs were expensive—pine that had been surface-treated with a green substance that preserves and protects the wood from attacks by insects. In Austin, Texas, I have seen sandboxes of this sort constructed from old telephone poles. In Holland, according to a report by Paul Hogan, a proponent of playgrounds made from inexpensive or free materials, these sandboxes are constructed from "restrollen," the centers of logs that were used in plywood manufacture. If none of these wooden materials is available, do not give up hope. If you can locate a source of free or inexpensive concrete pipe or ceramic pipe, such as the sort used for water or sewer mains, you can set them on end and fill them with rubble, rocks, sand, or dirt. They do not have to be filled with dirt, of course, to hold in the sand. One of the beauties of this design is that the sandbox serves more than one purpose.

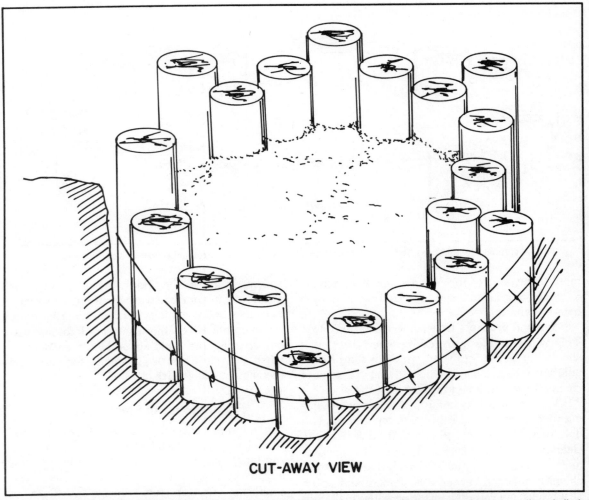

CUT-AWAY VIEW

Fig. 3-13. The vertical log sandbox—construction details. The logs are of varying heights so that kids can walk and climb on them for games of follow the leader. The line of dashes around the logs indicates the fill line. The line below it is a barbed wire stapled to each log to keep it in place and add stability and rigidity to the structure. Barbs were drawn on to distinguish the line of wire from the fill line, but plain wire is as good as barbed wire for the construction. The wire will be buried when the trench is filled.

I have already mentioned the use of this design as a double-duty retaining wall and sandbox side. A third use of this design is as a climbing apparatus that kids love to clamber over, alone or playing follow-the-leader, which can help them practice keeping their balance and improve eye-foot coordination. This activity will also exercise and develop gross motor skills. Therefore, if you can fill the concrete or ceramic pipes, the kids will be able to walk on top of the fill. Buying this fill material can be expensive, however, so scout around for a free source. Rocks, sticks, old cans, and building rubble may be available on your own building lot. If you live in the desert Southwest, you may be able to simply drive out into a field—with permission of the rancher, or course—and load up enough trailerloads of dirt to fill your pipes. If you live in a city, far from a desert region, drive around and try to find a site where a brick or rock building is being demolished. Much of the rubble turns to sand, and the wrecking company will usually not mind your taking several loads of material that it otherwise will have to haul away.

If the building rubble contains broken glass or other dangerous material, you should screen out at least that part that is going to go into the top of your pipes. Figure 3-18 shows the design for a screened sandbox cover intended to keep the neighborhood cats from turning your sandbox into a litter box, but the design is also useful as a screening device. The screen is actually hardware cloth. If you want a finer screen, you can rig one at home after screening out the biggest pieces of glass and brick rubble at the wrecking site.

Screening is a simple operation. You simply prop the screen up against anything that is handy, even a stack of broken bricks if nothing else is available, at about a 45-degree angle. Then, with your shovel, you throw the material on the screen. There is no need to drop it gently, unless your screen is delicately constructed, because throwing it helps bigger lumps of sandy mortar break up and fall through. When the screened pile gets big enough, set the screen aside and load the material into your trailer or boxes.

You don't need a trailer to haul sand, rocks, topsoil, or any other material for your yard or playground. Just get some boxes from your grocer and line them with doubled plastic garbage bags. Leave them in the trunk of your car or the back of your station wagon while you are filling them. If you try to pick up a filled box you risk injuring your back and breaking the box, which would cause all your work to go to waste. Keep an eye on how much your car sinks with the load. Sandy materials are deceptively heavy, and you do not want to overload your springs. It is better to make several trips with small loads than to make a few trips with loads too heavy for your vehicle.

Construction Method

When planning a vertical log sandbox, you must bear in mind that excavating for the logs will create a fairly large pile of dirt. Plan a place to put it. Dig a trench for the logs, rather than a big hole. In other words, leave as much dirt undisturbed in the center of the construction as you can. The depth of the trench depends on the length of your logs. The trench should go at least 3 feet deep if you plan to have the kids use the tops of the logs as a follow-the-leader trail and if the logs will rise as high as 2 feet above the ground. On the other hand, if the logs will rise no higher than 15 inches, a 12-inch trench will do.

If your design is for an irregularly shaped construction, now is the time to measure its distance. Even if you are constructing a circle or an oval, it is better to measure its circumference with a tape measure after you have dug the trench than to figure the circumference on paper before you have begun to dig because large rocks, tree roots, and other unforeseen obstacles may force you to alter the design as you dig.

Having measured the trench, you can now compute how many logs or pipes you will need by dividing the length of the trench by the diameter of the logs or pipes. Set all the logs in place, stand back, and have a good look. Now is the time to rearrange them, dig the trench slightly deeper in one spot to make the logs line up better, and make other such minor adjustments.

If the heights of the logs are irregular, as in Fig. 3-13, they will present a greater challenge to the kids using them as a footpath. Your only consideration will be to take care not to create too difficult a step for the youngest child using the construction. This irregular-height design will also save you some headaches, for the symmetrical pattern shown in Fig. 3-12 requires considerable log rearranging and trench deepening and filling.

When the logs are all in place, nail or staple a length of wire to a good sound log, one that is not splitting, surface flaking, or damaged so that it will hold the staple or nail. Figure 3-13 shows barbed wire being used for this purpose only because I wanted the wire not to be confused with the dashed line above it, which shows the level to which the trench will be filled. You can use barbed wire if you have it because it will go underground anyway, but it is much more expensive than plain wire.

Unless your soil is a nice, even sandy loam, with no rocks or roots in it, the sides of your trench will be less than straight. The trench will be bigger at the top than at the bottom; therefore, you will have to fill in some dirt on both sides of the logs. The inner side of the trench, for this discussion, means the side that will end up under sand; the outer side means the side that the wire goes around.

Take your shovel and lightly fill the inner side of the trench by the log with the wire nailed to it and the next three logs. Take a spirit level and check the first log. Make the log stand as straight and true as you can. Now get a piece of board and start tamping the dirt on the inner side. Check the log with your spirit level frequently. Compact the dirt from the bottom of the trench to the ground level. During this compacting process you will have to add more dirt.

Next compact the dirt around the bottom of the second log. Check for vertical standing with your spirit level. When the dirt is compacted about half way up the log, stretch the wire as tightly as you can and nail it onto the second log. Then finish compacting the dirt all the way up, checking frequently with your spirit level.

Follow the same procedure with the third and fourth logs. Then start filling in the outer side of the trench from the second log. Do not start with the first log because you will want to nail the wire to it when you have completed the circuit, and you do not want to have to dig it out again after going to so much trouble to compact and level in the first place.

Continue in this way all around the trench. Work slowly and carefully at first. As you discover how much each shovelful of dirt will compact and how much the compacting process moves the log and how much or how hard you have to shove on it to realign it vertically, you will be discovering what you need to know to speed up later. The most important point to make here is that the logs need to be kept vertical and solid from both sides, as you go around the circle. If you compact the entire inner side first, then the outer, you will almost certainly disalign some of the logs in the process.

It is not advisable to add water during this process. If it rains, and the trench fills, wait till most of the water has soaked through before completing your job. Slushy mud makes it very difficult to keep the logs properly aligned. The exception to this rule is a very sandy soil that makes compacting difficult, especially in a relatively narrow trench with a small tamping stick. In this situation, tamp as firmly as you can; then put in just enough water to dampen the sand. Add some more dry sand and retamp. Continue in this way, throwing in some rocks as well if they are available, until the trench is filled.

If you are making your sandbox from concrete or ceramic pipe, the construction method is exactly the same except that you will not be able to nail the wire to the pipes. The same strengthening and securing effect can be achieved, however, by tying the wire securely around every third or fourth pipe, depending on the diameter. To begin, encircle the first pipe with the wire and twist the end around the wire several times to secure it. Stretch the wire into place and wrap it loosely around the fourth and seventh pipes. As you reach the level of the wire in the compacting process, have someone hold the wire securely while you continue tamping. First pull the wire as tightly as you can around the fourth pipe, stretching it taut across the second and third pipes. If no one is available to hold the wire for you, nail it to a stake temporarily driven into the bottom of the trench. The compacted earth will not hold the wire in place, so you must keep it as taut as possible when moving it from one temporary stake to the next.

A satisfactory sandbox can also be constructed from solid concrete cylinders, used in some states to construct retaining walls. These cylinders typically are 18 inches long and 6 inches across. To make a retaining wall they are simply laid side by side as high as necessary, but the sandbox is constructed by erecting the cylinders in a trench, just as logs or concrete pipes are.

SANDBOX SCREENS

As pointed out in the introduction, an attractive danger, like the hot but highly chromed and shiny exhaust pipes on a motorcycle, ought to be screened from a sandbox if the sandbox has to be located near the danger. Screens can serve other purposes at the same time, of course, as the designs that follow will show.

The Easel Pegboard Screen

Figure 3-14 shows a screen that can have a child's painting easel or other toys attached to one side, and polishing cloths, screwdrivers, wrenches, or other motorcycle gear attached to the other.

Materials

Two pieces of 1-inch-by-2-inch pine, 6 feet long.
    Two pieces of 1 × 2, 4.5 feet long.
    Four pieces of 4-inch-by-4-inch pine, 1 foot long.
    One 4-foot-by-6-foot sheet of pegboard.
    Nails.

Construction Method

Nail a 6-foot 1 × 2 to the top of the pegboard; this piece is labeled A1 in the perspective drawing in Fig. 3-14. Lay the pegboard flat. Place a 4.5-foot 1 × 2 into position (B1 in Fig. 3-14) and lay one of the 4 × 4 (C2) pieces on it. This will show if the B1 piece is too long. If so cut it to length.

Nail B1 and B2 into place. Nail A2 (the other 6-foot long piece) into place. Note that A2 goes on one side of the pegboard and that A1 went on the other.

Lay the construction on its side, with A2 on the bottom. Place the 4 × 4 pieces C2 and C4 into position. Nail through B1 into C2 and through B2 into C4.

Stand the construction upright and place C1 and C3 into position. Nail them into place by driving nails at an angle through B1 into C1 and through B2 into C3. Finish the project by painting it with a good quality outdoor enamel.

The Sewer's Special

Figure 3-15 shows an easily made screen that has other advantages. It is easily moved, and it can contain any number of pockets for such things as hammers, nails, a saw, and a bottle of glue. It can also be made at almost no cost from scrap or found materials.

Materials

Two pieces of 1-inch-by-4-inch lumber, 5 feet long.
    Two pieces of 4 × 4, 4 inches long.
    One broomstick.

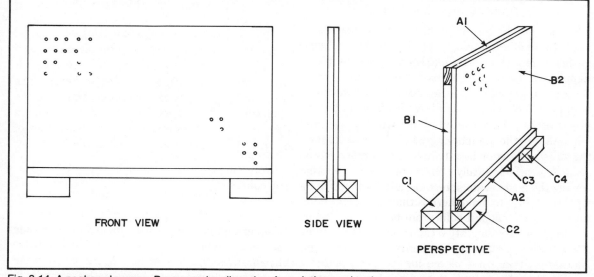

FRONT VIEW   SIDE VIEW   PERSPECTIVE

Fig. 3-14. A pegboard screen. Paper can be clipped on for painting, and tools can be attached for woodworking projects.

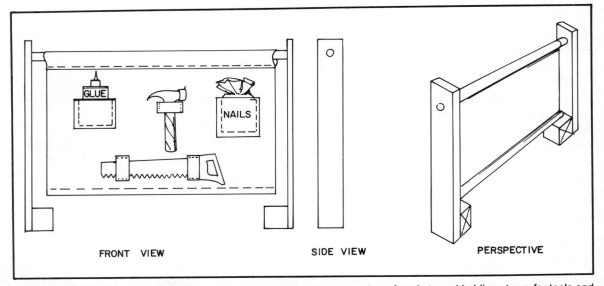

Fig. 3-15. The sewer's special—a screen that can be made with any number of pockets and holding straps for tools and materials such as nails and glue.

One length of pipe, 6 inches shorter than the broomstick.

One piece of fabric, approximately 3 feet by 5 feet.

Several pieces of scrap fabric.

Nails

Construction Method

Sew a hem in the bottom of the fabric large enough to accommodate the length of pipe, which will be pushed in to provide weight to keep the screen from flapping in the wind. You may also have to tie the corners to the bottom of the frame. Sew a second hem at the top large enough to accommodate the broomstick.

Using the scrap fabric, lay out the pockets for the nails and glue, straps to hold the hammer, saw, screwdriver, and other pieces of equipment. Before sewing the pockets and straps on, pin them in place with straight pins or safety pins and try them out for size and ability to hold the tools.

Measure the height of the screen against the 1 × 4 upright pieces and cut them off as necessary. Nail through the 1 × 4 pieces into the 4 × 4 pieces.

Drill a hole in the 1 × 4 pieces large enough to allow the broom handle to be fitted into it. If you lack a drill, cut a V-shaped piece from the top of each upright; the broom handle will fit in the V-shaped cuts, although it may also have to be tied down to keep it from slipping around.

Assemble all the wooden pieces and paint with a good quality exterior enamel. Put the screen on the broomstick and assemble after the paint is thoroughly dry.

This screen need not be used outdoors only. Set it up on a sheltered porch or patio on a rainy day and let the kids hammer and nail and saw to their hearts' content. Figure 3-15 shows pockets on one side only, but pockets can, of course, be put on the other side as well. If you have two kids who often fight, you can put identical items on both sides of the screen and keep them out of each other's way.

The Artist's Special

Figure 3-16 shows a screen on which an adult has had a hand at painting a Roman soldier, a fortune teller, and a copy of the *Mona Lisa*. You can leave the painting to the kids, of course, one way of occupying them when they get bored with the sandbox.

Materials

Two large, empty cans, such as 5-pound coffee cans or lard cans; the bigger they are the better.

Concrete.

One piece of fabric such as an old tarpaulin, an old tent, or the old cover of a pickup truck.

Two pieces of pipe, or PVC (plastic pipe), 12 inches longer than the length of the fabric, and two pieces of pipe 12 inches longer than the width of the fabric.

Two elbow pipe fittings for the top corners.

Two Tee fittings for the bottom.

String or cord for holding the fabric in place on the frame.

Construction Method

If you already have steel pipes for use in this construction, measure them and the fabric. Cut the fabric if necessary to fit the finished frame. On the other hand, two or more smaller pieces of fabric can be sewn together to make a piece big enough to fit the frame.

If you have the fabric and not the pipes, get them from a plumbing supply shop. The PVC or plastic pipe is easily cut with a wood saw; the fittings can be glued in with a tube of cement that the supplier also handles. Assemble all the pipes and allow the cement to harden.

Mix up enough concrete to fill the cans, or fill them when you have mixed up concrete for some other job. Place the frame in the cans. Use a spirit level to check that the frame is perfectly vertical. If necessary, prop boards up from either side against the elbow fittings to hold the frame vertical. Wet the concrete in the cans every 12 hours for the next 3 days to help it cure and harden properly.

If the fabric does not already contain enough holes, punch them out with a leather punch, a large nail, or an ice pick. If the fabric is nylon, you can carefully use the flame of a match to melt the edges of the holes to prevent fraying. Cotton material must be stitched, or you must use grommets. This step can be omitted if your frame will not be subjected to high winds that tend to make the cord tear

Fig. 3-16. The artist's special—a screen that takes advantage of old tarpaulins or pieces of nylon or canvas. Adults or children can provide the artist's touch.

through the fabric. Lace the fabric onto the frame with the cord. If you have trouble tightening it, cut the cord into three or four smaller pieces and tie it at several places on the frame. Neither galvanized pipe nor PVC pipe needs painting to protect it from the weather. You may want to paint the cans to protect them from rust and to make them look prettier.

The Gardener's or Plant Lover's Special

Figure 3-17 shows a less mobile screen. It is attached to two 2-inch-by-4-inch wooden stakes driven into the ground. The plants growing up the trellis can be planted directly into the ground or can be grown in pots. If placed in an exceptionally windy spot, the top of the trellis should be nailed to a handy corner of the house or garage.

Materials

Two 2 × 4 stakes, 14 inches long.
   Two new or scrap pieces of 1-inch-by-4-inch lumber, 6 feet long.
   Four 2-inch screws, and 16 1-inch screws.
   One piece of ready-made trellis.
   Paint.

Construction Method

You can make your own trellis, but the measurements and placements of the rivets is demanding, so we recommend a ready-made, relatively inexpensive one. You can expand it like an accordian, although the height diminishes as you increase its width. There is usually a fair coat of paint on it when you buy it in the garden-supply or hardware shop, but an extra coat won't go astray.

Stretch the trellis out as wide as necessary to provide the screen. Prop it against a wall and hold the 1 × 4 pieces up against it to check their height. Cut them as needed, saving the cut-off pieces, which will be screwed onto the bottom of the long pieces and onto the 2 × 4 stakes.

Lay the 1-×-4 pieces on their edges. Cut the pieces of scrap to 4-inch squares. Drive two screws through each of these squares down into the longer pieces of lumber that are lying on their edges.

Drive the stakes into the ground, leaving 4

inches above ground. Place the 1 × 4 lengths into position and drive screws through the smaller pieces into the stakes. Stretch the trellis into position and tie it to the uprights. Drill guide holes; then drive 1-inch screws through the trellis into the 1-×-4 uprights. Remove the strings. Paint the entire structure with a good-quality outdoor enamel. Plant vines or a climbing rose between the stakes, or bring out potted plants to grow up the trellis.

SANDBOX COVERS

Animals need to be kept from the sand so that it stays clean and the kids stay healthy. Three simple sandbox cover designs follow. Their dimensions will have to be changed to meet the size of your sandbox and their designs can be changed to meet other needs. Sandboxes do not have to be attached to their covers. The covers can be propped against convenient trees to become slides or hiding places, or they can be laid across two large boxes to become the roof of an almost instant cubbyhouse.

The Screened Cover

Figure 3-18 shows a simple wooden frame with "hardware cloth" stretched to cover it. Hardware cloth is a misnomer, for it is not cloth at all. It is made up of individual wires woven to produce squares about 3/8 inch on a side. It is then dipped in zinc to galvanize it to keep it from rusting. It is stiffer than screen wire and, therefore, holds up better. Children must not be allowed to sit or stand on it, however, because their weight will cause the wires to become unglued, creating holes for a cat to get through.

Materials (for a 5-foot-square sandbox)

Two 1-inch-by-3-inch pieces of lumber, 5 feet long.
   Two 1-inch-by-3-inch pieces, 4 feet-8 inches long.
   One 1-inch-by-3-inch piece, 7 feet long.
   Two pieces of 1/4-inch plywood or timber scrap, large enough to be cut into right triangles at least 7 inches on the smallest side.
   One 5-foot-square piece of hardware cloth.
   Nails, 2-inch and 1-inch.

Fig. 3-17. The plant lover's or gardener's special—a screen that can provide shade and shelter, beauty and fragrance.

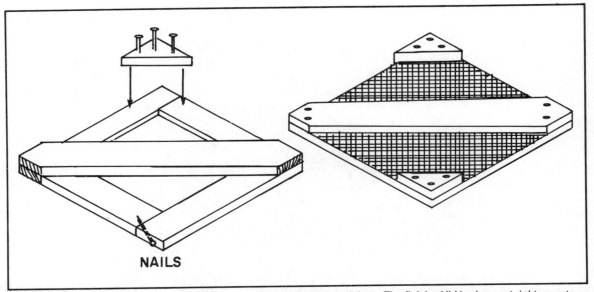

Fig. 3-18. A sandbox lid covered with hardware cloth to keep out cats and dogs. The finished lid is shown at right, construction details at left. The top method of attaching the corners (with three nails) is better than the single-nail method shown at the bottom.

Construction Method

Lay the four pieces of 1-×-3 lumber down to form a square (Fig. 3-18 on the left), making sure to put the shorter pieces between the longer pieces. One method of attaching the corners is shown at the bottom on the left. Drive a nail diagonally through a 5-foot piece into the shorter piece. We do not recommend this method, however, as it tends to split the lumber and drive the shorter piece inward, distorting the square. A better way to connect the corners is shown at the top. Nail on a triangular piece so that the sides of the triangle are flush with and parallel to the 1 × 3 pieces.

Before nailing down the triangle, however, lay the piece of hardware cloth into place. Now nail through the triangle down into the 1-×-3 pieces. This sequence will hold the hardware cloth in place and secure the corners of the square. Nail the other triangle down as shown in the drawing on the right in Fig. 3-18. Lay the 7-foot piece from corner to corner, as shown. If you are very handy with a handsaw, nail this piece on now and trim it later.

If you are not that handy, mark the saw cuts to be made; then cut the piece so that its ends are

pointed and it fits down flat and flush on the square. Nail it into place, taking care to push the 5-foot 1 × 3 piece firmly against the shorter piece until the nail catches; failure to follow this step may result in the two pieces not butting against each other firmly and creating a gap between them. Use the 2-inch nails to secure the 7-foot piece to the square. Use the 1-inch nails to fasten the triangles. Use them also to nail the hardware cloth down on the square between the triangles and the 7-footer. Paint or stain the wood to protect it from the elements; the hardware cloth needs no coating.

A Happy-Faced Cover on Thin Wood

This cover of thin wood is a good sandbox protector that can be made with salvaged materials. Once I made a cover like this from one side of a large packing box. The wood was 3/8-inch plywood that had bits missing here and there but that was still basically sound. You can also use 1/4-inch plywood or even Masonite, if you paint it.

Materials (for a 5-foot-square sandbox)

Two pieces of 1-inch-by-3-inch wood, 5 feet long.

One piece of 1 × 3, at least 6 feet long.

One 5-foot-square piece of plywood, Masonite, or similar material.

Nails.

Paint.

Optional: hinges and screws.

Construction Method

The N-shaped (or Z-shaped) placement of the 1 × 3 pieces gives this cover its strength. Lay the two 5-foot pieces on the square of plywood with the longer piece laid diagonally on top of them. The distance from the edge of the plywood to the edge of the 1 × 3 pieces depends on the length of the diagonal piece, for the shorter it is, the closer to the center the two 5-footers must go. Use a pencil to mark saw cuts on the diagonal for neat trimming so that it will fit true and square against the other two pieces.

When all the pieces are cut to size, turn them over so that you can nail through the ply. If the ply is poor quality, or if you are using another, softer material, it is very important to use nails with large heads, not almost headless finishing nails. Also, do your best to drive the nails in at an angle.

Nail in this sequence: a 5-footer; then the diagonal, held firmly up against it; then the other 5-footer, holding it firmly against the diagonal at the bottom. If your materials are at all flimsy, I recommend that this cover be hinged onto the sandbox and that the sandbox be placed close enough to a tree or a wall or a fence to allow the cover to rest against it at about a 45-degree angle. This will prevent the hinges from being stressed and broken. It also creates a secret place for little kids to hide for 30 seconds or so. A third advantage is that it holds the cover in relative rigidity, preventing it from being tossed around and broken and chipped. Finally, when the cover is lowered into place, it will contact the sandbox on its 1-×-3 pieces, not the plywood or Masonite.

Keeping in the inexpensive frame of reference, you can create a rainbow sandbox by cleaning out all those dabs of paint left in the almost empty cans on the shelf in your garage. You can paint all the sides of the sand box a different color, the underside of the cover a fifth color, and the top a sixth color. If your kids are old enough to handle the job responsibly, let them paint the box and cover. They will probably come up with a design you never

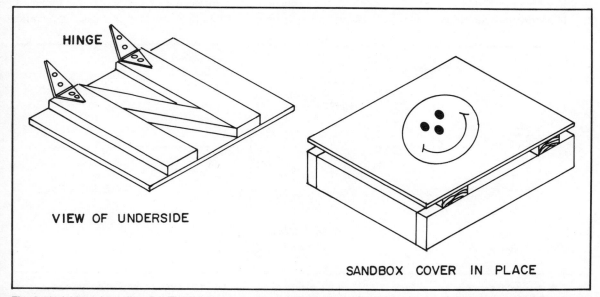

HINGE

VIEW OF UNDERSIDE

SANDBOX COVER IN PLACE

Fig. 3-19. A hinged sandbox lid. The lid or cover can be painted with a happy face, a checkerboard, or with a game such as parchesi, snakes and ladders, or backgammon.

dreamed of. You can also paint the top as a checker-board and then cut big checkers off a log with a chain saw. If your children are old enough, encourage them to play chess outdoors on this big chessboard. The chessmen can be made from papier-maché or simply be large (9 to 14 inches high) offcuts of 2-inch-by-4-inch wood with the suggestion of the chessmen painted on them. You can also use a combination of the two materials. Build the traditional shapes on the 2 × 4 pieces with papier-maché, let them dry thoroughly, and then paint them to make them waterproof.

Instead of the 64 squares of a checkerboard, you might try other ideas for the multiple use of this sandbox cover: paint on a chutes and ladders game; paint on a parchesi game; or paint on a giant backgammon board. (Figure 3-19).

A SUNKEN, HIDEAWAY SANDBOX

Figure 3-20 shows a sandbox that can be built right into the ground and completely closed. The ground around it can be put into grass or finished on top with paving stones or concrete patio pavers. I recommend paving the area because it allows the ground to become and stay dry, which helps preserve the sandbox timbers.

This construction takes quite a bit of work, so you should consider several factors before undertaking it. A good quality, rot-resistant wood is needed, and such wood can be expensive. Will your kids be using the sandbox long enough to justify the expense? Similarly, how long will you be in your present house? Long enough to justify the time and expense this sandbox requires?

Materials

The sandbox itself is a simple one, like the one in Fig. 3-3. Therefore, get four planks of the dimensions needed to suit your site plan. The planks should be at least 2 inches thick. For a box with a hinged lid (Fig. 3-20), 2-inch by 6-inch planks will do, but for a box with a gable cover (Fig. 3-21) 2-inch by 10-inch or wider is desirable because this sandbox requires more depth. This box has little head room at the sides. Therefore, the level of the sand must be dropped by using wide timbers to construct the box. An alternative method is to dig the box itself deeper. This may be necessary if your kids are already getting tall or if they suffer from claustrophobia.

Redwood and Pacific red cedar are long-lasting timbers, but you can also consider ash, cypress, spruce, and white cedar. A soft wood like pine can be used if it has been treated to resist water and

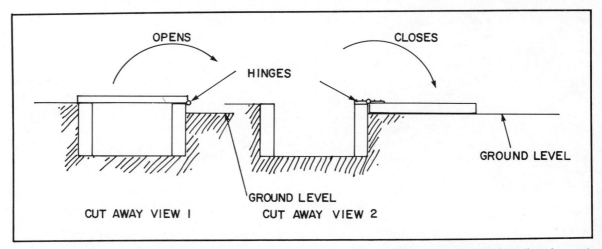

Fig. 3-20. A sunken sandbox with a hinged lid. When the sandbox is open, the lid becomes a convenient place for sandbox pies, buckets, shovels, and other implements. It can also be opened partially and propped up with a stick to provide a lean-to or part of a tent.

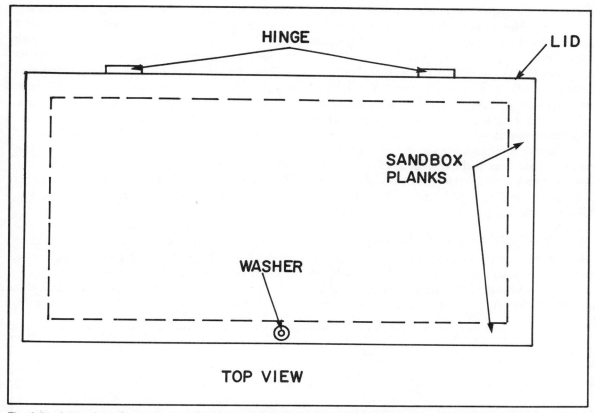

HINGE

LID

SANDBOX
PLANKS

WASHER

TOP VIEW

Fig. 3-21. A top view of a sunken sandbox, showing how all four sides of the sandbox help support the lid when it is closed. The washer on the left edge of the lid is fitted over a hole drilled part way through the lid; epoxy glue is used to hold the washer to the lid, and the glue is also spread with a match or toothpick on the sides of the hole. When you want to prop the lid open, use a short pole with a piece of steel rod glued into its end; the rod fits into the washer and hole in the lid.

insects. Such woods are light green because the preservative has been forced into the surface at high pressure. Be sure to use galvanized nails.

The tops for these sandboxes should be a good-grade exterior plywood, 3/4 inch thick. Inspect the sheets carefully and insist on sheets without splinters and any loose places in the top ply. Kids like to sit on the closed lids, and the gable-roofed model (Fig. 3-21) can even be a slide.

You will also need big, strong galvanized hinges. Use 1 1/2-inch galvanized screws. If the wood is soft, get 2 1/4-inch galvanized nuts and bolts for attaching the hinge to the box and 1-inch bolts with acorn nuts for the lid. For the finish use paint, stain, or a two-part epoxy.

Construction Method

Dig the site out to the required depth before assembling the box to avoid constructing a box that won't fit because of an unforeseen tree root or boulder.

Cut the planks to size and assemble the sandbox as described in Fig. 3-3. Apply paint or wood preservative if necessary. Put the box into the hole and, using a spirit level, level it. Put rocks under the box at various places to keep it level; then pack in dirt under the planks with a board. You want to eliminate pockets under the planks that the sand could run into.

The lid must be fitted true and square on all four sides of the sandbox. The cut-away views in Fig. 3-20 don't show this clearly, because the planks that would be nearest you, as the viewer, seem to be missing. Figure 3-21 clearly shows how the lid is to fit squarely on all four planks that make up the sandbox.

Smooth any rough spots on the sheets of plywood, on both sides, because the kids will use one side when the lid is open, the other when the lid is closed. Finish the plywood with paint, stain, or a hard-wearing epoxy finish.

Screw or bolt the hinges to the lid. Lay the lid beside the sandbox, in the position it will be in when opened. Mark spots for the guide holes on the sandbox plank. Drill the guide holes and attach the hinges to the sandbox.

A GABLE-ROOFED MODEL

For a gable-roofed sandbox, get good quality exterior plywood, at least 3/4 inch thick, and smooth out any rough spots with sandpaper. When the paint or epoxy finish is on these boards, they can be slip-pery, so smooth out some 1-inch-by-2-inch strips and screw them onto one sheet, as shown in Figs. 3-22 or 3-23. These will serve as toe- and hand-holds for the kids as they clamber up to the top. If you intend for the kids to use the other side of the roof as a slide, don't put any of these toe-hold strips on it.

If your roof is going to be long, or if the sandbox is going to be located in a shaded or dark spot, some skylights are advisable. They can be on either or both sides of the roof. Figure 3-23 shows two skylights with toe-hold strips between them; the other side of the gable roof could have a skylight in the middle, with the kids sliding on either side of it.

Skylights are easily made. Mark off the rectangle with pencil, making it 2 inches smaller, on all four sides, than the corrugated plastic cover that will form the pane.

Drill a hole in one corner. Insert a key-hole saw, or use a jigsaw, to cut the four sides of the rectangle.

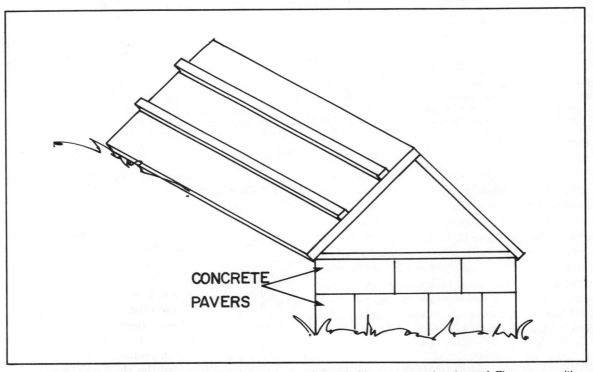

CONCRETE PAVERS

Fig. 3-22. A sunken sandbox with a gable roof. Strips of wood for toe-holds are screwed to the roof. The area on either end of the sandbox is paved with concrete paving stones, but grass is left on both sides of the box.

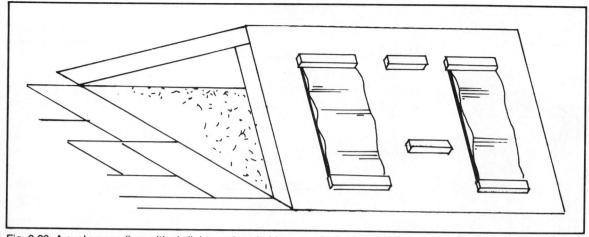

Fig. 3-23. A sunken sandbox with skylights and toe-holds on one side of the gable roof. The ground is paved at the end of the box.

The pane is held at top and bottom with strips of wood. If you want the pane to be watertight, put a strip of butyl mastic caulking compound between the pane and the roof. To waterproof the sides, get strips of sponge rubber. Put them in place between the roof and the pane. Use screws with rubber washers to fasten the pane to the roof.

Use galvanized screws to hold the strips of wood at top and bottom to the roof. You won't need rubber washers with the screws, but you should be sure to countersink them or use roundhead screws that won't hurt bare feet. The strips of wood should be sanded smooth before you screw them down on the roof.

When all the skylights and toe-holds are in place, give the underside of the roof a coat or two of white, exterior grade house paint; the paint will help brighten the sandbox when the roof is in place, and it will be an improvement even on plywood that is already a light color. When the paint is dry, screw the two sides of the roof together and set it in place on top of the sandbox. Attach it with long screws through the roof into the planks that make up the sandbox. Finish the outside of the roof with paint, stain, epoxy, or a combination.

SAND PLAY

To fully understand the importance of sand play in your child's development, imagine a young child at the beach. After overcoming his initial fears—the sound of the waves hitting the shore, the seemingly endless expanse of sand and water, beach balls flying, children running and splashing—the child begins to build his repertoire of beach experiences that we adults began years ago and have long since made a part of our total experience.

DIFFERENT TEXTURES, DIFFERENT TEMPERATURES

Imagine the child feeling the hot, dry sand between his toes. Stepping cautiously at first, his confidence begins to build until he is able to scamper across the hot sand towards the water's edge. The tide is moving out, and the child's running takes him from the hot dry sand onto cool, hard sand. Running is easier until he approaches the mushy, wet sand when his feet seem to sink into the ground.

When he enters the water, he is presented with a multitude of challenges. Shells, rocks, weeds, driftwood, and other materials are mixed in with the sandy bottom of the sea. It will be more difficult to walk because of these obstacles, and the child may well lose control and stumble. The combination of the wet sand and the waves constantly pushing against him will probably force the child to turn and move toward the shore once again.

He'll see the sandy beach from a different

45

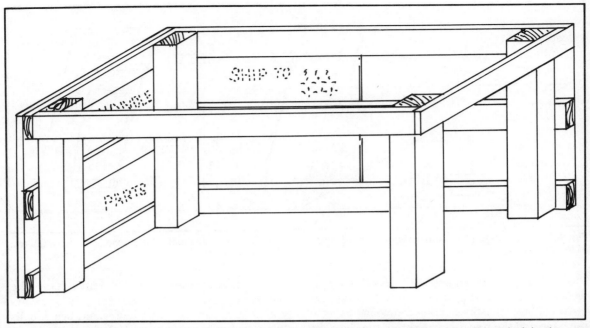

Fig. 3-24. A free-standing wind shelter. The four corner posts are sunk in concrete. Strips of 2-inch-by-4-inch lumber are then nailed to the posts on two sides. Sheets of plywood from old packing crates are nailed to the 2 × 4 strips to deflect the wind away from a sandbox placed in the center of the shelter.

perspective now. In retracing his steps he'll be more aware of the waves as they move across the sand, making it very wet and then disappearing again, allowing the sand to become "dry" until the next wave comes to wet it again.

SCULPTING AND CONSTRUCTING WITH SAND

Out of the water, the child is presented with a realm of possibilities for play. As his repertoire of beach experiences increases, he will learn that there are certain possibilities presented by wet sand. He will learn he can mold the sand into castles and sculptures. He'll draw lines in the wet sand, later creating full pictures. He'll use his hands and feet to dig trenches toward the water, which the waves will then fill with water. He'll find that by wiggling his foot back and forth in the sand, he'll dig a hole and, if he keeps wiggling, his foot will strike water, and he'll have made a well.

The child will find that dry sand offers other

possibilities. He'll lie in the sand on his back, moving his arms up and down in the sand, and his feet apart and together. When he stands up to see the silhouette of the "sand angel" he created, he'll find the sand easily brushes off his clothes and his body. He'll scoop the sand into piles, large ones and small ones. He'll run, clumsily, across the dry sand, jumping and sliding through the piles.

DISCOVERING AND USING SANDBOX ACCESSORIES

The child will discover seaweed, shells, sticks, stones, and rubble as he scavenges along the beach. He will incorporate these into his play as his play dictates. He may find that a stick is easier to draw with than his fingers or that a shell makes a particularly interesting imprint in the sand. Seaweed is good for landscaping a castle, and the waves will carry driftwood back out to sea for another wave to bring back to shore.

The key to this kind of learning is that the child

46

is making the discoveries for and by himself. The child discovers and makes productive any additional "equipment" he needs to extend his play. His need is fulfilled by his experimentation, testing, and discovery. The unique properties of each adjunct (added piece of equipment), are then compared with the properties of sand and water. Naturally, you wouldn't expect the child to put all of his discoveries into a verbal form, but he may well verbalize some of his comparisons and question others. His direct involvement and repeated involvement with the elements is the key to his increasing understanding of sand and water at the beach.

BEACH PLAY IN YOUR OWN BACKYARD

You may say this is well and good, but you live hundreds of miles from the nearest beach. Remember, our hypothetical child's initial exploration involved only himself and the sand, which your child can do in a sandbox in his own backyard. Touching, scooping, and digging with his hands and feet will enable your child to become fully acquainted with the properties of sand. He'll want to wriggle his bare toes in the sand. He'll lie on his stomach and crawl

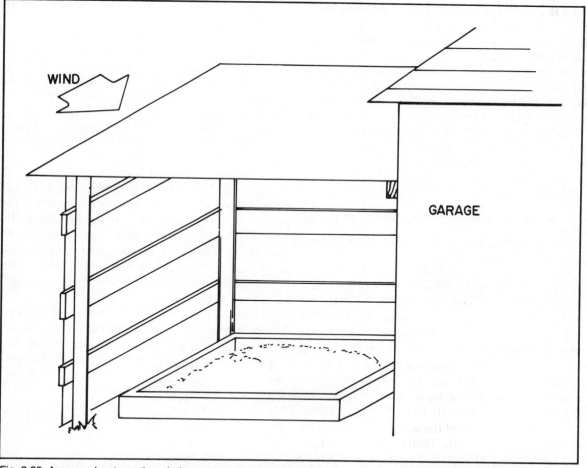

Fig. 3-25. A covered wet-weather shelter attached to a garage. Two sides are enclosed with sheets of corrugated plastic nailed to strips of 2-inch-by-4-inch lumber that is nailed or bolted to the corner posts and side of the garage. Note that the roof overhangs the wall enough to allow some air and light in, while preventing rain from entering. The roof is galvanized steel.

like the caterpillars and worms he's observed in your garden. He'll roll in the sand, getting it into his hair, perhaps his eyes. He'll experience the sensation of throwing the sand and feeling it prickle as it hits his bar skin. He'll be cautioned of the dangers of this throwing; he'll experience the pain of sand in his eyes. Your child will spend weeks, maybe months, in exploratory play before he gets bored with it. Boredom occurs only when further possibilities for play have been exhausted.

You can also duplicate some of the elements needed to enable your child to discover for himself the relationships created by the interplay of sea and sand and the simple properties of wet and dry sand. Give your child access to a hose, or provide him with a container of water. (Caution: Children should always be supervised when playing with water. Children have actually drowned in buckets of water.) Another good idea is to give your child experiences of playing in the sand on a warm, dry day and of playing in the sand right after it has rained. What adjuncts are at hand? What are some of the treasures for play your child can scavenge for himself in your backyard? Are there stones, feathers, flowers, grass, sticks, and seeds waiting to be discovered and used?

WHEN TO PROVIDE SANDBOX TOYS

Adults commonly give children toys and equipment before the children want or need them because adults see play from an adult's point of view, with an adult's years of experience and learning. How many footballs have been given to little boys on their first birthdays? How many two-wheel bicycles without training wheels have been given to three year olds who are simply fascinated by the wheels? When your child is ready for you to provide adjuncts for his extension, he will let you know by becoming restless in the sand, avoiding the sandbox altogether, asking certain questions, or just indicating the sand has no further interest for him. That is the time for you to introduce new equipment, but go slowly.

Give him several different sized spoons and two different sized containers, for example. Think of the mathematical discoveries your child will be faced with by these simple additions. How many big spoonfuls will it take to fill the small container? How much sand does the big container hold compared to the smaller container? How can he use the containers and/or spoons to mold a form? How much sand will it take to fill a hole? These are just a few examples of mathematical concepts your child will work out for himself when he is given the adjuncts and plenty of time to experiment.

Your child will gain a concept long before he acquires the language that he will use to explain the concept to you. Therefore, don't expect verbal precocity; be satisfied with your child's continued interest and repeated experimentation, for it is the raw material from which his concepts are being formed.

Your child will experience the difference in scooping sand with his hands and scooping with a spoon. It may be obvious to you, the adult, but your child doesn't have your years of experience. Each new experience of your child's must be lived to its fullest and repeated over and over again.

Sand and water go hand-in-hand, and you'll find that as your child gains confidence and experience with sand play, he'll not want to have one without the other. Remember, he is experimenting, trying things out and making his own observations, a procedure basic to the scientific method. You will probably be oversupplied with sandcakes and sandpies for a while, and there'll be a few tears when your child discovers that the cakes and pies he made on Monday and carefully placed on the side of the sandbox are dry and crumbly, possibly blown away by the wind, on Tuesday.

Rivers will be dug, often a very long and involved process. You may be asked to help fill them, or the child may fill them alone. If, at first, he decides to use a cup for transporting the water from the bathroom to the sandbox, what will he learn about sand's ability to retain water? An older child, having discovered that sand will not retain water, may reinforce his river with stones, pieces of wood, or bricks and demand a constant flow of water from a hose. He may want to create a current to float his boats from one point to another. Dams, canals, moats around castles—all are possibilities for developing play with sand and water.

As your child gains experience, he will often ask for what he needs. Cars and trucks are natural adjuncts to sand play. Colanders, sieves, pots, pans, and ice cube trays all extend the play and create little, if any, expense to you.

Junk materials provide another means of extension and enable your child to create what he needs. By providing him with the opportunity for self-discovery, you are giving him a firm basis from which to develop physically, cognitively, and socially. Never underestimate your child's ability to develop his own play and cater to his own needs.

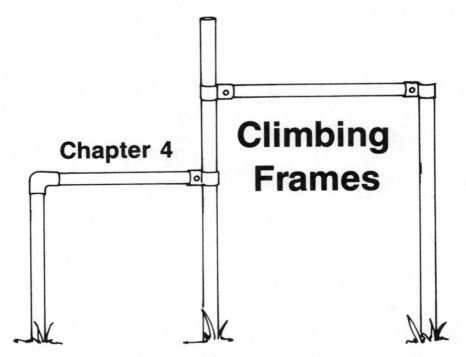

Chapter 4   Climbing Frames

A CLIMBING FRAME IS JUST THAT, A FRAME
that kids can climb all over. It offers
numerous opportunities for the kids to alter it, shape
it, modify it, or add to it—in short, to use their imaginations and create the kind of play environment
they want. The designs that follow all begin with
one relatively simple piece of equipment, and they
all wind up much more complicated. The beauty of
the designs, however, is that you can start simply
and inexpensively and build on later as your pocketbook and your children's needs make it possible and
desirable. The designs also enable you to use the
structural members of the original piece of equipment as components for the next piece of equipment, thus saving a few dollars.

Figure 4-1 illustrates the concept of the well-
integrated climbing frame. It started out with the
monkey bars. Then it acquired a trick bar and a seesaw. The climbing frame proper came next, fol-
lowed by a swing or trapeze. Don't be daunted by
the complicated nature of Fig. 4-1. You won't need
six swings, seven sandboxes, or three cargo nets.
They were only sketched in to show the possible

locations, not the desired ones. The seventh place
for the sandbox is under the climbing frame itself.

A few definitions are in order. By monkey bars,
I mean a horizontal ladder placed high enough off
the ground that the kids can swing from rung to
rung, using alternate hands. Figure 4-2 shows a
good set of monkey bars. Figure 4-3 shows the
climbing frame, a platform fastened to four tall
posts. The solid sheet leading from the ground to
a board halfway between the ground and the platform isn't part of the climbing frame; it is a sandbox cover doubling as a slide and as a set of steps
or toeholds (the small pieces of wood going up one
edge of the sheet).

A cargo net is just that, a net used for holding
cartons and boxes of cargo as they are being lowered
by crane from a ship to the ground. The plank referred to in Fig. 4-1 isn't fixed to the climbing frame.
(You can see an illustration of such a plank in the
next chapter, Fig. 5-1.) Such planks can be moved
all over the playspace by the children.

A trick bar is a bar, usually a pipe, placed
horizontally, high enough from the ground for kids

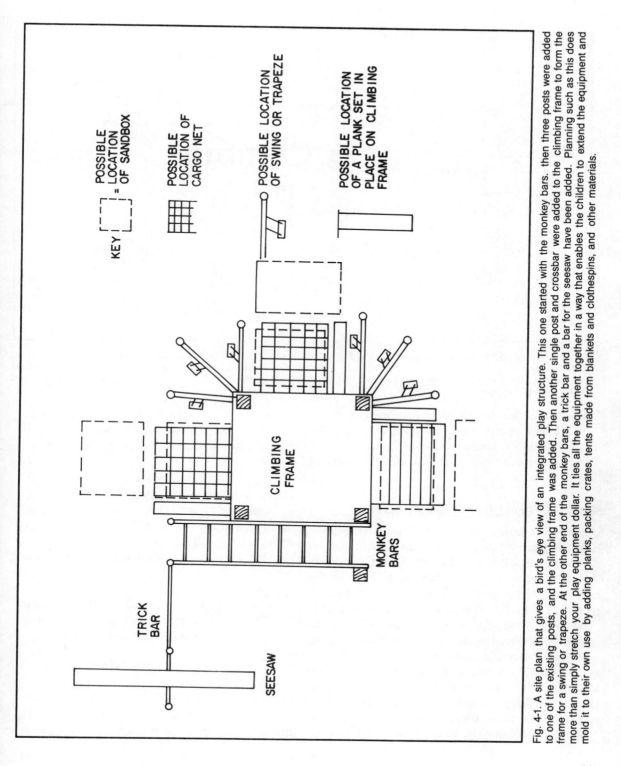

Fig. 4-1. A site plan that gives a bird's eye view of an integrated play structure. This one started with the monkey bars. then three posts were added to one of the existing posts, and the climbing frame was added. Then another single post and crossbar were added to the climbing frame to form the frame for a swing or trapeze. At the other end of the monkey bars, a trick bar and a bar for the seesaw have been added. Planning such as this does more than simply stretch your play equipment dollar. It ties all the equipment together in a way that enables the children to extend the equipment and mold it to their own use by adding planks, packing crates, tents made from blankets and clothespins, and other materials.

51

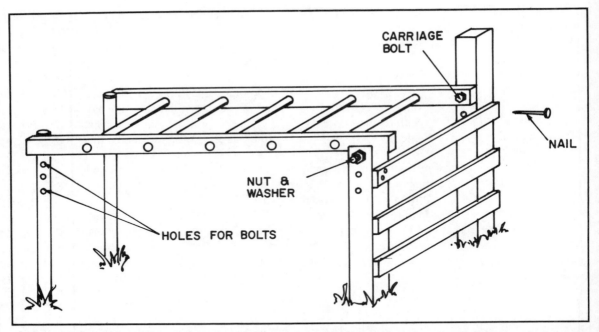

Fig. 4-2. A basic set of monkey bars. The horizontal ladder has been raised to its maximum height. Note the bolt holes in all four posts. A climbing frame can be added to this structure by using three more posts, each as tall as the tallest post shown. The floor of the climbing frame will rest, on one side, on the horizontal ladder. Safety rails will be fastened to the tops of the four posts.

to use as a chinning bar, as something to hang by their knees from, to turn flips from, and to use for other tricks. I assume that swing, seesaw, and trapeze are self-explanatory, although illustrations of them follow.

BUILDING MONKEY BARS

Few of the drawings in this book are done to scale, but they are all done to show details of the steps you need to follow to construct the various pieces of equipment. Therefore, don't be daunted by the seemingly huge posts at the near end of the monkey bars in Fig. 4-2; they are actually only 4-inch-by-4-inch timbers. The taller one will hold the guardrails (Fig. 4-3) that keep kids from tumbling off the platform.

At the other end of the monkey bars I recommend that you use two pipes, each set in 2 feet of concrete. When the kids swing across the monkey bars to these pipes, they can then slide down them, fireman's pole fashion. Note the caps on top of the

two poles; they keep rain out.

Details for constructing the ladder part of the monkey bars are given in Chapter 5.

Materials

One 4 × 4 post, 9 feet long.
    One 4 × 4 post, 11 feet long.
    Three or four pieces of 1-inch-by-2-inch wood, approximately 30 inches long.
    Two steel pipes, 2- or 2 1/4-inch diameter, 9 feet long.
    Nails.
    Sand, cement, gravel, and water for concrete.
    Paint or outdoor wood stain.
    Four carriage bolts, nuts, and washers.

Construction Method

When you buy the steel pipes, be sure they have caps to keep out the rain. Have the supplier drill a number of holes in the top end of each pipe. The first hole should be 2 inches below the cap; the second hole should be 6 inches below the first one; the third, 6 inches below that; and the fourth, another 6 inches down. These holes are for the carriage bolts, and they will enable you to lower or, as is usually needed, to raise the height of the monkey bars as the children grow.

Inspect the 4 × 4 poles for splinters and rough spots. Use a wood rasp to smooth them as necessary and to round the corners of the pole that won't be underground.

If the wood hasn't been treated for protection against bugs and decay, you should do so now. You can use a commercial preparation, such as creosote. We have used bituminous paint, with sand sprinkled on while it is still sticky. Or, if you change the oil in your car, save it to soak the posts in, adding 1 or 2 quarts of kerosene to assist the oil in penetrating the wood.

When all four posts are ready to be set in place, dig the four holes and mix up the concrete. A good mix is one shovelful of portland cement, six of gravel, two of sand, and just enough water to make it all stick together, not enough to make it runny. When thoroughly mixed, the concrete should be like cookie dough, not like pancake batter. Mix enough concrete to fill the holes to within 6 inches of the ground level. At the pipe ends, this will enable the kids to slide down and land on dirt rather than concrete. At the timber ends, you don't want the concrete to come up to ground level for a different reason.

During the first 12 to 18 months the posts are in the ground, the wood will shrink. If the concrete comes all the way to the level of the ground, this shrinkage will produce a miniature well around all four sides of the post. Rain water will fill these lit-

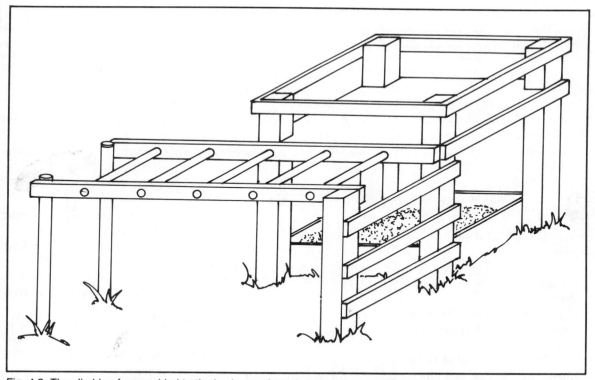

Fig. 4-3. The climbing frame added to the basic set of monkey bars. For the sake of simplicity, the ladder rungs nailed to the square posts of the monkey bar frame have been omitted from this drawing. Ladder rungs could also be nailed to the posts of the climbing frame. A solid sheet of plywood is shown in place at one end of the climbing frame. The sheet contains strips of wood for toe-holds on one side, but the other side has been left plain, to serve as a slide.

tle wells, and the posts will be standing in water, which won't do them any good, even if you have treated them with a rot-proofing compound. Dirt around the posts at ground level will enable the water to drain away, and the concrete under the ground will hold the posts in place. Just be sure to dig the holes at least 2 feet deep initially.

Put the posts into their holes. They will lean crazily and not stand upright till you shovel in about 8 inches of concrete. When they stand up on their own, twist each one as necessary to line up the holes for the carriage bolts. Carefully measure the distance between the posts, both length and width, and adjust as necessary.

Shovel in about 6 inches more of concrete to hold the posts steady. Then carefully put the ladder in place between the poles with the carriage bolts and nuts. Stand back and take a good look from all angles. If you find that the ladder has drawn the tops of the posts closer together than the bottoms, you will have to shift the bottoms in their holes. This is why you've put in only enough concrete to hold the posts in place.

Shift the posts in this way. If the post has to be shifted northward, shove a long pipe or steel bar down the post hole on the south side of the post. Now, heave back on the pipe or bar, using the side of the post hole for leverage, and the post should shift (Fig. 4-4).

Now take a broomstick, steel bar, or piece of pipe and poke it down into the concrete on all sides of the posts. This helps it settle and fill in all the little pockets of air. Fill the holes to the desired level, poking and settling the concrete as necessary. After 24 hours the kids can start using the monkey bars, although a wait of two or three days is better. Fill the holes with dirt and thoroughly wet it 12 hours after pouring the concrete. This will keep the concrete damp for several days, helping to cure it to a hard perfection.

While the concrete is curing, measure and cut to size the 1 × 2 pieces of timber for the rungs that will be nailed to the 4-×-4 posts. Use a wood rasp to round off all the sharp edges. The most secure way to attach the rungs to the posts is with long screws, provided you use roundhead screws. If you

Fig. 4-4. How to shift a post in its hole after concrete has already been poured in the hole. This is tricky work at best, so you should always put in only enough concrete to hold the post upright, to begin with, then check for distance between other posts. After all the necessary adjustments have been made, pour in the rest of the concrete.

use flathead screws, countersink them. If you use screws, you will have a fairly easy time removing them to alter the distance between the rungs as your kids grow.

If you choose to nail the rungs into place, use very long nails and drive them downward at an angle of about 30 degrees. This is most important on the top rung. As the kids launch themselves off it, their feet will exert a backward force against it, and if the nails have been driven in horizontally, it won't take much of this force to push the nails right out of the post. This problem is illustrated in Fig. 4-5, on the left. The drawing on the right shows how the nails driven in at an angle must be drawn up, as well as back, to loosen in the posts.

Double check to see that the heads of the carriage bolts are on the inside of the ladder, or, to put it another way, check that the ends of the bolts don't

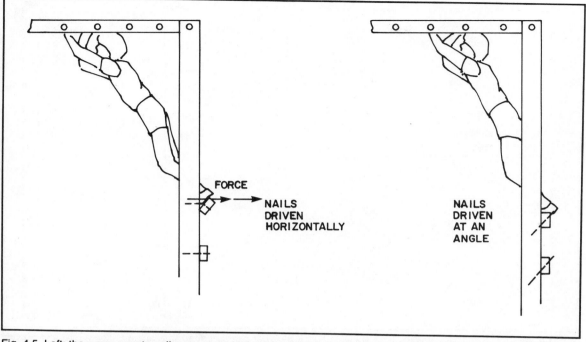

FORCE

NAILS
DRIVEN
HORIZONTALLY

NAILS
DRIVEN
AT AN
ANGLE

Fig. 4-5. Left: the wrong way to nail rungs onto the posts of the monkey bars. The force of the children's leg movements will force the nails out of the wood. Right: the correct way to drive in the nails. At this angle, the nails have to be drawn up as well as out, so they stay in the wood.

stick inward where they will scratch the kids' arms when they swing between the posts.

Finish all the wood with a good paint or an exterior stain.

ADDING A TRICK BAR AND SEESAW BAR

Figure 4-6 shows a trick bar connected to one of the steel posts holding up the monkey bars. For simplicity's sake, I haven't drawn in the 4-×-4 wood posts or the rungs behind the steel posts, but I have drawn in the wooden parts of the ladder of the monkey bars.

Figure 4-7 shows an alternate method of placing the trick bar and the seesaw bar. It has several advantages over the method shown in Fig. 4-6. One, the seesaw bar can be raised, lowered, or removed; if raised, it can become a second trick bar. Two, the bars are connected with pieces of hardware called tees, which tighten up with a simple wrench, requiring no welding. Three, none of the connections re-

quires threaded pipes. Our only caution is one you might already have considered. Figure 4-7 shows an arrangement that would put one end of the seesaw parallel with the monkey bars. Should the seesaw skew to one side, it might put its occupant under another child using the monkey bars. Therefore, I recommend that the trick bar be placed between the monkey bars and the seesaw bar.

Materials

For Fig. 4-7, buy two 9-foot steel pipes, capped to keep out the rain.

Two 2-inch diameter steel pipes, one 4 feet long for the trick bar and one 3 feet long for the seesaw.

Four tees.

For Fig. 4-6, you need only one 9-foot steel pipe.

Two 2-inch diameter steel pipes.

One 4-foot long steel post.

Three tees.

One elbow or a fourth tee.

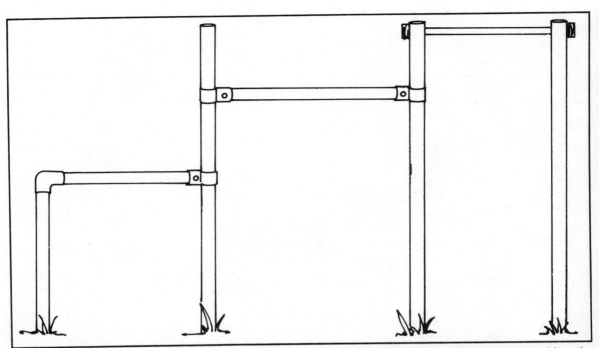

Fig. 4-6. An end view of the monkey bars showing how a trick bar can be added with one additional post and how the bar for a seesaw can then be added to the trick bar.

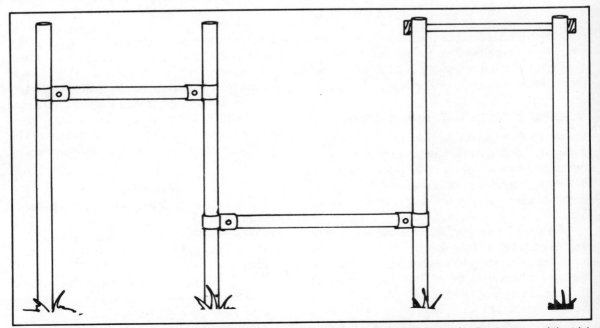

Fig. 4-7. Another end view of the monkey bars, showing an alternate means of adding a bar for the seesaw and the trick bar. Their positions could be reversed, of course, to put the trick bar between the monkey bars and the seesaw.

Construction Method

Dig the holes and prepare the concrete to hold the posts in place, as described with Figs. 4-2 and 4-3. If you are using the scheme shown in Fig. 4-7, put the posts in place, pour the concrete, poke it with a stick or pipe to settle it, and leave it to cure and harden.

After 24 or 36 hours, attach the two horizontal bars as shown in Fig. 4-8.

If you are using the scheme shown in Fig. 4-6, thread the 4-foot post and the 3-foot long steel pipe into the elbow before you put the post into the hole. Partially fill the post holes with concrete. Settle the concrete with a stick or pipe. Attach the seesaw bar (the 3-foot steel pipe) to the 9-foot post with a tee. Fill the post holes to the desired level and allow the concrete to harden. Attach the trick bar to the posts with the tees, and the apparatus is ready for use.

When the kids start giving the trick bar a workout, they may complain that the trick bar revolves inside the tees, giving them a scary or giddy sensation. This often happens when the diameter of the trick bar is 1/2 inch or 1 inch smaller than the diameter of the steel posts. If it happens, disassemble the trick bar tees and wrap the ends of the trick bar pipe with sticky black electrician's tape. Build up the ends of the pipe even further with flattened pieces of old garden hose or some other plastic material that can be slightly compressed. Then reassemble the tees, and the bar should be perfectly steady.

ADDING A CLIMBING-FRAME PLATFORM

There's nothing to prevent your building a whole set of equipment at once. You don't have to complete the monkey bars before you add the trick bar and the climbing frame platform. You can do the lot in one go, if you like. I've usually done my kids' equipment in bits and pieces for two reasons, money and time. I had enough money for a single project, which was usually completed on a weekend. Assuming you've completed the monkey bars and trick bar, you should be ready now to add the platform.

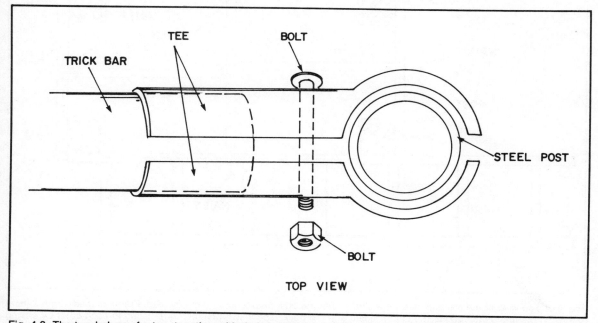

Fig. 4-8. The two halves of a tee, together with their bolt and nut. If the trick bar rotates within the tee, the nut can be loosened and the trick bar wrapped with tape, flattened garden hose, or some other material to build up its diameter. This should prevent rotation after the nut is retightened.

Materials

Three 4-inch-by-4-inch posts, 9 feet long.

Sand, cement, gravel, and water for concrete.

Two 2-inch-by-4-inch pieces of lumber, 8 feet long.

Three 2-inch-by- 4-inch pieces, 4 feet long.

25 feet of 1-inch-by-2-inch lumber.

One 4-foot-by-8-foot piece of exterior grade plywood, 3/4 inch thick.

A ladder, or some other means of getting the kids from the ground to the platform.

Nails and 4-inch lag bolts.

Construction Method

Dig three post holes for the new posts. One will be parallel with the monkey bar ladder, which will be nailed to the new post. The other two new posts are to be placed approximately 44 inches apart, by their outer dimensions, from the two posts nailed or bolted to the monkey bar ladder. Similarly, the longer dimensions should be 92 inches (8 feet minus 4 inches). When the 2-×-4 pieces are nailed to the posts, they will form a rectangle measuring 4 feet by 8 feet, the size of the platform floor.

Figure 4-9 is a top view of the frame work, with the 2 × 4 pieces attached to the posts with lag bolts. Note how the larger rectangle has been divided into three smaller rectangles by the three 2-×-4 pieces that will help support the platform floor. Note also how these 2 × 4 pieces are offset so that you can drive the nails straight through the middle width of one 2-×-4 piece into the end of the piece that butts against it. This arrangement does away with

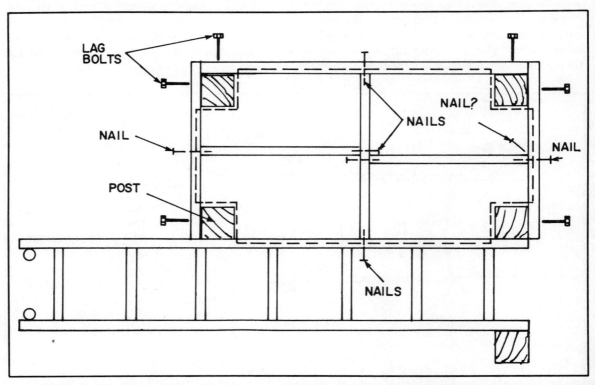

Fig. 4-9. Top view of the framing plan for a climbing frame built onto a set of monkey bars. Frame is made from 2-inch-by-4-inch members attached to the corner posts with lag bolts. The 2 × 4 members are nailed to each other by driving nails through one 2 × 4 into the end of another 2 × 4 butting against it. Nails can also be driven in at an angle, but this is more difficult and not quite as strong. The line of dashes shows how the climbing frame floor must be notched at the corners to allow room for the corner posts.

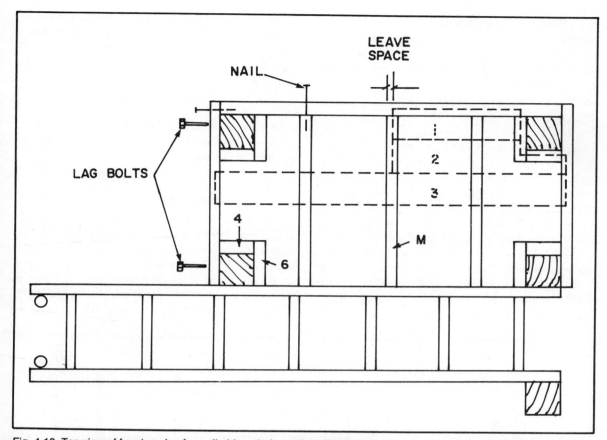

Fig. 4-10. Top view of framing plan for a climbing platform when the floor is to be constructed of planks. Position of three planks is indicated by lines of dots.

the need for a more difficult nailing job, driving the nails in at an angle, as indicated by the word "nail?" at the lower end of the platform. This means, however, that the center of one 2-×-4 piece running parallel with the ladder will be 23 inches from the outer edge, and the center of the other will be 25 inches; you must make allowance for this difference when you nail the floor onto these pieces.

Measure the actual thicknesses of the four corner posts. If you bought them as 4 × 4 pieces, they'll probably measure close to 3.5 inches or 3.75 inches on a side. This measurement will give you the dimensions of the squares you must now cut from the four corners of the floor sheet. The position of the floor sheet is indicated in Fig. 4-9 by the line of dashes, although these lines run down the

middle of the 2-×-4 pieces and the edges of the floor piece should come right out to the outer edges of the 2 × 4 pieces, not stop at their centers. Similarly, the floor sheet should fit snugly up against each post; the corners have been notched too large in Fig. 4-9 only for the purpose of illustration. If this drawing is confusing, look at Fig. 4-3, which shows how the floor platform goes all the way to the outer edges of the supporting 2-×-4 members. Figure 4-11, an end view of the apparatus, shows how the floor sheet fits on top of one side of the monkey bar ladder.

An Alternative Platform Floor

Figure 4-10 shows that the platform floor can be made of planks instead of a single sheet of plywood.

This floor might be desirable if the planks are inexpensive or free—provided they aren't full of splinters and provided they are durable or can be treated to make them durable. If you live in an area of high rainfall, you might choose the plank floor, leaving a small space between each plank to allow the rain to drain off the platform.

For the longer supporting pieces of 2 × 4 lumber, you'll need 28 feet just for the solid sheet platform floor. This design requires an extra 40 inches, however, to be cut into four 4-inch-long pieces and four 6-inch-long pieces. These will be nailed onto each corner post (indicated in Fig. 4-10 by the circled figure 4 and the circled figure 6 in the lower left corner of the platform drawing).

The position of three planks has been indicated by lines of dots. Planks 1 and 2 show how to use shorter pieces of free material to best advantage; plank 3 shows how to use the longer pieces, if they are available. The lines of dots have been drawn down the middles of the 2-×-4 pieces for convenience, except for the middle supporting member, marked with a circled M. The right ends of planks 1, 2, and 3 and the left end of plank 3 should go all the way out to the outer edges of the supporting members, not stop in the middle of them. The left ends of planks 1 and 2 must stop in the middle of supporting 2 × 4 member M, however, to leave space for the planks that will be laid from the upper left corner post to the center member M.

Adding the Safety Rails

Whether you've built the platform floor from a solid sheet or from planks, you now need to add the rails at the top of the platform to keep kids from tumbling off. Figures 4-3 and 4-11 show only a single rail going around all four sides, but that is for the sake of simplicity in the drawings. If the distance from the platform floor to the top of a cor-

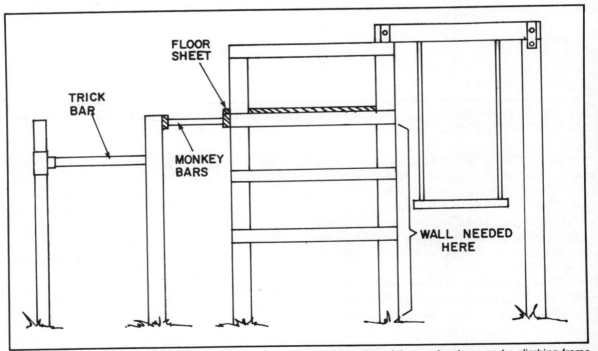

Fig. 4-11. An end view showing how a trick bar has been added to one side of the monkey bars, and a climbing frame to the other side. With the addition of one more post and a crossbar, a trapeze can be added to the climbing frame. Note that a wall is needed to prevent children's darting out from under the climbing frame and being struck by a child on the trapeze.

60

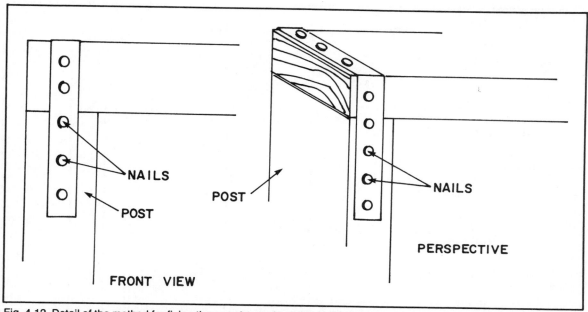

Fig. 4-12. Detail of the method for fixing the crossbar to the posts for the trapeze or swing frame. Nails are driven through a strap of steel into the posts and the cross bar, tying the three together.

ner post is greater than 24 inches, you might consider putting two rails around the top, especially if children below the age of five are going to use the climbing frame.

These rails will withstand considerable pulling, hanging onto, and rolling into, so they must be well fastened onto the corner posts. Therefore, you should put them on with nuts and bolts, lag bolts, or countersunk flathead screws or roundhead screws. You can also nail them on as indicated in Fig. 4-5.

Adding a Swing or Trapeze

One of the beauties of a climbing frame is that it is also half the frame for a swing or trapeze. Figure 4-11 shows how this equipment can be added to one corner of the trapeze, using one of the existing corner posts of the climbing frame and one additional post. The swing or trapeze can actually be placed in six different positions as indicated in Fig. 4-1.

Materials

One 4 × 4 post, 9 feet long.

One 4 × 4, 6 feet long.
Plumber's strap.
Nails.
One swing or trapeze.

Construction Method

Sink the post in concrete in the usual manner and allow the concrete to harden and cure. After the concrete has hardened, put the 6-foot 4 × 4 across the tops of the new post and the corner post of the climbing frame. Using about 30 inches of plumber's strap for each post, and a lot of nails, secure the top piece to the posts (Fig. 4-12). The top piece can also be fixed in place with pieces of wood nailed diagonally across the corners formed by the top piece and the posts (Fig. 4-13).

Attach the swing or trapeze. Details for constructing swings and trapezes are given in Chapter 7.

The last thing you need to do for the apparatus is to add a barrier between the swing or trapeze and the climbing frame (Fig. 4-11). Imagine a child playing happily in a sandbox under the frame and a second child contentedly swinging on the trapeze. From

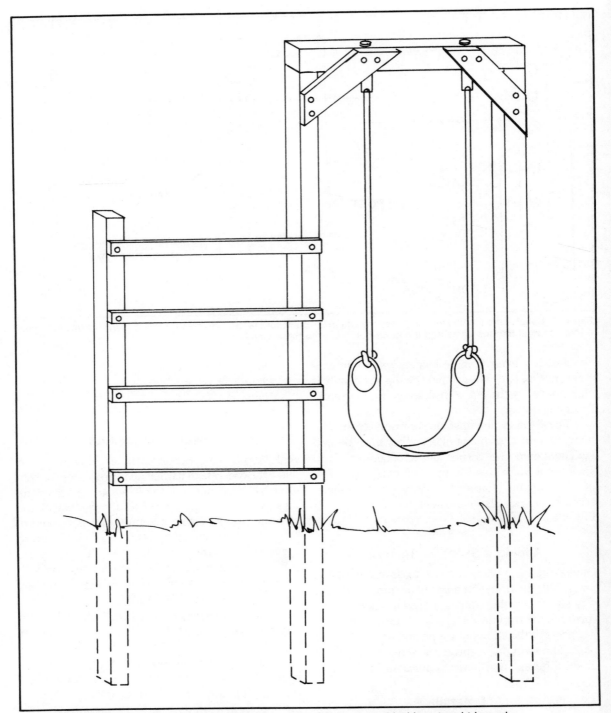

Fig. 4-13. A basic swing and ladder. The swing is made from a tire turned inside out and trimmed.

the house, to the right of the climbing frame, the mother of the family calls the child in the sandbox. This child dutifully leaps up and heads for the house and collides with the kid on the trapeze. The "wall needed here" (Fig. 4-11) should be either a solid wall or a series of horizontal boards nailed between the posts. Such boards can double as steps to the top of the frame when no one is swinging.

A STARTER LADDER AND SWING

Figure 4-13 shows a simple swing made from a tire turned inside out with a ladder alongside. I call it a starter for several reasons. It can be made relatively cheaply. It can provide plentiful play for a very young child. And, it can be added to, like our previous designs, and eventually be part of a climbing frame, swing, slide, what-have-you integrated piece of play equipment.

Materials

Two 4-inch-by-4-inch posts, 10 feet long.
    One 4 × 4 post, 8 feet long.
    One 4 × 4 piece, 6 feet long.
    Cement, sand, gravel, and water for concrete.
    20 to 25 feet of 1-inch-by-2-inch lumber.
    12 feet of 1-inch-by-3-inch lumber.
    Nails.
    One tire swing.

Construction Method

I recommend that this apparatus be set 3 feet in the ground to keep it steady and stable when the kids use the swing. In sandy soils you may also have to add supporting members at 45-degree angles (Fig. 4-14).

Smooth out all the rough spots and remove splinters from the three posts. Round off all corners and edges of the top of the 8-foot-long post, which a small child may want to hug for support upon reaching the top of the steps or rungs.

Dig the post holes and prepare the concrete as described earlier for the monkey bars. Before filling the post holes with concrete, however, you should smooth out all the rough spots, remove splinters, and round the edges of the 1 × 2 lumber that will form the ladder rungs. These will serve to hold the posts in place while the concrete sets.

Put the posts in their holes and shovel in just enough concrete to keep them upright. Twist or shift them as necessary to make their front faces parallel. Directions for shifting a post are given along with Fig. 4-4. Use a spirit level to ensure the posts are vertical. Lightly nail 1 × 2 pieces across the face of the posts, leaving the heads of the nails protruding, so that they can be drawn out easily after the concrete has set (Fig. 4-15). Lining up the posts and tacking on the 1 × 2 pieces may have moved them out of their vertical lines, so recheck with a spirit level.

Fill the post holes to the desired level, 6 inches from ground level, and settle the concrete as described along with Figs. 4-2, 4-3, and 4-4.

Make the swing as described in Chapter 7. Drill the holes in the 6-foot 4 × 4 piece for the swing hardware.

After the concrete has hardened and cured, put the ladder rungs on the posts. Use roundhead screws, flathead screws which you countersink, or nail them on as described along with Fig. 4-5.

Cut four diagonal pieces from the 1 × 3 lumber and nail them onto the 6-foot top piece. Put the top piece in place on the posts, and nail the diagonals onto the posts.

Finish the equipment with paint or wood stain. Fill the post holes with dirt. Attach the swing at the top, and turn the kids loose on the apparatus.

Adding a Climbing Frame

Figures 4-16 and 4-17 show two views of a climbing frame added to the starter swing and ladder. On the assumption that smaller children will be using the frame, I've put two guardrails around the top. The perspective in Fig. 4-16 allows me to show the solid wall along one side of the climbing frame. This prevents kids from darting out from under it and being hit by the swing. For simplicity's sake, the diagonal connecting pieces at the top corner of the swing have been omitted from the drawing on Fig. 4-16. Details for the plank shown in Fig. 4-16 are

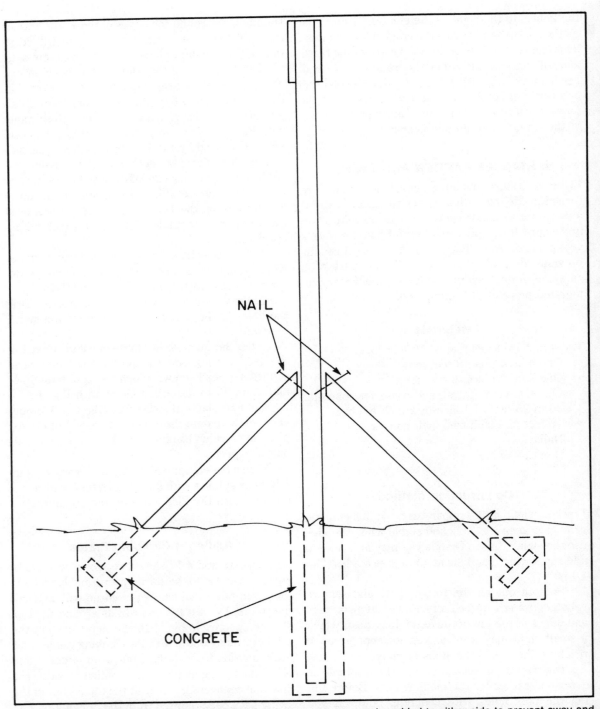

NAIL

CONCRETE

Fig. 4-14. A side view of the swing and ladder, shown how supports can be added to either side to prevent sway and to strengthen the structure.

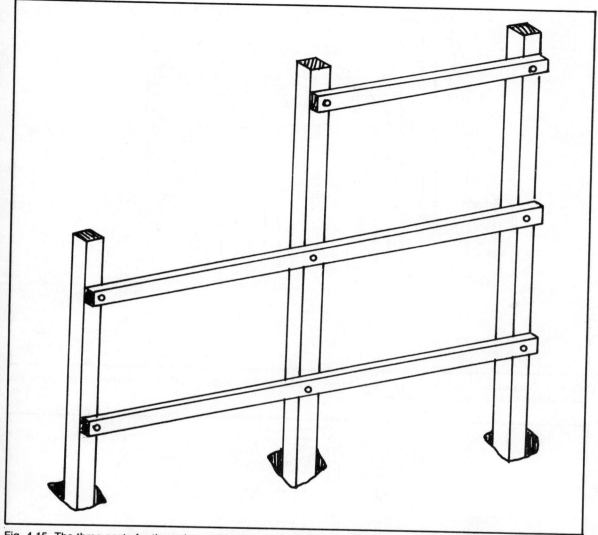

Fig. 4-15. The three posts for the swing and ladder put in place and held vertical by long pieces of wood tacked onto them. Nails aren't driven all the way in and can easily be pulled out after the concrete sets in the post holes.

given in the next chapter; it isn't fixed in place, and the kids can move it around at will. The children in Fig. 4-17 have grown, so the tire swing had been replaced by one with a more conventional seat.

Materials

Three 4-inch-by-4-inch posts, 9 feet long.

Two 2 × 4 pieces, 7 feet, 8 inches long.

Two 2 × 4 pieces, 4 feet, 4 inches long.

Three 2 × 4 supporting members, 3 feet, 9 inches long.

Lag bolts.

Nails.

Cement, sand, gravel, and water for concrete.

One 4-foot-by-8-foot sheet of exterior grade plywood.

25 or 50 feet of 1 × 2 lumber (for guard rails).

12 to 24 feet of 1 × 2 lumber (for rungs).

Fig. 4-16. The swing and ladder with a climbing frame added. Note the wall to prevent children from running under the climbing frame into the path of the swing.

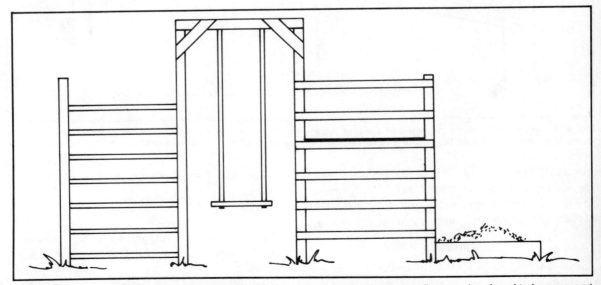

Fig 4-17. An end view of the climbing frame added to the swing, showing how a sandbox can be placed to become part of the play structure.

66

Rounded timber offcuts, sheets of plywood, or planks (for the separating wall).

Construction Method

Dig three holes for the new posts so that (Fig. 4-18) they form a rectangle using one existing post that was put in for the swing. For mixing the concrete and pouring and settling it around the posts, follow the directions given with the monkey bars.

Attach the longest 2 × 4 pieces to the posts with lag bolts (Fig. 4-18). Then nail or lag bolt the 4-foot, 4-inch 2 × 4 pieces onto the ends. The outer dimensions of the rectangle thus formed will be 8 feet by 4 feet. Put the three supporting member 2 × 4 pieces into place; nail through the rectangular frame pieces into the ends of these supporting members.

The position of the floor sheet is shown in Fig.

4-18 by lines of dashes. Although these dashed lines are shown in the center of the 2 × 4 pieces, in reality the floor sheet should go all the way to the outer edges of the 2 × 4 frame. Note that two corners of the floor sheet must have squares cut out to accommodate the corner posts. An alternative to the solid sheet floor for the climbing frame platform is described along with Fig. 4-10.

When the floor has been nailed into place, cut guardrails from the 1 × 2 lumber and attach them with nuts and bolts, screws (either roundhead or countersunk flathead screws), lag bolts, or nails driven in at an angle of approximately 30 degrees.

The separating wall indicated in Fig. 4-18 and shown in Fig. 4-16 has been made from the offcuts of pine logs, available free from a lumber mill near my home. As many of you might not have a lumber mill so conveniently located, I've suggested some

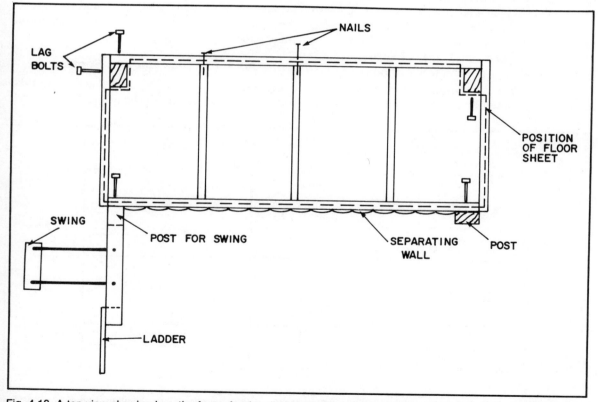

Fig. 4-18. A top view showing how the frame for the climbing frame is built onto the swing. Lag bolts are used to hold the 2-inch-by-4-inch framing members to the posts. The position of the floor sheet is indicated by the line of dashes.

alternative materials in the materials list. I dug a shallow trench, buried the bottom ends of the offcuts, and nailed the top ends to the 2 × 4 forming the frame for the climbing frame floor. If you use another material, you'll probably have to nail one or two more 2 × 4 pieces to the corner posts, parallel with the platform floor. Figure 4-19 shows two such pieces nailed in place; three sheets of plywood, salvaged from packing crates, nailed into place form part of the separating wall.

The last part to add to the climbing frame is a set of ladder rungs for the kids to climb up and get to the platform. If you put only three rungs on one end, as shown in Fig. 4-16, you'll need three pieces of 1 × 2 lumber, each a shade shorter than 5 feet; if you put three rungs on the other end as well, you'll need 3 more 5-foot pieces. That's why the materials list was deliberately vague in stating that you needed 12 to 24 feet of lumber for these rungs. They'll take a beating, so put them on with screws (roundhead or countersunk flathead), lag bolts, nuts and bolts, or nails driven down at an angle, as described with Fig. 4-5. Finish the climbing frame with paint or exterior wood stain.

I had built many things from pine offcuts, including play equipment, when a friend, who is also a real estate valuer, warned that the offcuts invite termites. I wasn't willing to dismantle all the equipment, so I bought a commercial preparation from the local hardware store and treated the ground around the equipment with it, to discourage termites from invading our playspace. It was poisonous, and I didn't like having to use it, so I chose one that would have to be consumed in vast quantities to be harmful to a child or a pet.

You don't have to avoid offcuts from timber mills or drench the earth with poisons if you want to use this free material. If you are considering using offcuts, it would pay you to call the building inspectors in your local city hall and ask them if you are likely to be troubled with termites and, if so, what you should do to prevent a termite problem. Building inspectors usually won't recommend products by brand name, but they will give you advice on the types of chemicals you will need. If you would just be wasting your money with a ground treatment, the building inspectors will tell you that, saving you time, expense, and worry.

Adding a Trick Bar and Seesaw

Figure 4-20 shows a trick bar added to the post that forms part of the ladder of the original ladder and

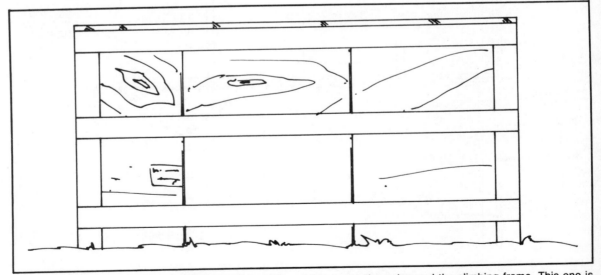

Fig. 4-19. An alternative method of building a separating wall between the swing and the climbing frame. This one is made from sides of shipping crates, which can often be obtained at little or no cost.

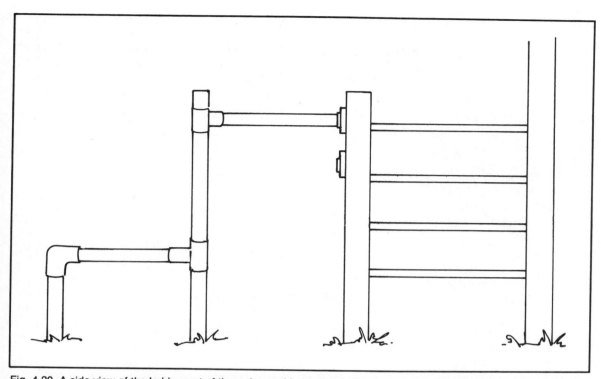

Fig. 4-20. A side view of the ladder part of the swing and ladder basic structure, showing how a trick bar can be added with one more post and the use of flanges and tees. A bar for a seesaw has been added to the trick bar post.

swing (Fig 4-13), although the swing itself is out of the picture, to the right. The trick bar fits into a flange on the post, and it is held to a steel post on the other side with a tee. The tee can be moved up and down the steel post. Flanges can also be moved up and down, but in this case the old flange was left on the post, at about the height of the third rung, and a new flange was put on when the trick bar was moved up.

Figure 4-21 shows how to attach the threaded flange to the post with screws. Do that step first; then twist the threaded end of the trick bar into the flange. The final step is tightening the tee around the post, taking care to check that the bar is level before you tighten the nut and bolt.

The seesaw bar added to the left of the trick bar (Fig. 4-20) shows only one method of adding this valuable piece of equipment to the apparatus. Figure 4-7 shows another method, which is superior, because the bars are both adjustable.

What shall you add to the apparatus the next time you have a long weekend? Look back at Fig. 4-1. Monkey bars, planks, cargo nets, and sandboxes are a few suggestions.

BUILDING A CLIMBING FRAME, PURE AND SIMPLE

The two previous designs started out with monkey bars and a ladder-swing. This design is for a climbing frame with nothing on it, to begin with, such as might be needed by a family that already has a swing set and some other equipment but needs something to give height (the vertical dimension) to the playspace.

Figure 4-22 shows a simple climbing frame with a section cut out of the floor to accommodate high-rising kids using the rope ladder. Figure 4-23 shows the same simple climbing frame, on top, but with a ladder of rungs on one side, a ladder of tires on

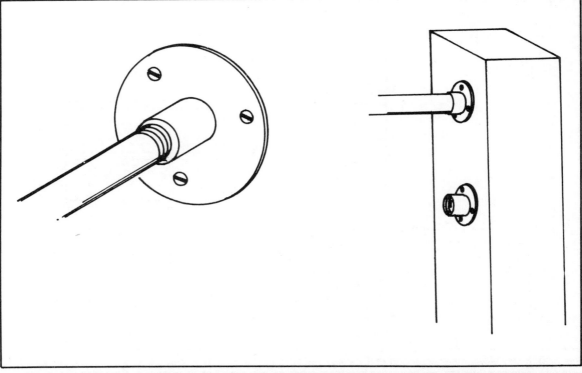

Fig. 4-21. Left: detail of a threaded flange attached to the post with wood screws, with the threaded end of the trick bar just outside the flange. Right: two flanges on a post, to indicate how the height of the trick bar can be adjusted by threading it into flanges at different levels.

another, a climbing rope on a third side, and a trick bar on the fourth side.

Materials

Four posts, 11 feet long.

Four 7-inch carriage bolts, four washers, four nuts.

Two 7-foot 2-inch-by-4-inch pieces of lumber.

Three 2 × 4 pieces, 3 feet, 8 inches long.

Sand, cement, water, and gravel for concrete.

One 6-foot-by-4-foot sheet of 3/4-inch thick exterior grade plywood (for the floor).

25 to 50 feet of 1-inch-by-2-inch lumber (for the guardrails).

50 to 75 feet of 1-inch-by-3-inch lumber (for the rungs that go around the four sides of the frame).

Nails.

Paint or stain.

Construction Method

When finished, this climbing frame will be 8 feet tall, with a floor 5.5 or 6 feet above ground level. The floor will be approximately 4 feet wide by 6 feet long.

Dig four post holes so that each is at the corner of a rectangle that measures 4 feet by 6 feet. Make the holes 3 feet deep. Mix the concrete and fill the holes, settling the concrete and straightening the posts, as necessary, and as described along with Figs. 4-2, 4-3, 4-4, and 4-5.

Bolt the 7-foot-long 2 × 4 pieces to the posts as indicated in Fig. 4-24. The top edge of the 2 × 4 pieces should be 5.5 or 6 feet above the ground, depending on your preference and the ages of the kids who'll use the climbing frame.

Nail through the 7-foot 2 × 4 pieces into the ends of the 3-foot, 8-inch pieces. You should wind

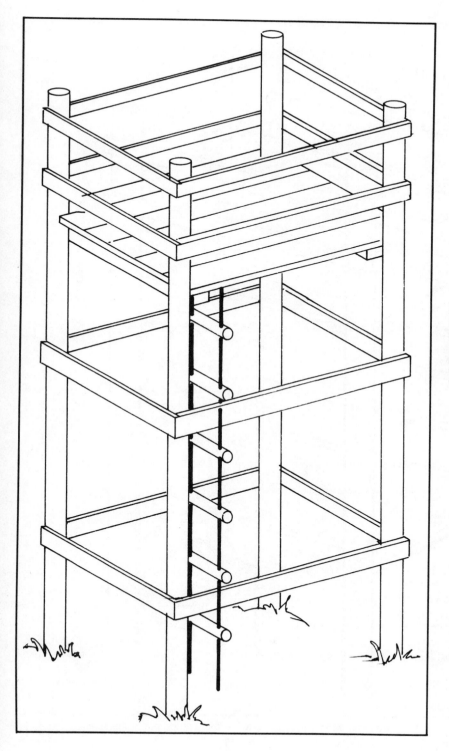

Fig. 4-22. A climbing frame unattached to a swing or set of monkey bars. The rope ladder is optional, for other means can be devised to get the kids to the climbing frame floor.

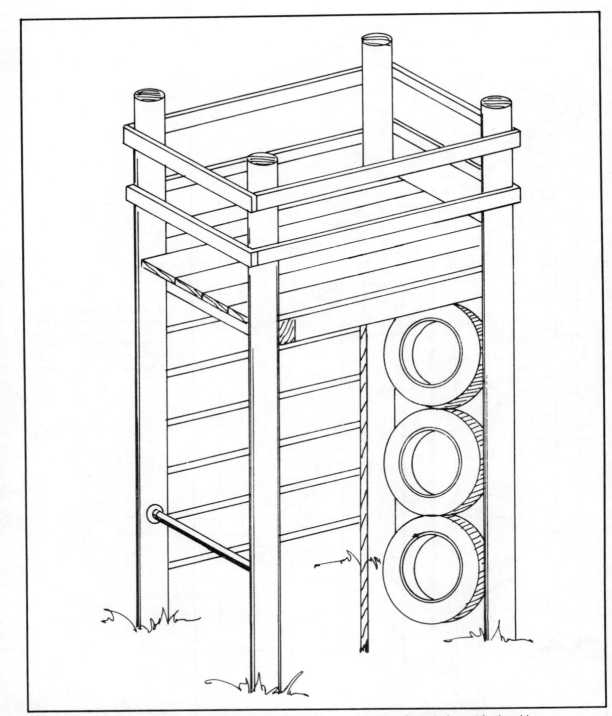

Fig. 4-23. Another independent climbing frame showing a range of devices that can be put in the sides.

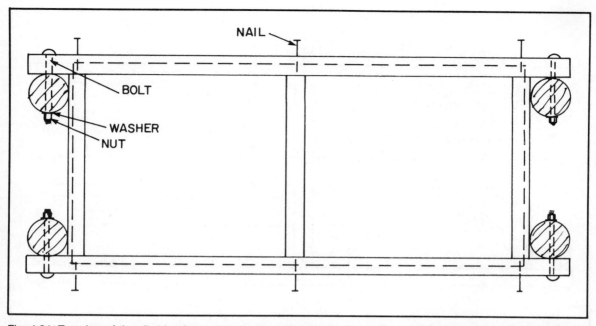

Fig. 4-24. Top view of the climbing frame showing the way to frame for the floor. The position of the floor is indicated by the lines of dashes.

up with a rectangle that measures 4 feet by 6 feet. The plywood floor can now be nailed onto this frame of 2 × 4 pieces as indicated by the lines of dashes on Fig. 4-24. The dashed lines have been drawn down the centers of the 2 × 4 pieces for convenience of illustration; in reality, the edges of the floor sheet should go all the way to the outer edges of the 2 × 4 frame.

Figure 4-25 shows an alternative method of making the floor. If you can get free or cheap planks, they can be nailed on as indicated by the lines of dots marked 1 and 2 in the drawing. You can leave space for rain water to drain off between the planks.

The materials list was deliberately vague about the amount of lumber you need for the guardrails. If you want a single rail, you'll need about 25 feet; if two rails, 50 feet. Although the rectangle measures 6 feet by 4 feet, or a minimum of 20 feet around, you need to make the guardrails about 5 feet and 7 feet long, to leave plenty of wood to nail to the corner posts. Put the guardrails on with nuts and bolts, lag bolts, countersunk flathead screws,

roundhead screws, or long nails driven in at about a 30-degree angle.

If you want two rungs all the way around the climbing frame (Fig. 4-22), the 50 feet of 1 × 3 lumber will do; 75 feet would give you three such rungs. Attach them with the same hard-wearing connections used for the guardrails, as both must withstand pulling and climbing on. If you put on two rungs, they will be approximately 24 inches apart, assuming a climbing frame floor 6 feet off the ground. Three rungs will be about 18 inches apart.

Details for the rope ladder and climbing rope are given in Chapter 5 . Details for the ladder of tires are given in Chapter 7.

Finish the climbing frame with paint or exterior stain.

A Few Possible Additions

Figure 4-26 shows three ways a plank can be used to make the climbing frame be more than just a climbing frame. Junior has his plank high enough for a slide. Susie Q puts hers on the first rung and on a packing case, and she's now pretending to be

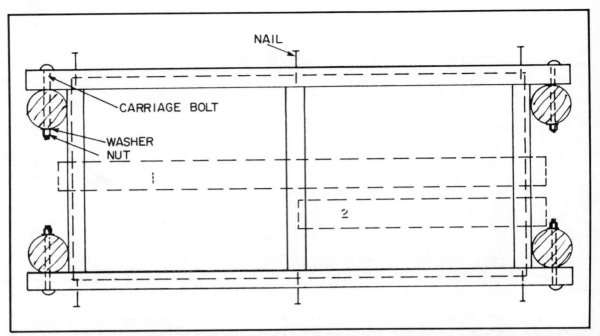

NAIL

CARRIAGE BOLT

WASHER
NUT

1

2

Fig. 4-25. Top view of the framing plan if planks will be used for the floor. The position of two planks is indicated by lines of dots.

Fig. 4-26. Three ways kids can use planks to extend their basic climbing frame with the use of planks.

an Olympic gymnast doing a beam routine. Bubsy-Boo, pacifier and all, thinks he's on the way to Mount Everest, even though the plank is on the lowest rung. Details for the planks are given in Chapter 5. You can see at the bottom ends of these three the ends of the small pieces of wood that are screwed on the underside of the planks. These pieces hook over the rungs on the climbing frame and, in Susie Q's example, over such things as packing crates.

Figure 4-27 shows how easy it is to add a table to the climbing frame. The table can be any length you want it, and it can be as wide as the rung it fits on. Make the legs as follows. Assuming a table that will sit on a rung 2 feet from the ground, cut the two leg pieces (marked L in the drawing) 24 inches long. Make the foot piece (F in the drawing) 6

inches shorter than the width of the table. Assuming this table will be 3.5 feet wide, piece F should be 3 feet long. The diagonal piece (marked D in the drawing) will have to be about 4.5 feet long to begin with and be cut to fit properly.

Nail the F piece onto both L pieces, then measure and cut the diagonal D and nail it into place. This leg structure can now be attached to the table top. Figure 4-28 shows three methods: (A) You can nail through the top down into the leg structure. (B) You can use rigid, L-shaped pieces of hardware (called bent angles) with holes cut into them for screws. I prefer this method to (A) because it will hold the structure more rigidly and it avoids holes in the table top. (C) You can glue and, using small nails, nail a piece of quarter-round lumber on the bottom of the table top; then put screws through this

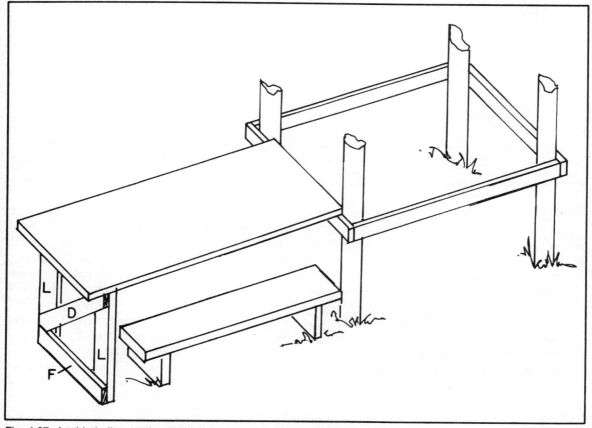

Fig. 4-27. A table built onto the climbing frame, with a bench under the table.

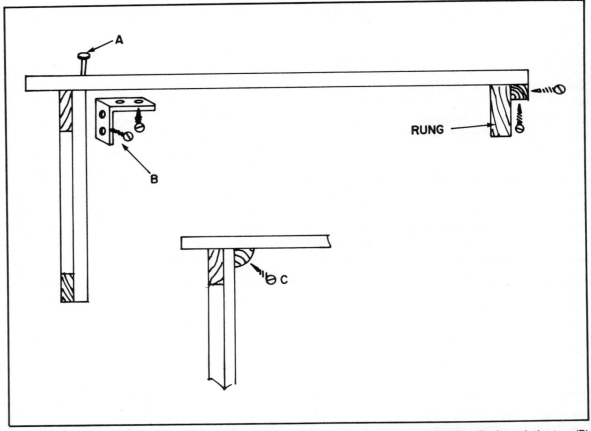

Fig. 4-28. Side view of the table, showing three methods of fixing the leg to the table top: (A) nails through the top; (B) screws and a bent angle; (C) screws and a piece of quarter-round wood. At the right side is shown the rung that is part of the climbing frame, together with a strip of wood and screws, for attaching that end of the table top to the climbing frame.

piece into the leg structure. This is my second choice for attaching the table top; it is especially attractive if you already have the quarter-round and the screws and your budget is tight.

Figure 4-28 also shows a good method of attaching the table to the rung of the climbing frame. first, glue and screw a piece of lumber onto the bottom of the table top; a piece with a square profile is shown here, but quarter-round would also do. Second, put screws through the square or quarter-round lumber into the rung of the climbing frame.

Figure 4-29 shows the simplest kind of bench you can make, two legs attached to a plank with shelf brackets. The bigger the shelf brackets, the sturdier the bench, so don't get small brackets just

because small people will be using the bench. The wide pieces of lumber shown in the top drawing of Fig. 4-29 can be expensive, so an alternative bench is shown in Fig. 4-30. The seat is formed by two planks of 1-inch-by-3-inch lumber, but other combinations are possible. For example, three pieces of 1 × 2 lumber would also do. Smaller pieces of the same lumber are screwed to the planks to keep them together, or apart, as your preference may be. If you are making a long bench, use at least three of the small pieces, as shown, especially if you are butting the long planks up against each other. The long planks can be very limber, and they will pinch the bottoms of the kids sitting on, and squirming on, them unless you have these smaller pieces in the middle as well as at both ends.

The legs of this cheaper bench can be made the same way you made the legs for the table. The legs can be attached to the bench seat with self brackets. If you have spare pieces of lumber and you want to save yourself the price of the brackets, you can use the method shown in Fig. 4-30. A piece of 2 × 4 lumber, instead of the 1 × 3 used for the bench seat, has been used to hold the planks in place. Screws driven through the leg into the 2 × 4 piece make the bench very sturdy.

Adding a Trapeze

Figure 4-31 shows how easily a trapeze can be added. Just sink another 11-foot-long post into the ground about 6 feet from an existing corner post. While the concrete is setting and curing, build the trapeze (details Chapter 7) and drill the holes in the crosspiece that will go on top of both poles.

When the concrete has set, put the top piece on with plumber's strap (Fig. 4-31). Although Fig. 4-31 shows square posts and a square top piece, you can use round posts and a round top piece and hold

it securely and safely with the plumber's strap.

The Tree and the Fireman's Pole

Figure 4-32 shows an imaginative bit of apparatus you can easily make from an old telephone pole or a log of similar diameter. Use a chain saw to cut the notches for hand and foot holds. Consult Chapter 10, "Making Your Own Designs," for the distances apart these toe-holds ought to be; the distance will vary according to the size of your child.

Figure 4-33 shows details of how the fireman's pole is attached to the tree. On the top is a front view of a 6-inch-by-7-inch piece of 1/4-inch steel plate with four holes drilled in for the lag bolts. The pipe the boy has both hands on, much like a trick bar, is welded directly onto the steel plate. The other end of this trick-bar-pipe is welded onto the vertical piece that forms the fireman's pole proper (the bottom drawing, Fig. 4-33).

The telephone pole ought to be set at least 3 feet in the ground and held in place with concrete. The fireman's pole can go 3 feet into concrete as well. As mentioned above, put the steel plate onto the telephone pole with 3-inch lag bolts.

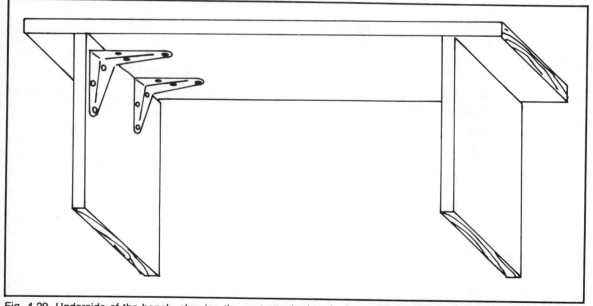

Fig. 4-29. Underside of the bench, showing the seat attached to the legs with the use of shelf brackets and screws.

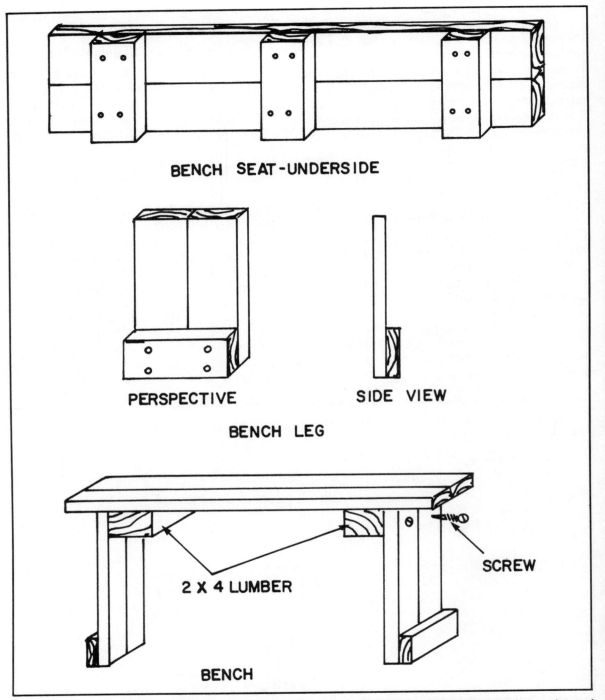

BENCH SEAT-UNDERSIDE

PERSPECTIVE

SIDE VIEW

BENCH LEG

SCREW

2 X 4 LUMBER

BENCH

Fig. 4-30. How to build an inexpensive bench. Top: the bench seat built by three short pieces and two longer pieces of scrap lumber. Middle: a perspective and a side view of the construction of a leg. Bottom: the bench assembled.

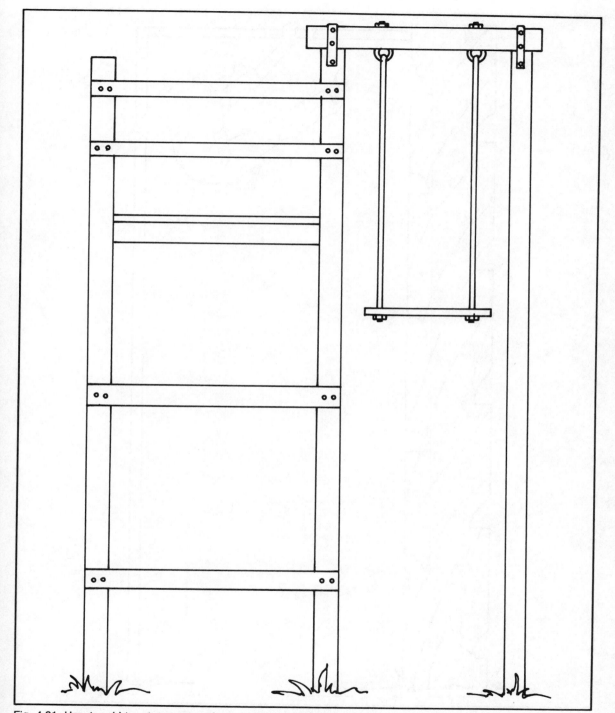

Fig. 4-31. How to add to a trapeze to a free-standing climbing frame.

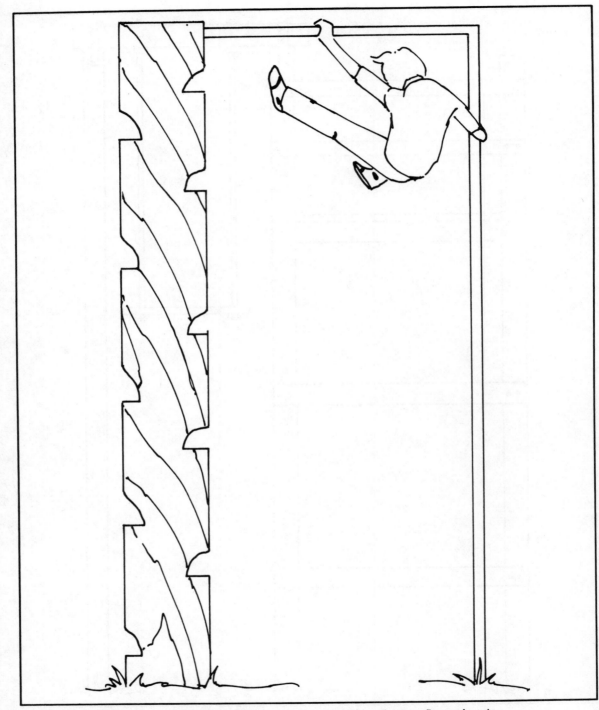

Fig. 4-32. A climbing tree, notched with a chain saw, and connected by pipe to a fireman's pole.

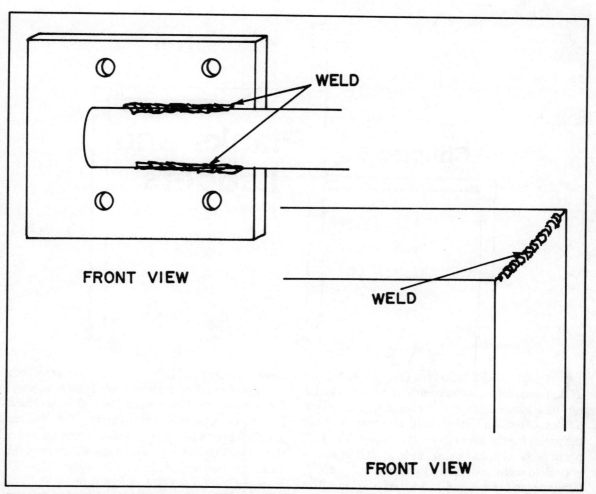

WELD

WELD

FRONT VIEW

FRONT VIEW

Fig. 4-33. Left: a plate of metal with four holes drilled in it and the horizontal bar welded on. The plate will be attached to the climbing tree with lag bolts. Right: the horizontal bar welded to the fireman's pole.

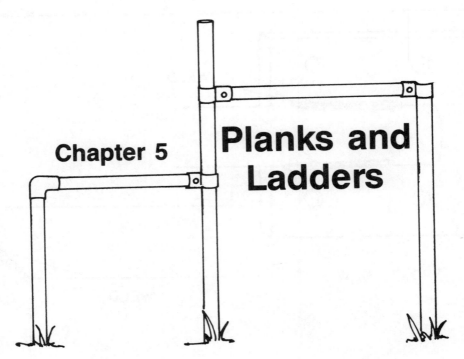

Chapter 5

Planks and Ladders

A LONG BOARD MAY BE ONLY A PIECE OF construction material to you, but to a child it can be a balance beam, a diving board, the plank pirates make their victims walk, or a pathway from the ground to the top of a climbing frame. The best plank is the simplest plank, as long as it is strong enough to withstand the uses children will put it to. The top plank shown in Fig. 5-1 is such a plank. The small pieces attached to either end form hooks to keep the plank from sliding off rungs on the climbing frame or the tops of boxes and crates. Take your supplier's advice when choosing wood for planks. Show him pictures in this book and tell him exactly how many kids may be scrambling onto and over the planks. The plank shown in the center and bottom of Fig. 5-1 is for a seesaw. It should be rigid, strong, and thick enough for two kids on either end.

Seesaws don't necessarily need handles, but if you want them they can be made in many ways. The bottom drawing in Fig. 5-1 shows a nylon rope knotted on the underside of a plank to make a handle. Figure 5-2 shows five other handle styles. Number 1 shows the sides of the plank sawn and rasped away to create hand holds. Numbers 2-5 are all end views showing three handles made from dowels and one of rope. The dowels should be 1.25 inches thick. Drill holes in them as shown in Fig. 5-8. You can get pipes precut to the proper size at your hardware store. Don't cut the rope till you have tightened the knots on the underside of the plank. Use the overhand knot described in Fig. 5-10.

THE SIMPLEST LADDER

Figure 5-3 shows part of a ladder that is the simplest, easiest ladder for the beginner. It is also strong and will last a long time if properly looked after.

Materials

Two 1.25-inch-by-3-inch pieces of wood for side rails, 6 to 12 feet long, or two 1-inch-by-2-inch pieces for side rails, 4 to 6 feet long.

1 × 2 inch wood (for rungs).

Screws.

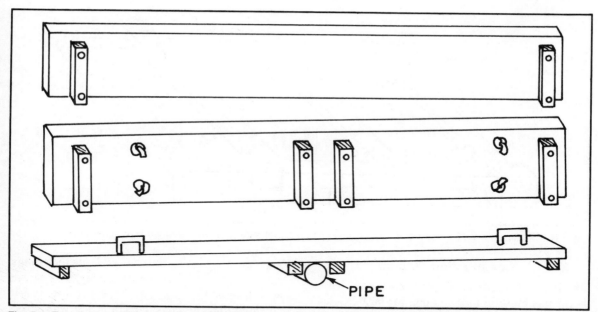

Fig. 5-1. Top: the underside of a plank, showing how two small pieces of wood should be screwed on to form "hooks" that keep the plank from slipping off climbing frames and other pieces of play equipment. Center: the underside of a plank that can be used as a seesaw as well. Bottom: the same plank shown in position on the pipe to form a seesaw. Handles are of nylon rope.

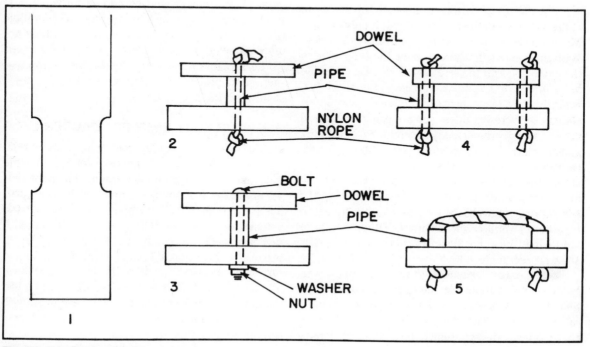

Fig. 5-2. Handles for seesaws.

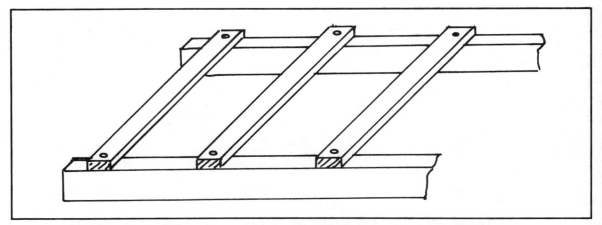

Fig. 5-3. The simplest ladder you can make—rungs laid on top of side rails and attached with screws.

Construction Method

Two kinds of side rails are listed above, one obviously for use by little folk and one for large. Consult Chapter 10 to determine how far apart the rungs should be, given the ages of the users of the ladder. Figures 10-12 to 10-14 will also give you a good indication of how long each rung should be.

Cut the rungs to size and lay each one on top of the side rails in the position it will finally occupy. Mark these positions with pencil or felt-tip pen. With the rungs still in place, mark the rungs where the guide holes for the screws will go. Drill the guide holes for the top and bottom rungs. Put these two rungs back in place, prepare the holes for countersinking the screws (unless you are using roundhead screws, which are perfectly acceptable for this job), and attach the top and bottom rungs. This will keep the side rails the proper distance apart while you attach the other rungs. If you start from one end and work toward the other, you risk attaching the second rung with the rails either slightly squeezed together or slightly spread apart. Either way, your ladder will be more in an A-shape than a neatly squared rectangle.

Some extra steps are worth considering if your ladder is going to be outside or if it is going to get heavy use. One, you can put four screws in some of the rungs. With only two screws in each rung, the ladder can eventually be distorted into a parallelogram. If you are in a hurry, you can drive long finishing nails into several of the rungs. Adding nails will be faster than driving extra screws and will serve the same steadying purpose. A second thing you can consider is putting waterproof glue between the rungs and side rails before you attach them with screws and nails. To decide if this step is necessary, have a look at the garden sheds, garages, and playground equipment in your area. Rain and variations in humidity and temperature make wood swell and shrink, and some areas are more affected than others. If parks department workers, plant nursery staff, woodsmen, groundsmen, and others in the know advise glue as a steading influence, use it.

THE NEXT SIMPLEST LADDER

Figure 5-4 shows a ladder exactly like that just described, except that the rungs are set into the side rails inside of sitting on top of them. The materials list is the same as for the simplest ladder. Figures 5-5 and 5-6 show two methods of cutting out the notches for the rungs. Both methods start out with saw cuts made parallel to each other across the entire width of the notch. If using a chisel, you should turn it bevel-side up (Fig. 5-6). Tap easily at first till you get the feel of how deeply the chisel bites; then tap with more force. You may have to smooth the bottom of the notch with a wood rasp or coarse sandpaper.

If you have a table attachment for your saw (a

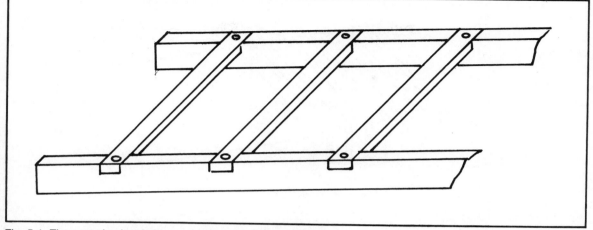

Fig. 5-4. The next simplest ladder—rungs inset into the side rails.

Fig. 5-5. Cutting notches with an electric saw. Two completed notches are shown at the handyperson's right. Notches are made by sawing a number of parallel cuts then running the board at right angles to these cuts to knock out the little ridges of wood between the cuts.

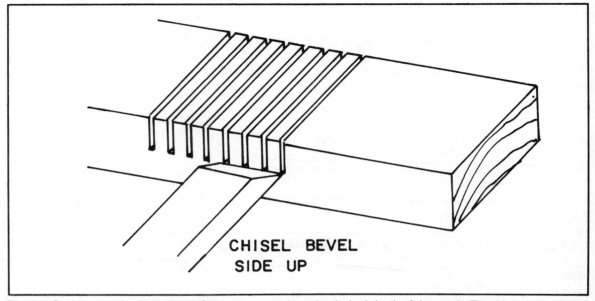

Fig. 5-6. Cutting a notch with a chisel. Saw cuts are made to the desired depth of the notch. The ridges between the cuts are then removed with the chisel.

saw driven by an electric drill is shown in Fig. 5-5), set the blade for the desired depth. Make the series of parallel cuts carefully, and don't leave more than 1/16 inch between them. Next, carefully saw out the little ridges of wood between the cuts. If you take care in this operation you can smooth out the entire notch and not have to use a rasp at all; if you don't take care, you can cut the notch too big, leave humps to be rasped off, and bend your saw blade.

When the notches have been cut, cut the rungs to size and drill guide holes for the screws. If the bottoms of the notches are rough, put in some filler, such as plastic wood, then attach the rung. As you tighten down the screws, the rungs will squeeze the excess filler out, which you can scrape off with the blade of a screwdriver or filling knife. This treatment prevents the formation of little pockets under the rungs where water can collect and decay can start.

LADDERS WITH ROUND RUNGS

Figure 5-7 shows a ladder with round rungs set all the way through the side rails. These are tricky projects for the home handy person for several

reasons. They require a larger diameter hole in the side rail than a beginner will have a bit for in his starter tool box. The diameter of the dowel must be exactly the same as the diameter of the hole; too big, and the run will slip around and be loose; too small, and the dowel for the rungs must be carefully rasped off to fit the hole. If you rasp off too much on one side, the dowel may seem to fit, but after it starts it journey through the hole you'll find it going in at an angle, which makes it bind as it goes farther in. If you can overcome these problems, go ahead and build the ladder.

Materials

Two side rails, 1.25-inch-by-3-inches by 8 to 12 feet long.

Dowels, 1.25-inch thick.

Construction Method

Cut the rails to size and drill holes for the rungs. Cut the dowels square on one end and at an angle of about 10 degrees on the other. This slanted end will help you assemble the ladder (drawing 1, Fig.

5-7). Assemble the square ends of the rungs into the side rail as shown. Then lay the slanted tip of each rung into its proper hole in the other side rail. With all rungs started in their proper holes, lay a board beside the side rail (drawing 2, Fig. 5-7) and hammer this board as shown. Put your C-clamps around the two boards to hold them together. Brace the other side rail against the side of the garage or some other solid structure. Don't hammer on one end only. You must drive the side rail onto the rungs evenly by knocking the rail on about 1/4 inch along its entire length, by frequently moving the hammer from one rung, or a spot in line with one rung, to another. When the rungs are well started in their holes, unclamp the boards. Drive the rungs the rest of the way through by hitting the first side rail, which was braced against the side of the garage. When the rungs are all the way through, rasp off their slanted edges to make the rungs flush with the side of the side rail.

Figure 5-9 shows other methods of making a ladder with round rungs. Each method involves cutting a notch for the rung. You can use the techniques described above (Figs. 5-5 and 5-6). The rungs may not fit snugly in their notches, and, even if they feel snug, they may eventually loosen enough to rotate when the ladder is set in place horizontally to be used in monkey bars. This rotation is prevented by the use of long screws (drawing 1) or long nails (drawing 2) or by short screws and a thin capping piece (drawing 3). Combinations of these methods are also possible.

Note how the rung in drawing 2 has been flattened so it will sit squarely in the bottom of the notch. This is easily accomplished if you nail together a holding device as shown in Fig. 5-8. The dotted line on the end of the dowel in Fig. 5-8 indicates the depth to go with your wood rasp to flatten the dowel. The X marked between the end of the dowel and the C-clamp is where you would drill a hole for a rope ladder.

If you live in the dry Southwest, you can use

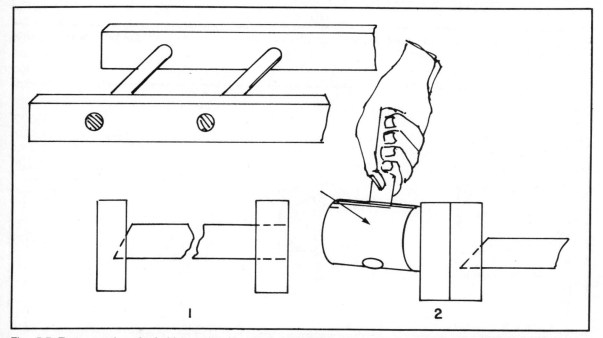

Fig.. 5-7. Top: a section of a ladder made with round rungs fitted all the way through the side rails. Rungs should be cut square on one end, slanted on the other. After the square ends are fitted into the side rails, the slanted end is started in the hole in the other side rail, as shown in 1. The side rail is then driven onto the rungs by hammering a third board, as shown in 2. When the rungs are all the way through, the slanted ends can be rasped flush with the side rail.

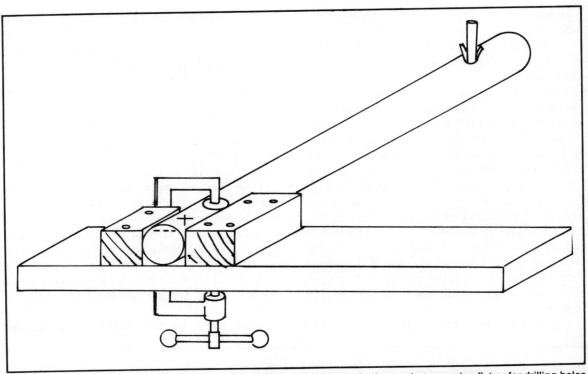

Fig. 5-8. A simple device for holding round pieces of wood, such as dowels, for rasping one edge flat or for drilling holes for rope ladders.

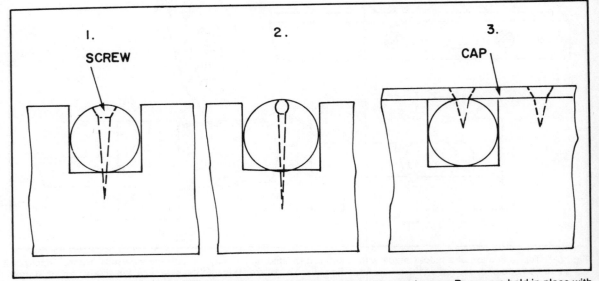

Fig. 5-9. End views showing three other methods of constructing ladders with round rungs. Rungs are held in place with screws or nails. A cap of wood as long and as wide as the side rail can be put on top.

your ladders as shown in Fig. 5-9. It is still advisable, however, and it is essential in other areas, to fill in the triangular-shaped holes between the notch and the rung. Any good filler for external use will do.

The cap shown in drawing 3 of Fig. 5-9 is a strip of wood as long and wide as the side rail and at least 1/2-inch thick. It should be put on the side rail with screws set close enough to each other to prevent gaps between the cap and rail. A screw between each rung is usually sufficient.

All of these designs are good for constructing ladders to go in monkey bars and climbing frames. Be sure to plan enough length at each end of the side rails to bolt the ladder to the posts. The distance from the posts to the first rung in the monkey bars is not really very critical, for kids very quickly start skipping rungs as they go from one end to the other.

Climbing Ropes

Figure 5-10 shows, at left, how to tie an overhand knot. A series of overhand knots in a thick rope can make a good climber, as shown in the center of Fig. 5-10. Pieces of fence post, logs, lamp posts, and other materials can be made into a climber as shown at the right of Fig. 5-10. Rope in such constructions can be thinner than that used alone.

Man-made fibers are the best, in my opinion, for play equipment. They don't rot like sisal or Manila ropes, and they are stronger. For example, rope of 1/2-inch diameter will hold about 325 lbs. if it is sisal, 3,000 lbs. if it is polyester, and 4,650 lbs. if it is polymide (or nylon). You can safely assume, therefore, that almost any polyester or polymide rope you buy will hold all the weight your kids put on it, regardless of the diameter of the rope. I saw four fair-sized kids stacked on one poor tire swing—a fifth kid tried to climb on but kept falling off for lack of hand holds—suspended from monkey bars with a single 5/8-inch-thick nylon rope. Of course, the rope had been marketed in a plastic package that said you could use the contents to pull cars and

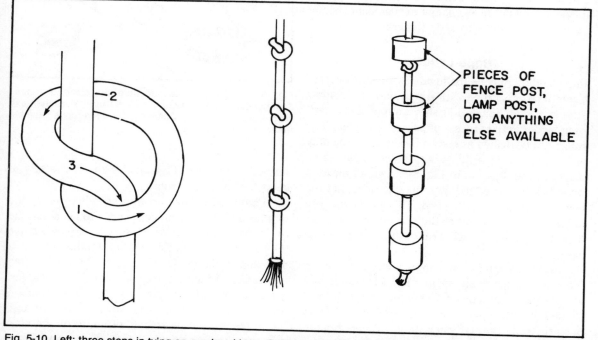

PIECES OF FENCE POST, LAMP POST, OR ANYTHING ELSE AVAILABLE

Fig. 5-10. Left: three steps in tying an overhand knot. Center: a thick rope with a series of overhands to form hand- and footholds. Right: pieces of lamp post, fence post, or even flat boards resting on overhands also give children something to rest their feet on when climbing ropes.

trucks, so I didn't hold my breath when the kids piled on the swing.

The disadvantages of man-made ropes are that some are affected by sunlight and that they become stiff with overwork and age. Nylon stretches under strains, but it recovers its strength well. Three times I had to shorten the rope holding the tire swing mentioned above. The best thing is to look at the ropes every few months to be sure they aren't fraying through anywhere and to replace them when necessary. You can stretch new rope by hanging it under a load. Sling one end over a tall branch and tie a heavy object on. Let it hang several days, moving the heavy object as necessary to stretch the entire length.

All ropes come unraveled if not looked after. You can prevent this by tying the end up tightly with string, tape, or wire. With man-made ropes you can also melt all the little fibers together with the flame of a match or cigarette lighter. You can also tie an overhand in the end of rope to keep it from unraveling, but I don't recommend it because it is big and unwieldy and because it sometimes presents an unnecessary challenge to little fingers.

Rope Ladders

Rope ladders may be made wholly of rope or from a combination of rope with rungs made from some other material. Figure 5-11 shows a rope and dowel-rung ladder in the process of being completed. The rungs can be drilled as shown in Fig. 5-8. The only pitfall may be in drilling both holes in the same plane. In the drawing in Fig. 5-8, a small piece of wood has been wedged with match sticks into the hole already drilled in one end. This will enable you to line up your drill bit at the end marked with an X so that ropes passed through the holes will be parallel.

Paint or stain all the rungs before assembling the ladder. Start as shown in Fig. 5-11, taking care to leave plenty of rope above the top rung to be tied to the limb, play house, or climbing frame. As you push the rope through each rung, tie the knots in it before putting the rope through the next rung. The third rung shown in Fig. 5-11 will have to be pushed down the ropes to meet the knot already

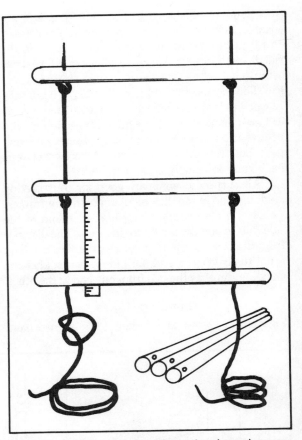

Fig. 5-11. Making a ladder from dowels and ropes. Overhands must be tied under each rung before the next rung is put on the rope. Distances between rungs must be measured carefully.

formed at the left. Tighten the knots carefully to keep the rungs horizontal.

Figure 5-12 shows an all-rope ladder being tied to a limb with two smaller ropes. You can also tie the ladder to the limb with the same rope you make the ladder from, but this entails standing on a ladder and judging from angles that are often misleading. When you buy the rope for this ladder, get five times the length of the proposed ladder. Start from the bottom and work toward the top. Leave plenty of rope at the bottom to tie onto the post or ring to keep the ladder from swinging. Then tie a double overhand. Pull it tight. Tie the next double overhand, but don't pull it tight before careful-

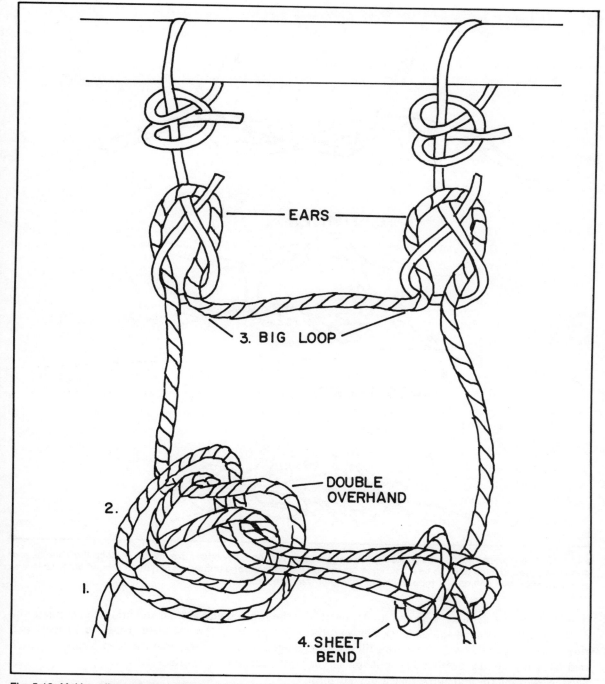

EARS

3. BIG LOOP

DOUBLE
OVERHAND

2.

1.

4. SHEET
BEND

Fig. 5-12. Making all-rope ladder. You start (1) by making the first double overhand near the end of the rope. Continue by making double overhands as far apart as the rungs are to be. At the top of the ladder (3) leave a big loop, from which the two ears can be formed. Then (4) tie a sheet bend into each loop of the double overhands to complete the ladder.

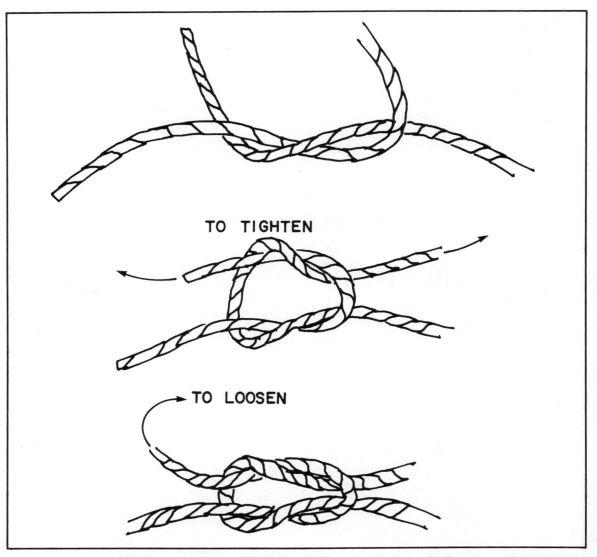

TO TIGHTEN

TO LOOSEN

Fig. 5-13. The square knot. Start by looping the ends of rope around each other, exactly as you loop the ends of your shoe laces around each other to tie a bow knot. Next, loop the ends of rope around each other a second time. To loosen a square knot, pull one end of rope back (3), then pull the ropes apart.

ly measuring the distance between knots, for this distance will determine the distance between the rungs. Continue in this way up the rope till you have tied as many double overhand-rung-loops as you need. Now bring the end of the rope around to form what is called the "big loop" (Fig. 5-12); make it big enough to form the two "ears" that will be tied to the ropes going around the limb. To complete the ladder, using the end of the rope, tie a sheet bend (step 4 in Fig. 5-12) into the loop formed by each of your double overhands.

Selecting knots

Some useful knots are shown in Figs. 5-12 to 5-17.

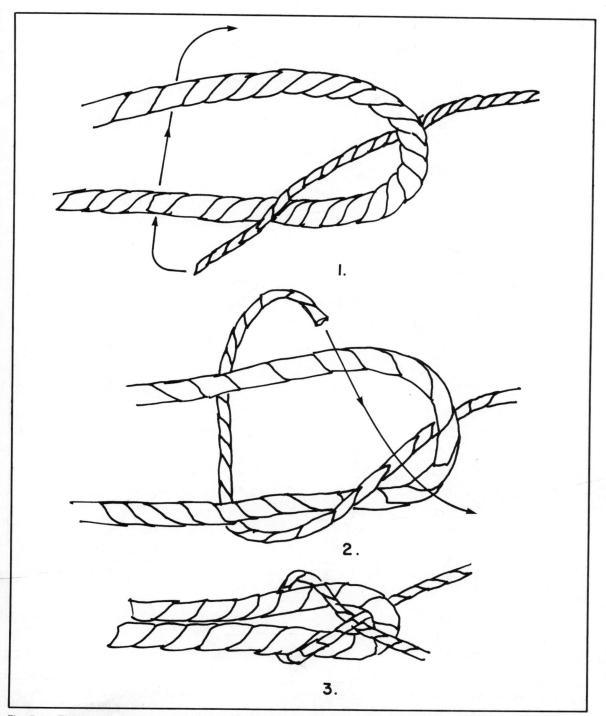

I.

2.

3.

Fig. 5-14. Three steps in tying a sheet bend, the best knot for joining ropes of unequal diameters.

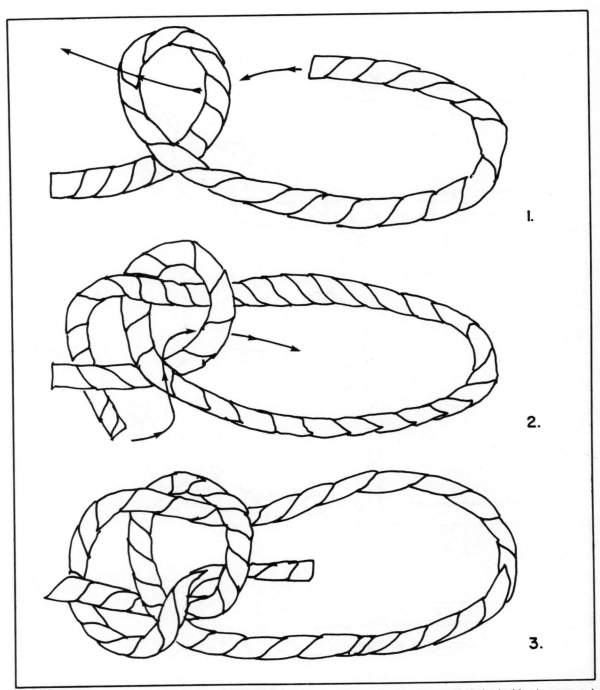

Fig. 5-15. Three steps in tying a bowline. A little story helps with this knot. (1) A rabbit in his hole decides to come out for a breath of air. (2) Outside, he nibbles a bit of grass and goes around a tree, but he hears a hound coming, so he (3) dives back down his hole.

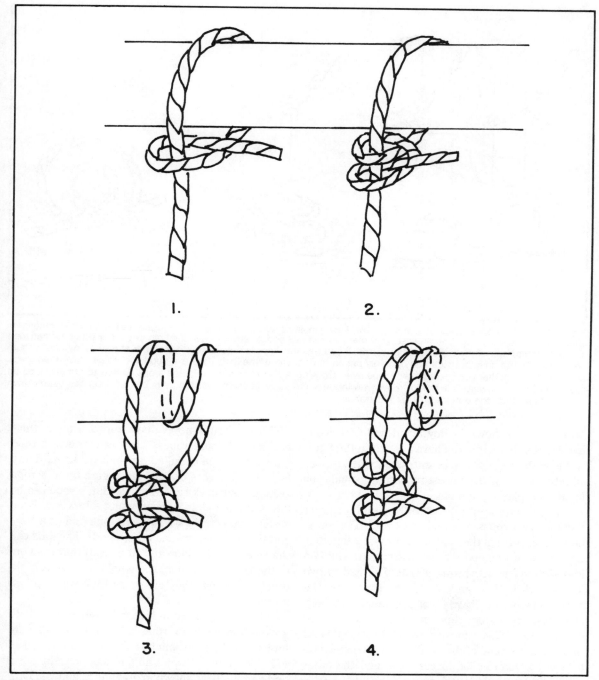

1.

2.

3.

4.

Fig. 5-16. How to tie two half hitches. Start out by making a single half hitch (1); then make another just like it (2). Two half hitches are as strong as you can make this knot, so there's no need to add a third or fourth half hitch. The drawings in 3 and 4 show a couple of twists you can give the rope to give it greater holding power while you tie the half hitches.

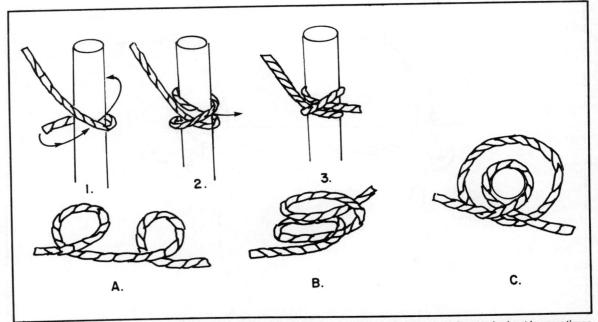

Fig. 5-17. Two methods of tying a clove hitch. This knot almost never slips, and, when the rope is wet, the knot is sometimes almost impossible to untie. The finished knot that you see in 3 should always have the limb or post or whatever between it and the other end of the rope. In other words, if you use this knot to tie a swing to the limb of a tree, the knot should be on the top, not on either side and certainly not on the bottom, of the limb. This is a good knot to tie around tent pegs and other objects that you can slip two loops over. Drawing A shows how to make the loops; B how to put one loop on top of the other. Drawing C is the top view showing how the loops fit down over the peg. The top loop has been drawn much smaller than the bottom only for illustration.

Most are also shown in Boy Scout and Girl Scout handbooks. In fact, if you have a Scout in the family, he or she can usually be entrusted with responsibility for tying the necessary knots to make or fasten the play equipment.

The square knot (Fig. 5-13) is useful for tying together two ropes of equal thickness. The sheet bend (Fig. 5-14) is the best knot for tying together two ropes of unequal diameter. Compare the two knots. Notice how the square knot is formed by two loops, with both strands of the dark rope on the same side of the lighter colored loop, and both strands of the lighter rope on the same side of the darker loop. This contrasts with the sheet bend because one strand of the smaller rope is on the bottom of the loop in the larger rope, and the other strand is on top of that loop.

A bowline is shown in Fig. 5-15. The wonderful thing about this knot is that it doesn't slip.

Children should never have ropes around their necks, even loose ropes. They can receive a rope burn if the rope is pulled off their necks hard and fast. The dangers of getting tangled up in a rope around their necks are obvious. But, a rope can be tied around a child's waist, using a bowline. Even better, you can tie a bowline in one end of a rope and tie the other around a high limb. The kids can then step into the loop and sit on it. If they hold onto the rest of the rope, the whole becomes an all-rope swing that they sit on as they would a tire swing.

The knots shown in Figs. 5-16 and 5-17 are both good knots for tying rope ladders or swings onto limbs. A single half hitch is shown in drawing 1 of Fig. 5-16; alone it won't hold much, but add a second half hitch, as shown in drawing 2, and you have a knot that won't slip and that will hold as long as the rope stays good. A third half hitch is unnecessary; two half hitches will form as strong a knot as you need. If you are ever suspending something heavy by yourself, without someone to hold the weight while you tie the knot, loop the rope around the limb as shown in drawing 3 or 4 before you tie the half hitches. Loops parallel to each other, as in 3, look neater, but loops wrapped over each other as in 4 hold better.

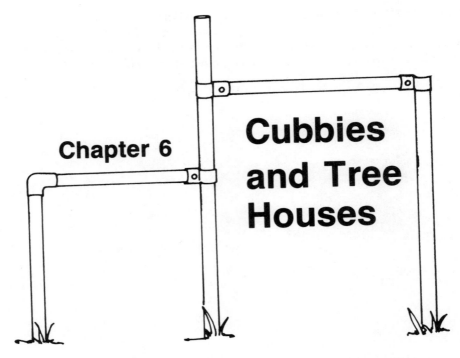

Chapter 6

Cubbies and Tree Houses

P LAYHOUSES FURNISH CHILDREN WITH places to get away from others for a while, to store some of their play furniture, to visit or to invite their friends to visit, and to carry on with the important business of experiencing life. Children should be encouraged to get on with this important function even before the cubby or playhouse is built, for the suggestion of a cubby is enough to get them into the activity. They will make their own cubbies from limbs you trim from trees or from sticks and brush in parks and reserves and along creek beds. You can often make a 5-minute cubby with an old blanket or quilt tied or pinned or tacked to a tree or fence or poles of a patio and stretched out to the ground and held in place with bricks or large stones. Later on, when you have the time, energy, and money, you can build a more permanent cubby. Several designs follow.

AN A-FRAME CUBBY

Figure 6-1 shows an A-frame cubby that is fairly easy to build, is sturdy, and can contain a surprising amount of room. The sturdiness comes from its triangular frame; it cannot be distorted. The frame can be covered with planks or with sheets of plywood. The disadvantage of the A-frame is that it requires considerable height to leave enough headroom for even fairly small kids. Figure 6-2 shows half of the space available in A-frames of three heights, 6, 7, and 8 feet. The total width of the cubbies would be double the amounts shown, that is, 6, 7, and 8 feet. Note that a cubby 6 feet high and 6 feet wide at floor level leaves little more than 2 feet of horizontal head room for a three-year-old, about 1 1/2 feet for a six-year-old, and 6 inches for a nine-year-old. Put another way, three year olds and six year olds can walk the length of a 6-foot-by-6-foot A-frame cubby, but nine year olds might bump their heads even on the highest part of the cubby. Increasing the width of the cubby won't appreciably increase the head room, so be sure to plan a cubby that is tall enough to accommodate your childrens' heights.

I recommend using 2-inch-by-6-inch timbers for the sides and 2-inch-by-4-inch timbers for the bottoms of the frames. Figure 6-3 shows how long these

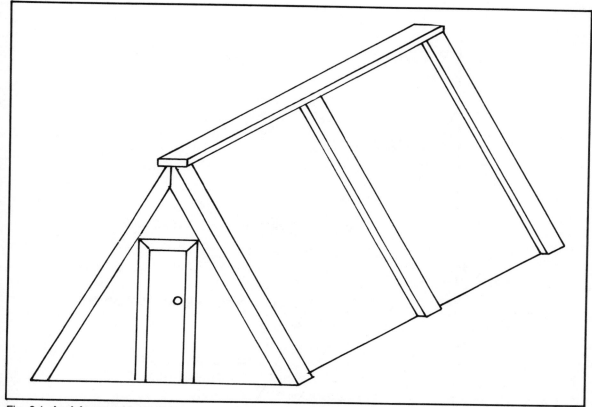

Fig. 6-1. An A-frame cubby house.

2 × 6 and 2 × 4 pieces must be, assuming inside dimensions of 6 feet wide by 6 feet high, 7 feet wide by 7 high, and 8 by 8. To make five frames, you'll need ten pieces of 2 × 6 and five of 2 × 4 timber.

Lay three pieces in place on the floor of your patio or garage or in the back yard and mark the 2 × 6 pieces so that they will butt together after being cut (Fig. 6-4). You can nail through one 2 × 6 into the other or connect them with triangular pieces of plywood, as shown, provided the plywood is at least 1/2 inch thick. The 2 × 4 bottom piece should be laid in place on these 2 × 6 pieces, marked, cut, and then nailed to them as shown in Fig. 6-5.

Preparing the Foundation

When the five frames are finished, you are ready to assemble the cubby, but you should prepare the foundation first. Provided you have good drainage away from the cubby site, you can put the cubby right on the ground. If you are worried about drainage, build the site up so that the cubby sits several inches higher than the rest of the yard. If the site is subjected to strong winds, there are several things you can do to anchor the cubby. You can sink four treated posts in about 18 inches of concrete in the corners and then bolt the 2 × 4 bottom frame pieces to them. Another thing you could do is to nail galvanized chicken wire over the 2 × 4 bottoms, but don't stretch it tight. Step on the wire or press it down with your hands so that most of it is lower than the tops of the 2 × 4 frame bottom pieces. Next pour a concrete floor in the cubby, leveling it between the bottoms of the frames by dragging a board across the top of the wet concrete while pressing the board down onto the bottom frame pieces.

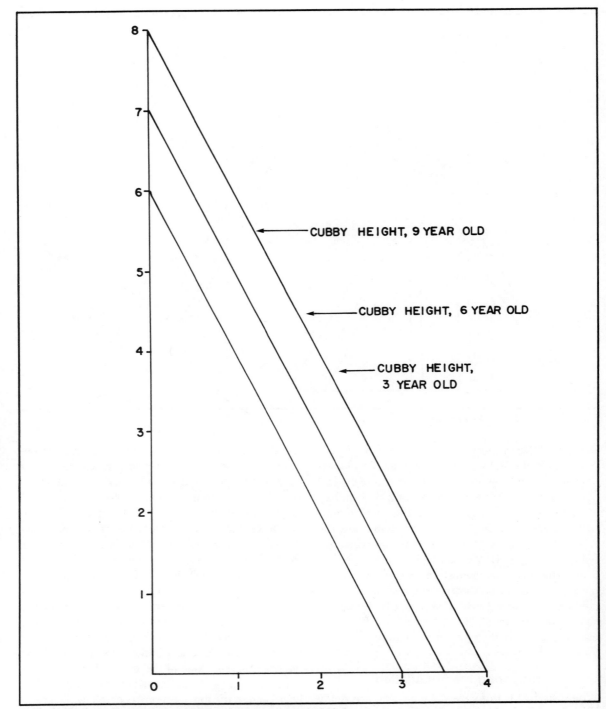

Fig. 6-2. Head room available in A-frame cubbies of various heights.

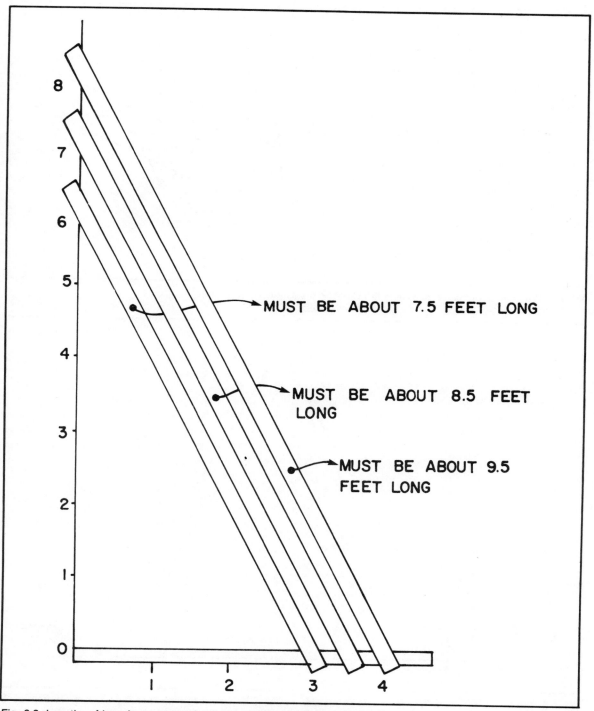

Fig. 6-3. Lengths of boards necessary for A-frame cubbies of various heights.

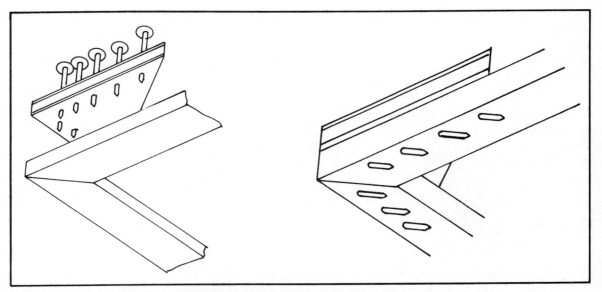

Fig. 6-4. Detail of one method for joining the two 2 × 6 side pieces at the top.

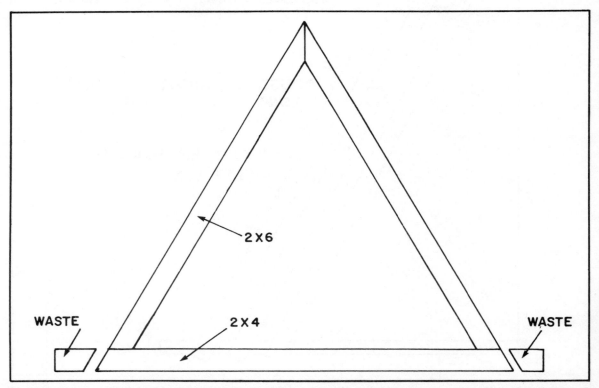

2 X 6

WASTE   2 X 4   WASTE

Fig. 6-5. The 2 × 4 bottom piece can be laid on the side pieces and marked so that when the waste piece from each end is removed, the bottom piece fits flush against both side pieces.

Of course, this assumes the frame has been assembled and is in place, so we had better consider that step next. The anchoring methods are illustrated in Figs. 6-7 and 6-8.

Squaring the Frames

Figure 6-6 shows the four frames held in place by two 9-foot boards lightly tacked onto each frame. As the cladding is nailed on, the cubby will become more and more rigid, and the 9-foot boards can eventually be removed. You can start the nails in these boards before attaching them to the first frame. Just remember not to drive the nails all the way into the frames, so that you can easily draw them out to remove the boards later.

Covering the Frames

These cubbies can be covered with planks or sheets of plywood. Some friends had a big stack of 5-foot-long, 1/2-inch-by-5-inch planks from an old fence around their back yard. The planks were well weathered but not rotten, and they covered the A-frame cubby beautifully when nailed onto the frames (part A of Fig. 6-9). If you have access to such planks, you can cover your cubby in the same way. Start at the bottom and work toward the top, using long nails, driven in at angles, as shown. Parts B, C, and D show, respectively, shiplap, chamfer board, and tongue-and-groove dressed lumber, all of which are used to cover houses and cubbies. Few people nail shiplap on incorrectly, but an absent-minded handy person can put chamfer board or tongue-and-groove on upside down. Turn Fig. 6-9 upside down for a moment, and you'll see how rain can run down into the grooves and next to the framing 2 × 6 pieces if the cladding boards are nailed on incorrectly.

If you use planks to clad the cubby, the distances between the frames is not too critical. If you want to use sheets of plywood, however, the distances are critical and the frames must be as square as you can get them. Figure 6-10 shows the distances between five frames to be clad with plywood of standard widths. Going from the top of Fig. 6-10 down, note that a sheet of plywood 8 feet long could go from

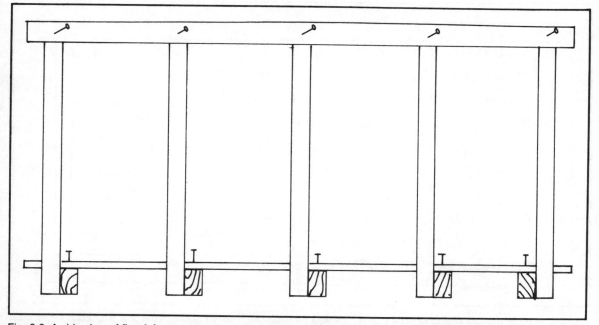

Fig. 6-6. A side view of five A-frames squared up and held in place by two long boards, one tacked on near the top and the other tacked onto the bottom 2 × 4 pieces.

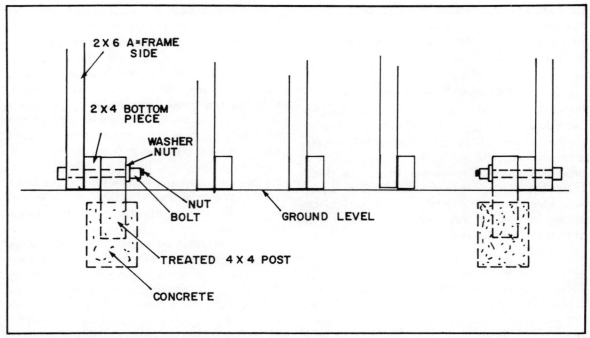

Fig. 6-7. Detail showing one method of anchoring an A-frame cubby.

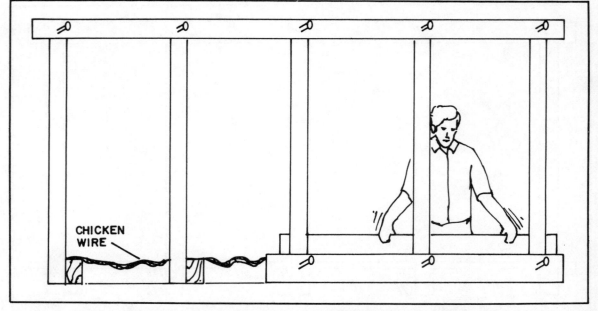

Fig. 6-8. Another method of anchoring a cubby. Chicken wire has been nailed between the 2 × 4 bottom pieces then covered with concrete. The handyperson is pulling a board across the tops of the bottom pieces to smooth the surface of the concrete. Note the board tacked onto the bottom of the A-frames to prevent the concrete from spilling out the sides.

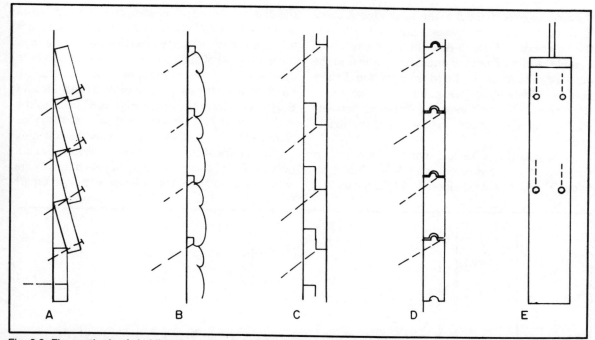

Fig. 6-9. Five methods of cladding the cubby. A-D show profiles of planks dressed in various ways and how they should be nailed to the A-frames; E shows a board covering the seam between two plywood sheets.

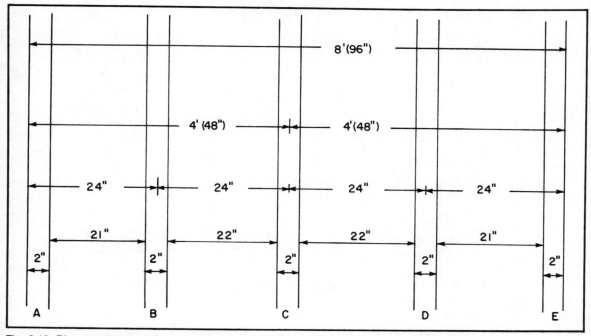

Fig. 6-10. Distances between five A-frames to be clad with plywood sheets of various widths.

the outer edge of frame A to the outer edge of frame E. Next, two 4-foot-wide sheets are used, one from the outer edge of frame A to the middle of frame C, and the other from the middle of frame C to the outer edge of frame E. Third from the top, I show how four 2-foot-wide sheets should be nailed onto the frames. Finally, I show the distances between the framing pieces, assuming each to be two inches wide.

A standard 2 × 6 is less than two inches thick; therefore, the distances between A and B and between D and E will be closer to 21.75 inches and

the distance between B and C and between C and D will be closer to 22.75 inches. I point this out not to confuse you but to warn you that measuring from the inner edge of one plank to the inner edge of the next is not the way to measure properly. Instead, measure from the outer edge of A to the middle of B or C and from the outer edge of E back to the middle of D or C. That way you guarantee that your planks will have frames to rest on and be nailed to.

If you use sheets of plywood to clad your cubby, you should cover the joints between the sheets with another board to keep rain out of the joint (part

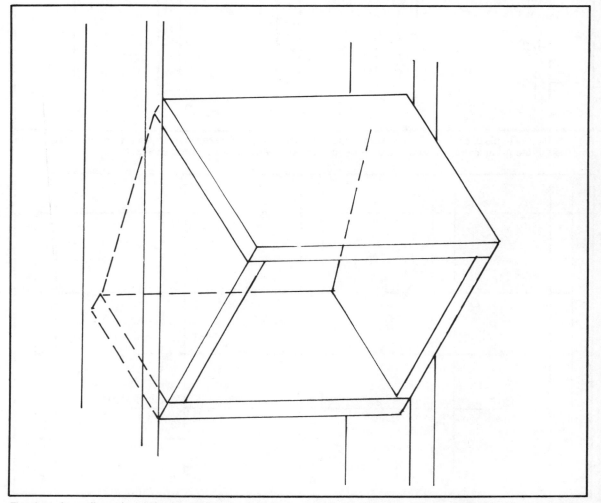

Fig.. 6-11. An easily made wooden box that can be nailed between side members of an A-frame to hold a ready-made window.

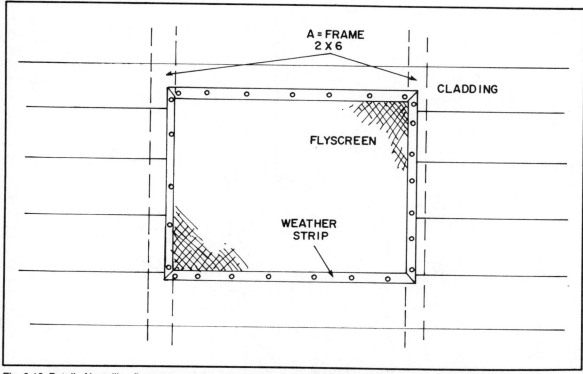

Fig. 6-12. Detail of installing fly screen over a window formed by omitting part of the cladding on the side of the A-frame cubby.

E of Fig. 6-9). The covering board is shorter than the joint for the purposes of illustration only. Once the sides of the cubby have been covered, the structure will be rigid and self-standing, so you can turn your attention to a door in one end and windows in the other.

Installing Windows

In the discussion above, I assumed that the sides of the cubby would be windowless. This doesn't have to be so. Hardware stores and timber dealers often carry a variety of sizes of ready-made windows, and some can be fitted into your cubby if you plan the space for them before hand. Nail the cladding on before installing the windows. The windows can serve the purpose of shelves, or their sills can be used as shelves. Because the width of the cubby decreases as it goes up, some means of providing shelf space without further decreasing the width of the cubby is welcome. Figure 6-11 shows one way

to achieve this aim. It is a box made of planks or sheets of plywood. The top slants down to allow rain to run off. The bottom serves as a shelf. The box should be built to accommodate a ready-made window, nailed into place between two 2 × 6 framing pieces, and the window installed last. The size shown in Fig. 6-11 is hypothetical and was made to fit the illustration. Your window box-frame might be many times taller than the one shown here.

Figure 6-12 shows a screened window that can be installed with almost no fuss and bother. You simply leave the space for it. Cut the fly screen to be slightly larger than the window. The weather strip can be of several sorts, but I recommend aluminum with a plastic bead down one edge to help ward off errant rain drops. Aluminum is easily cut with a hack saw, but you should take care to keep it as flat as possible, for once it is bent it is difficult to get it as straight as it originally was. Get aluminum strips with holes already cut for the nails or screws.

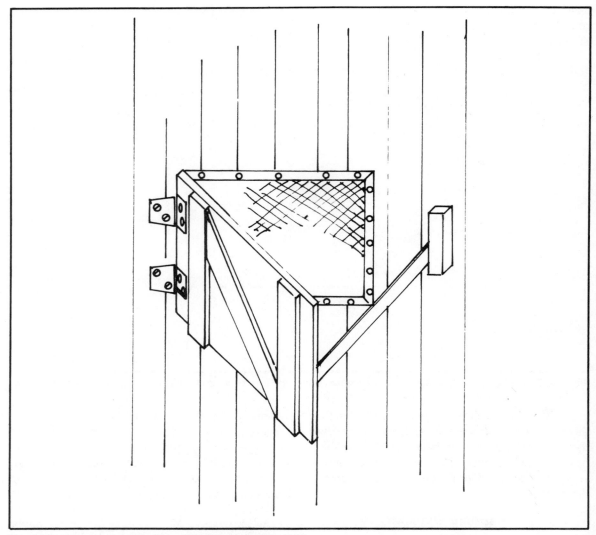

Fig. 6-13. A simple cover for the window shown in Fig. 6-12.

Figure 6-13 shows a cover that you can make to close the window when it looks stormy. A hook on the cover and an eye on the cubby side might be a good idea to keep the cover down in strong winds. The cover doesn't have to be made of three planks, as shown, or from any planks, for that matter. You can make it from a single sheet of plywood. However you make it, the Z-shaped reinforcing pieces are an essential to keep the cover flat. Several sorts of hinges will do to hold the cover in place.

Some fancy T-hinges that wrap over the end of the cover are shown, but plain T-hinges would do as well.

Figure 6-14 shows a simple frame you can nail together and fit into the back frame of the cubby to take two or three windows. Windows that are hinged at the top and swing out from the bottom, similar to the cover described above, work well in this sort of frame. Such windows are good for hot climates, for they project out into the breeze and help redirect it into the cubby. Windows that go up and down don't reach out into the breezes in the same way.

Cut the three crosspieces the same length so that they will fit between the long pieces and butt against them. Nail through the long pieces into the ends of the shorter ones. If you make this frame from 2-inch-by-2-inch timber, it will be strong enough for the windows, and it will nicely finish the end of the cubby frame. When the window frame is nailed into place (bottom of Fig. 6-14), the 2 × 2 pieces will be in the same plane as the 2 × 6 members of the cubby frame. This will enable you to nail on the cladding in a nice, smooth, easily flat-

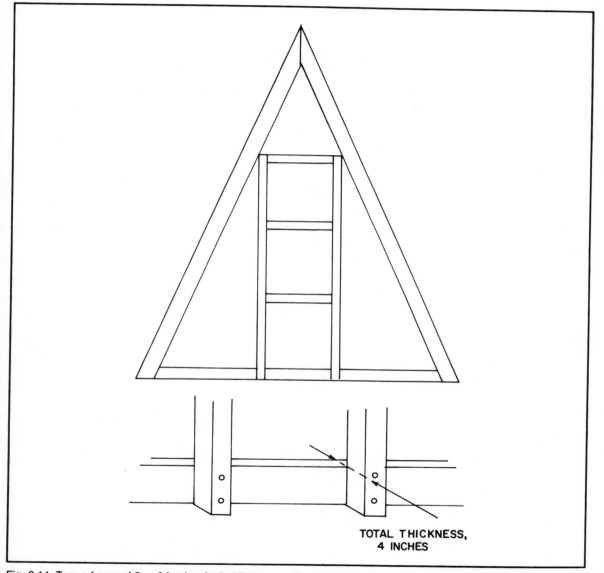

TOTAL THICKNESS,
4 INCHES

Fig. 6-14. Top: a frame of 2 × 2 lumber for holding two or three ready-made windows. Bottom: detail of how the frame fits flush against the 2 × 4 bottom piece of the A-frame.

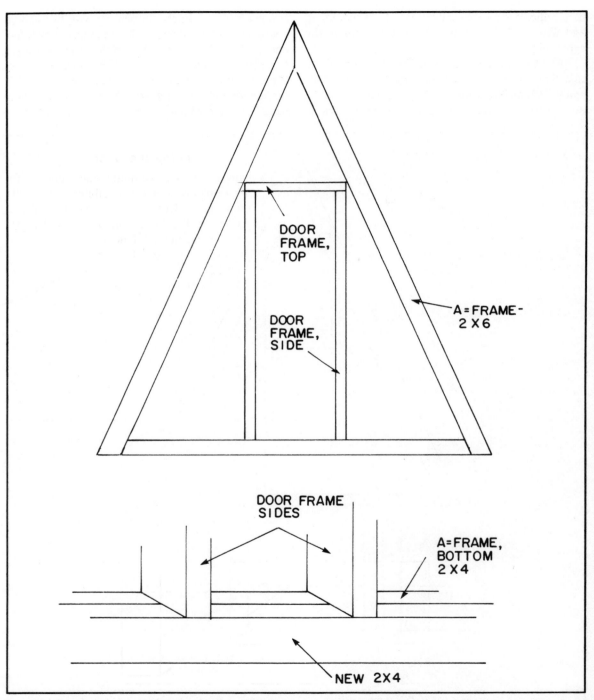

Fig. 6-15. Top: a door frame of 2 × 4 pieces set in place in the A-frame. Bottom: detail of how the door frame fits on the A-frame's 2 × 4 bottom piece and on a new 2 × 4 piece nailed to it.

110

tened plane. Swing-out windows aren't, of course, the only type of windows that can be used in window frames of this type. Nor do you have to confine yourself to two or three small windows. One wide swing-out window, a wide window that slides open horizontally, or even a long window that slides up and down in either a wood or an aluminum track would also do well in the end of the cubby. The 2 × 2 frame will suffice for most applications, but if you have an old window framed in wood almost as thick as your 2 × 2 frame, you'll have to modify your plan and use a 2 × 4 frame. It is as easily made, and it is what we recommend for installing the door.

Putting in the Door

Figure 6-15 shows a door frame made of 2 × 4 lumber set in place on the bottom 2 × 4 of the A-frame and another 2 × 4 nailed to it. The figure is drawn to scale and shows how narrow the door must be to get the necessary height. Better still, refer to Fig. 6-2 and lay a ruler at various places on it. You can barely squeeze a 2-foot-wide-by-5-foot,8-inch door into a cubby with a maximum inside height of 8 feet. You can make the door wider by lowering it, but don't make it so low that the kids

will bump their heads coming and going. Finally, consider what you want to put into the cubby before you completely close up both ends. Tables and chairs can usually be turned on their sides and maneuvered through narrow openings, but more solid pieces, like model refrigerators and cooking ranges, might better be moved into the cubby before the door frame is installed.

Finding the Door

With really good luck you might find a door to fit the cubby. Don't overlook the possibilities of installing two small doors, Dutch farmhouse fashion, if you can find two suitable doors from, say, an old wardrobe or storage cabinet. Such doors put on with fancy hinges might set your cubby off and make it the envy of the neighborhood. If you have to build your own door, Fig. 6-16 shows a good design. It is made from good quality tongue-and-groove lumber nailed onto a big reinforcing Z.

Figure 6-17 shows a cut-away view from the top. The top of the door frame has been cut away to allow us to look at how the door fits between the 2 × 4 door frame sides. The pieces of cladding will be nailed to these sides on one end, and to the 2

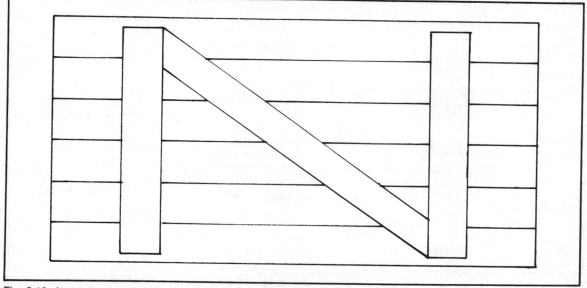

Fig. 6-16. An easily made door for the A-frame cubby.

× 6 A-frame side pieces on the other. The stopper strip is a long strip of wood nailed to the inside of the door frame for the door to stop against. Without it, the door would just keep on swinging into the interior of the cubby.

Figure 6-18 gives a side view of the door and door frame in place with several other structural details shown as well. From the bottom, we see the A-frame 2 × 4 with the new 2 × 4 flush up against it. Note that the grain of the new 2 × 4 is shown X-ray fashion in dotted lines because, from this view, we can't actually see the new piece because it is behind the 2 × 6 A-frame side member. Similarly, note how you can see half of the 2 × 4 piece that forms the top of the door frame and that the 2 × 6 A-frame side member hides the other half. The side of the door frame is actually sitting on both 2 × 4 pieces at the bottom, but this is better seen in Fig. 6-15 than here. The plywood plate at the top of this figure is that triangular piece shown in Fig. 6-4 to hold the two 2 × 6 side members together at the top. Cladding of planks is shown, but it can, of course, be of plywood sheets.

Make and install your door in this order. Nail the new 2 × 4 piece to the A-frame bottom 2 × 4 piece. Nail the three pieces of the door frame together and set it in place; nail it to the two 2 × 4

pieces it is sitting on. Tack a long board to both A-frame 2 × 6 side members and the door frame top to hold the door frame in place. Starting from the bottom, nail on the cladding. When you reach the long piece that you tacked on to hold the door frame in place, you can simply remove it, for the cladding will now be holding the door frame in place. When all the cladding has been installed, make or cut your door to size and install it with hinges (Fig. 6-17). Install the stopper strip (Fig. 6-17), door handle hardware, and the trim on the outside to frame the door nicely.

Finishing the Corners

As you nail on the cladding to the door and window ends of your cubby, you may cut the boards parallel with the 2 × 6 members (top of Fig. 6-19). Coming down the left side of Fig. 6-19, however, you can see how boards not quite long enough to fit all the way to the outer edge of the 2 × 6 members have still been made to cover the required space. If you compare the piece of waste cut off the cladding piece at the top with that cut off the piece of cladding at the bottom, you'll see how the bottom piece, although short, still suffices.

When the cladding has been nailed onto all four sides of the cubby, the corners should be finished

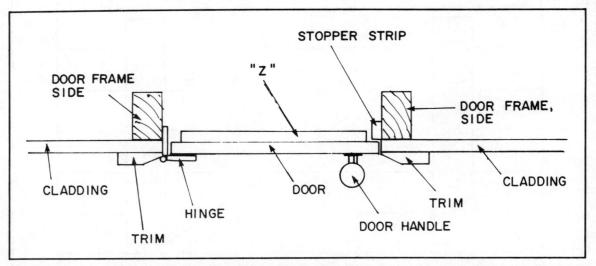

Fig. 6-17. A cut-away view from the top showing how the door fits into the frame and placement of the cladding, trim and hinges.

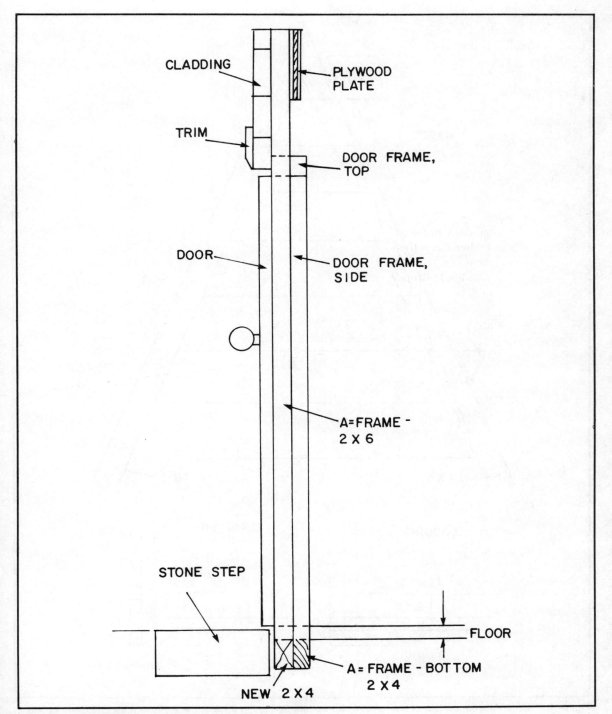

CLADDING

PLYWOOD PLATE

TRIM

DOOR FRAME, TOP

DOOR

DOOR FRAME, SIDE

A=FRAME - 2 X 6

STONE STEP

FLOOR

A = FRAME - BOTTOM 2 X 4

NEW 2 X 4

Fig. 6-18. A side view of how the door fits into the A-frame.

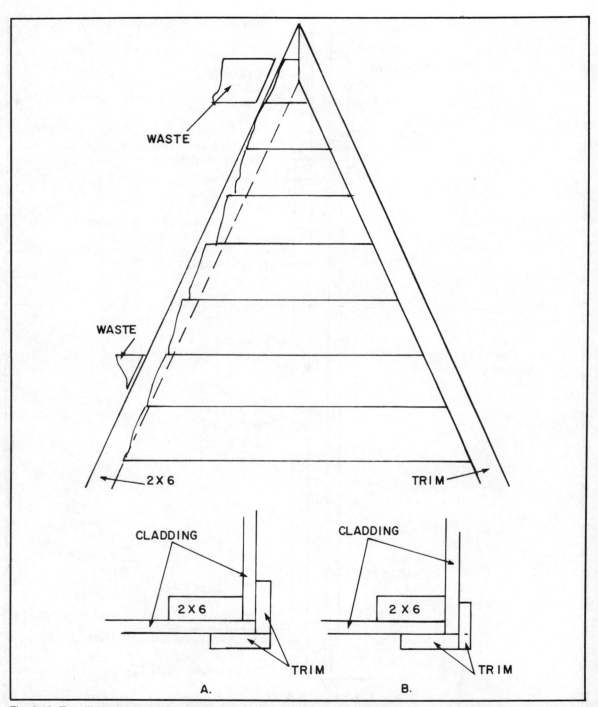

Fig. 6-19. Top: illustration, on left, of how planks can be trimmed at the ends of the A-frame cubby. Bottom: details of how trim should be nailed onto the corners to cover seams formed by cladding on sides and ends of the A-frame cubby.

with trim to make them neat and tidy and to help keep out rain. Two pieces of trim are needed for each corner. Nail them on as shown at the bottom of Fig. 6-19. Part A assumes that the side cladding has come just up to and flush with the edge of the 2 × 6 side member; part B shows the side cladding as slightly overshooting the edge of the 2 × 6 side member. Nail on the trim as shown, to cover the joint where one piece of cladding butts against the next.

Sealing the Top

Figure 6-20 shows three methods of sealing the top of the A-frame cubby to keep out rain, snow, or blowing sand or dust. At the top we see the end view of a piece of roofing iron that can be obtained from building supply houses and nailed on with widehead nails. This drawing shows the sides of the cubby clad with plywood; the cladding on the end and the trim have been omitted from the drawing for the sake of illustration only. When you seal the top of your cubby, do so only after installing all the cladding and the trim.

The cladding and trim have also been omitted from the drawing in the middle of Fig. 6-20 for the sake of illustration only. This shows an inexpensive

way of sealing the top of the cubby, assuming you have a free or low-cost supply of boards and sponge rubber or a similar material. Because the rubber will deteriorate rapidly in the sun and weather, this is the least desirable method of sealing the cubby. Nevertheless, over a short term, it works satisfactorily.

The top and middle drawings show how the cladding tends to flatten out the top of the A-frame cubby, taking the edge off the tip formed by the two 2 × 6 side members. The bottom drawing in Fig. 6-20 shows the trim nailed onto the end of the cubby, cut to fit the profile formed by the cladding. The top of the cubby is then capped with a plank nailed along its length. If there are big cracks between the top of the cladding and this capping piece, they can be filled with butyl mastic.

Installing a Floor

If you poured a concrete floor as one means of anchoring your cubby against strong winds, you might consider covering the concrete with a piece of linoleum or vinyl floor covering, floor tiles, or a piece of carpet. If you did not pour in concrete, you can put in a wooden floor by nailing it on to the 2 × 4 bottom pieces of the A-frame (Fig. 6-18). The floor

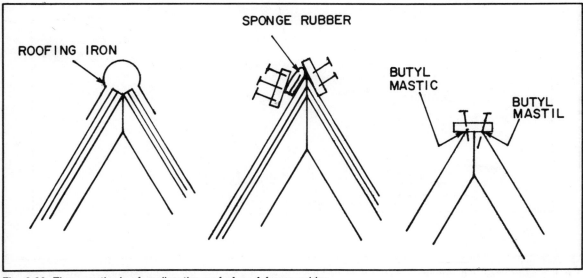

Fig. 6-20. Three methods of sealing the roof of an A-frame cubby.

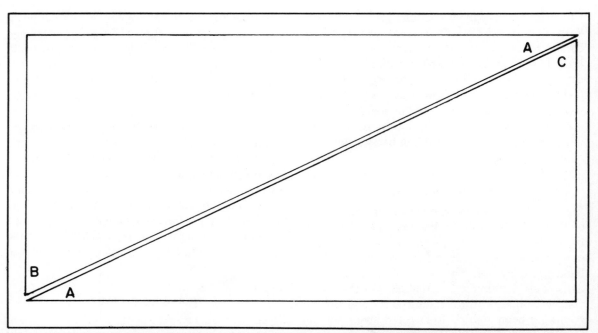

Fig. 6-21. The triangular ends of the A-frame cubby can be thought of as halves of a rectangle for the purposes of computing the cladding required to cover them.

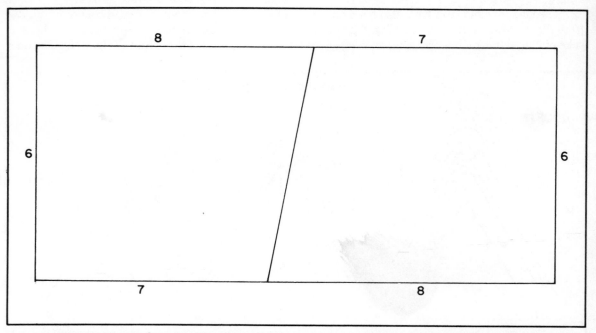

Fig. 6-22. The two sides of a cubby with a front wall taller than the back wall can be considered as forming one long rectangle for the purpose of computing the cladding required to cover them.

may be going over spaces approximately 8 feet long by 2 feet wide, however, so we recommend putting in some additional 2 × 4 pieces perpendicular to the bottom pieces to give the floor extra support. Use the techniques and placements illustrated in Fig. 4-9 and 4-10. A wooden floor should be painted, varnished, or covered with a floor covering.

Estimating the Area for Cladding

Figuring the area of the sides of an A-frame cubby is simple, but the ends might throw you. How do you figure the area of a triangle? You don't have to, for these triangles are, in fact, halves of a rectangle. Think of the triangle's parts as A at the top, B on the lower left, and C on the right. Now look at Fig. 6-21, and you'll see how we got the triangle from a rectangle, and how we can multiply the height of our A-frame cubby by half its base to compute the area of the front and back. In figuring the amount of cladding needed, don't forget to subtract the area occupied by the door and the windows.

Figure 6-22 shows how to compute the area of the two sides of a cubby shown in Fig. 6-23, where the sides are 6 feet long at the bottom, but 8 feet tall on one side and 7 feet tall on the other. The two sides can be thought of as one long, 6-foot-by-15-foot rectangle (Fig. 6-22).

A SIMPLE CUBBY OR SHED

The cubby shown in Fig. 6-23 is easily made and uses many of the techniques described in the chapter on climbing frames. Basically, it consists of four posts sunk in concrete, with the spaces between them filled in with cladding. The roof slants to allow the rain to run off. The plans call for a single window, in the back wall, rather than in a side wall as shown in Fig. 6-23. Walls can come all the way to ground level, or you can leave space between ground

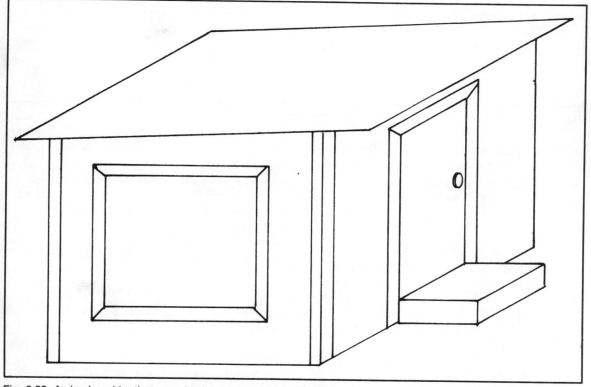

Fig. 6-23. A simple cubby that can also be used as a storage shed.

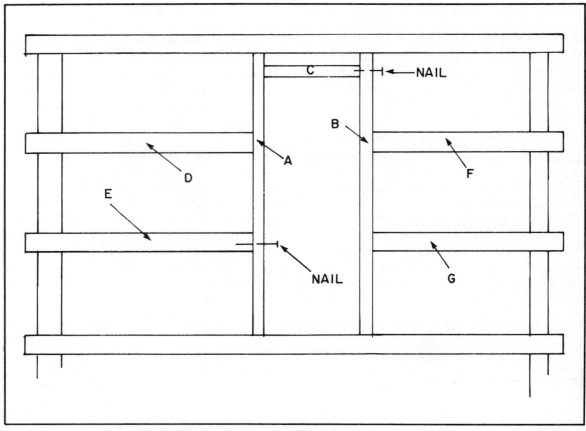

Fig. 6-24. Front view, showing position of framing members and door frame.

and floor for air circulation or storage. Ceiling height ranges from 7 to 8 feet, so that the structure can become a storage shed after the kids have outgrown the need for a playhouse, and adults won't bump their heads on a low ceiling.

Materials

Four 4-inch-by-4-inch corner posts, two at 12 feet long and two at 11 feet long. (These lengths allow for a 1-foot space between ground and floor.)

Approximately 137 feet of 2-inch-by-4-inch lumber, as follows: eight at 9 feet long, eight at 7 feet long, and three at 3 feet long.

One door, approximately 3 feet wide by 7 feet tall.

One window.

Four pieces of 1-inch-by-2-inch lumber, each to be 10 feet long.

Approximately 70 square feet of roofing.

Approximately 225 square feet of cladding.

Approximately 54 square feet of flooring.

Approximately 96 feet of 1-inch-by-4-inch lumber for trim. The finished cubby will be approximately 6 feet wide and 9 feet long.

Construction Method

Dig four holes 3 feet deep and sink the posts in them, filling with concrete to within 6 inches of the ground level. Square the posts and allow the concrete to set.

Nail the bottom 2 × 4 pieces on the front and back; then nail the side 2 × 4 pieces on so that they

118

overlap the front and back ones (Fig. 6-27). Nail on the top 2 × 4 pieces in the same order. Then trim the 4 × 4 corner posts if necessary so that no part of them juts above the level of the top of the 2 × 4 pieces.

Measure the width of your door. Nail in the two 2 × 4 pieces marked A and B in Fig. 6-26, taking care to make the distance between them the width of the door plus 1 inch. The door frame will actually stand directly on these two 2 × 4 pieces, although the door frame has been drawn slightly off their centers in Fig. 6-26 for the purposes of illustration. Nail in the remaining pieces of the floor substructure (C-H in Fig. 6-26), all of which are made of 2 × 4 lumber. These are offset to make it easier to nail through A and B into the ends of D, G, and so on.

Nail in 2 × 4 pieces A, B, and C in that order (Fig. 6-24) to form the door frame. Note that pieces A and B should be sitting directly on the floor substructure as described above. Be sure to cut piece C so that it is the width of the door plus 1 inch. Nail on 2 × 4 pieces D-G as shown.

Measure your window. Cut pieces A and B (Fig. 6-25) to allow for the height of the window and, if no sill is included in a ready-made window purchased from a building supplies store, the sill (Fig. 6-29). Nail 2 × 4 pieces C and D (Fig. 6-25) to the corner posts; then nail in pieces A and B. Next, nail on the 2 × 4 side pieces E-H, noting that they overlap the longer pieces (Fig. 6-27).

Nail in 2 × 4 pieces A and B (Fig. 6-27) to form the roof substructure. These should actually be cut at a slight angle so that they fit nicely between the longer 2 × 4 pieces, so follow this procedure. Lay a piece of 2 × 4 on top of pieces C and D so that it protrudes just over their outer edges. Holding a straightedge or a piece of wood flat against the in-

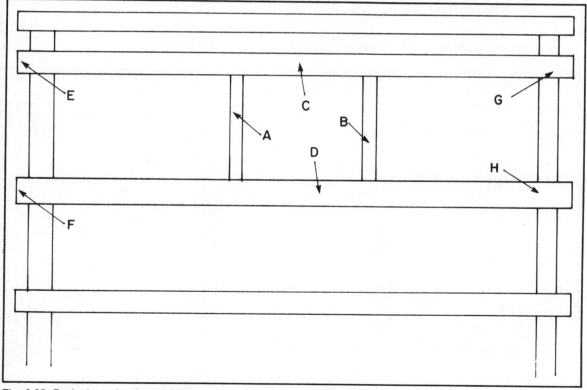

Fig. 6-25. Back view, showing position of framing members and window frame.

119

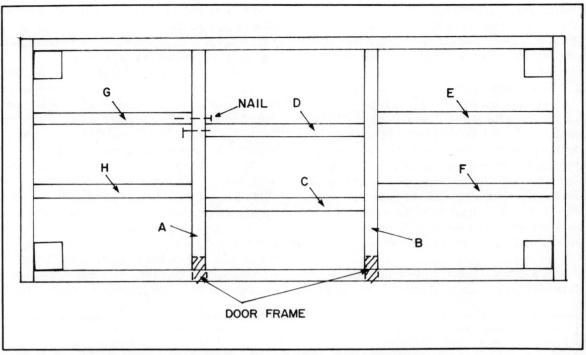

Fig. 6-26. Top view, showing position of support structures for the floor substructure.

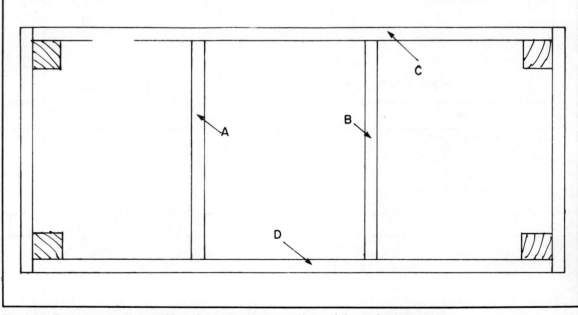

Fig. 6-27. Top view, showing position of 2 × 4 support members of the roof substructure.

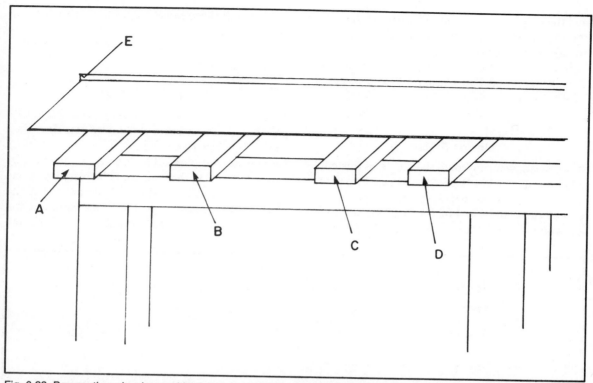

Fig. 6-28. Perspective, showing position of the 1 × 2 pieces to which sheets of roofing materials will be attached. These sheets are to extend 6 inches beyond the wall on all four sides.

ner edge of C and against the new 2 × 4 piece, mark the new piece with pencil or pen. Keeping the 2 × 4 piece in place, hold the straightedge against the inner edge of piece D and mark the new piece on that end. When the new piece is cut on these two marks, it should fit snugly and precisely between pieces C and D.

Nail on the cladding on all four sides.

Nail the 1 × 2 pieces A-D on for the roof (Fig. 6-28). Note that these pieces extend about 6 inches beyond the side 2 × 4 pieces but that they are flush with the longer 2 × 4 pieces on the top. Attach the sheets of roofing material (E in Fig. 6-28) to pieces A-D as recommended by the supplier. Screws and rubber washers are often recommended for fiberglass roofing material, special nails for roofing iron. This will leave a space about 1 inch high between the 1 × 2 pieces. Depending on the conditions where you live, you can do several things with this space. The first is simply to leave it there for a bit of air circulation. The second is to tack on pieces of fly screen over the space to let the air through but to keep the bugs out. The third is to cut pieces of 1 × 2 to size and put them in the space to fill it in if your climate is very cold.

Install the door in the frame. Figure 6-17 shows how all the pieces should fit together.

Install the window. If you need a sill, Fig. 6-29 shows a simple, easy-to-make sill. Nail a piece of 2 × 4 to the bottom piece of 2 × 4 that is already part of the window frame. The top of the new piece should be 1/2 inch higher than the top of the window frame piece. Nail on a piece of 1 × 3 as shown and a piece of 1 × 4 as shown. Fill the V-shaped space between the 1 × 3 and the 1 × 4 with a waterproof crack filler.

Install the floor.

Install the trim around the window, the door,

and the corners of the cubby. Figure 6-19 shows how the corners of the A-frame should be finished, and the same technique should be used here, bearing in mind that you have a 4 × 4 instead of a 2 × 6 corner piece, and that you have 2 × 4 pieces between the corner piece and the cladding. Paint or stain the outside of the cubby if necessary.

Interior Finishing

If you wish, you can finish the inside of this cubby much as you would a house. You can easily nail plaster board (gyprock), paneling, knotty pine, or other material to the 2 × 4 pieces that form the frame, and you can use interior trim around the door and window. But those same 2 × 4 pieces also form excellent starting points for the installation of shelves, cabinets, and even tables and benches, (Figs. 4-27, 4-28, and 4-29).

TREE HOUSES

A tree house can be different things to different people. There is no reason the cubby just described couldn't be built 10 feet off the ground between four suitably placed pines. The kids could get to it by a rope ladder. Or, the door could be installed in one corner, and boards could be nailed onto one of the trees to give access to the door. As a variation, the walls could go up only half way. As another, the roof

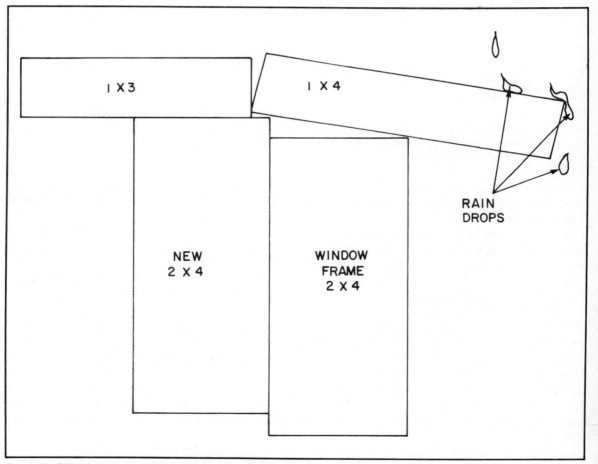

Fig. 6-29. Side view showing how a simple window sill can be constructed.

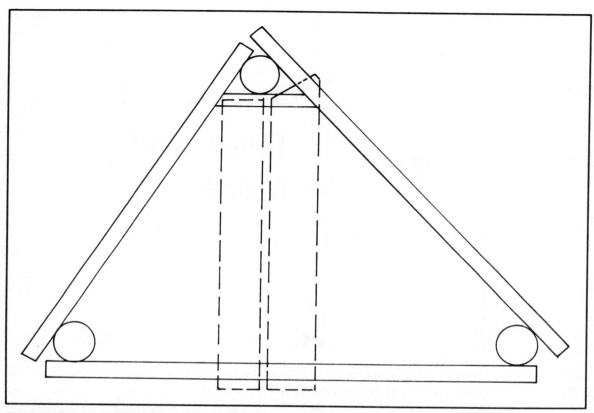

Fig. 6-30. Framing members for a tree house floor.

could be left off entirely, using the canopy of the trees for a roof.

Another good tree house is more a climbing frame in trees, or the branches of a tree, than a proper cubby. Many of the designs in Chapter 4 can be varied to form such a tree house. Figure 6-30 shows how 2 × 4 pieces can be nailed to three tree trunks or limbs and how planks, shown in dotted lines, can be nailed to them for the tree house floor. These flooring planks should have spaces between them for the rain to run through. Rather than walls, these tree houses should have several rails nailed around the sides so that the kids can sit on the floor and lean back against the rails. Finish the wood with stain or paint unless there is a natural preservative in the wood.

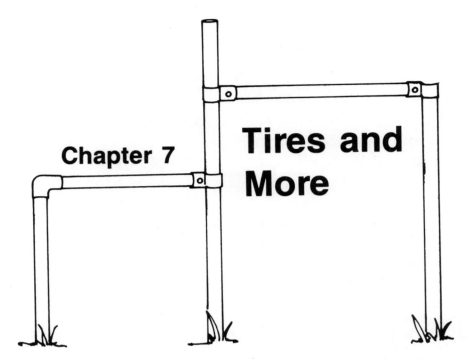

Chapter 7

Tires and More

THE VIRTUES OF TIRES ARE MANY. THEY ARE available, free, almost everywhere. They don't rot. They don't need to be painted, although they can be if you wish a special effect. They are durable. They are strong. And, kids like them. About the only disadvantages of tires are their propensity to hold rain water and their color in hot climates, as any of you who have touched a black tire on a 98° F. day would know. As for the water, you can drill holes as necessary for drainage, without weakening your tire play structure.

Plans follow for tire swings and tire climbing structures that can be free standing or part of a climbing frame. Loose tires around the yard can also be fun. Not only will kids stand them up and roll them, they can ride them, race them, toss balls through their centers, stack them up and jump over them, build igloos of them, and devise more games than we have room to describe here. Figure 7-1 shows a handy way to store the kids' tires—just throw them over a pole sunk in the ground for that purpose. Even stacked up this way the tires present a climbing challenge.

Figure 7-2 shows several bits of hardware that will be useful for working with tires. From the top, there is an eye bolt with a nut and washer on it and under it an eye screw. The item in the middle is called a cable clamp. As you tighten the two nuts, you force the part marked A tighter and tighter against cable inserted in the center of the clamp. The item under that is a U bolt. It is lying on its side here, but if you turn the page sideways, you'll see that it is U shaped, although it has a two-holed washer on it. The item on the bottom is also a U bolt, and it is very useful for swings and trapezes and hammocks.

SWINGS

Figure 7-3 shows one tire swing. A piece of metal bent to the contour of the tire should be inserted in the tire, with an eye bolt inserted through the tire and the metal. The washer and nut complete the assembly in the tire. A loose cable clamp is then put on the cable; the cable end is passed through the eye of the bolt and then through the cable clamp.

Fig. 7-1. Loose tires can be kept out of the way by stacking them on a pole.

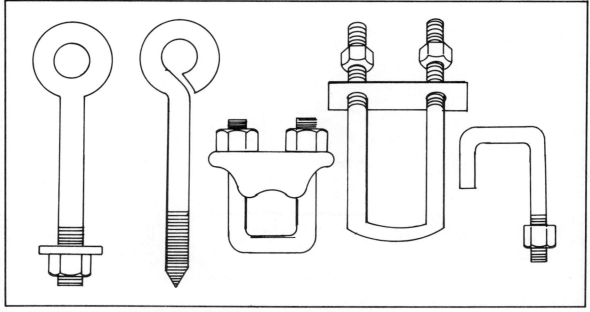

Fig. 7-2. Useful bits of hardware for assembling play equipment from tires.

A second cable clamp can be used to secure the cable around a tree limb.

Figure 7-4 shows another style of tire swing. Three blocks of wood are fitted in the tire, and eye screws are securely fastened into them. The tire can then be hung with cable and cable clamps (top left) or chain and shackles (top right). The enlarged drawing of the shackle shows it is a U-shaped piece of metal with threaded holes at the top. When the bolt is removed from these holes, the shackle can be put through the eye of the screw. The first link of the chain is then dropped into the U, and the bolt screwed into place through the link.

This tire swing can be hung in several ways. If you use cable rope, you can pass all three through a large eye bolt or eye screw and secure them with cable clamps. You might also consider a ready-made structure consisting of two steel rings and a swivel (top of Fig. 7-5). With the three lengths of chain already attached to the bottom steel ring, you don't have to worry about clamps or shackles. The top steel ring can be attached to a tree limb with a piece of cable and a cable clamp. The bottom drawing in Fig. 7-5 shows another ready-made device, an eye

bolt with three lengths of chain attached. A third method would be to use three shackles to attach the lengths of chain to an eye bolt.

CLIMBING STRUCTURES

Figure 7-6 shows cut-away views of (A) the way to fasten two tires together and (B) the way to fasten a tire to a post. These might make a bit more sense if you have a quick look at Fig. 7-7, showing four tires between the posts of a climbing frame. To fasten two tires together, drill holes in the two tires, put a big washer on a bolt, put it in the first tire, and push the end of the bolt through the hole. Bring the second tire into place and carefully work the bolt into the hole in it. Put the second washer and the nut on the bolt and tighten the nut. (Washers are indicated by a big W in a circle in the drawing.) That item marked "sleeve" in part B might be a short piece of steel pipe or aluminum pipe. Call the metal fabricators in your town and ask them if they will give away small off-cuts of pipes. Failing this free source, you may have to buy them. In assembling B, remember to put a washer on the bolt before you insert it in the tire to push it through the hole you

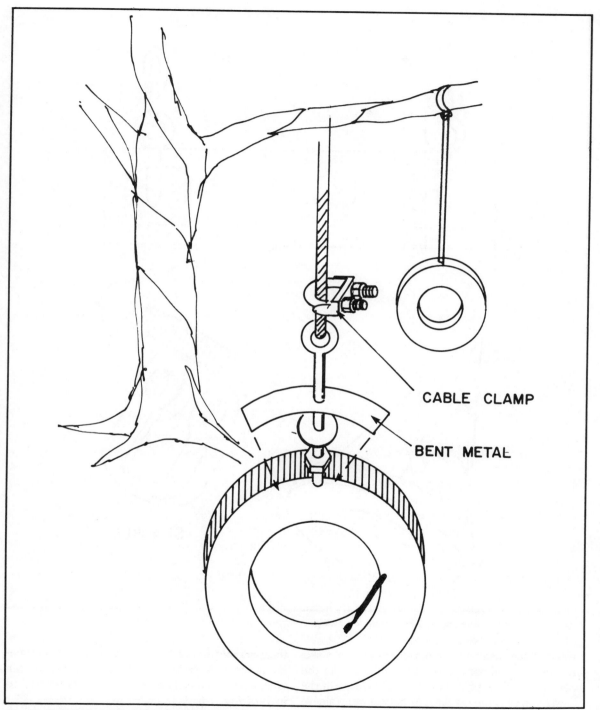

CABLE CLAMP

BENT METAL

Fig. 7-3. Details for assembling one type of tire swing.

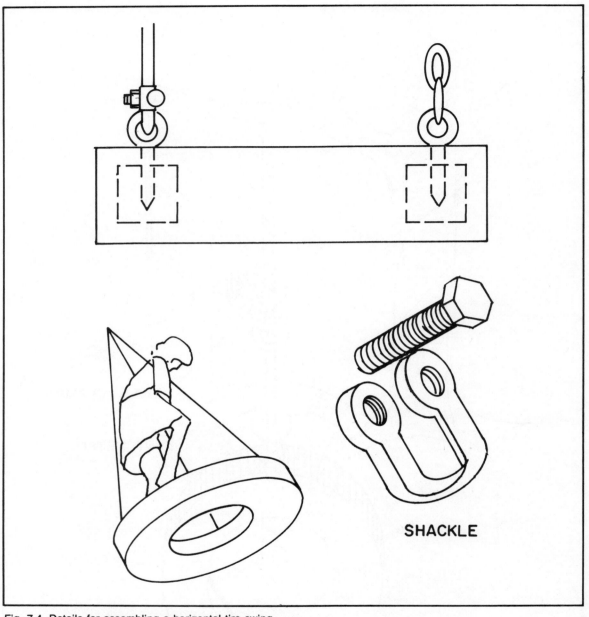

Fig. 7-4. Details for assembling a horizontal tire swing.

drilled. After pushing the bolt through, put on a second washer, and the sleeve. If the diameter of the hole drilled in the post is approximately that of the sleeve, you may need a washer between the sleeve and the post. A final washer and the nut complete the assembly. In Fig. 7-7 each A represents a fastening procedure described in A of Fig. 7-6, and each B represents the bolt and sleeve assembly described in B of Fig. 7-6.

Figure 7-8 shows an assembly of tires that can

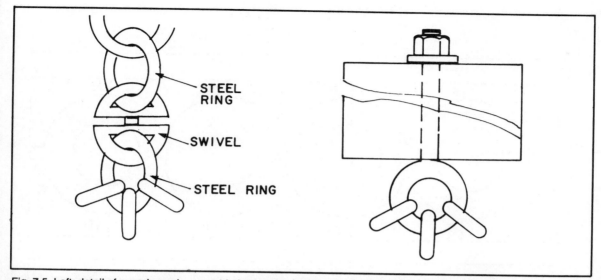

Fig. 7-5. Left: detail of a ready-made assembly from which three lengths of chain for a horizontal tire swing can be hung. Right: another ready-made assembly—an eye bolt with three lengths of chain for the tire swing.

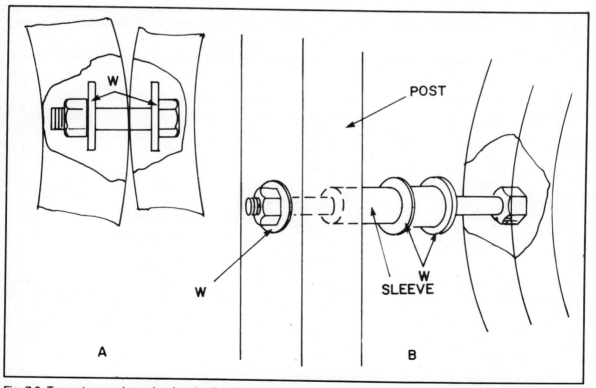

Fig. 7-6. Two cut-away views showing details of (A) assembly method of fastening one tire to another and (B) assembly method of fastening a tire to a post. A capital W in a circle indicates washer.

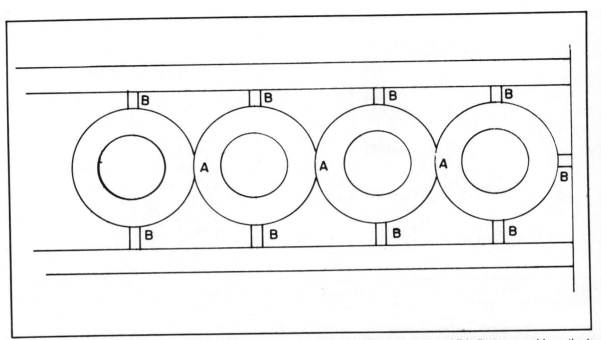

Fig. 7-7. Four tires forming a ladder between the posts of a climbing frame. The capitals A and B indicate assembly methods shown in Fig. 7-6.

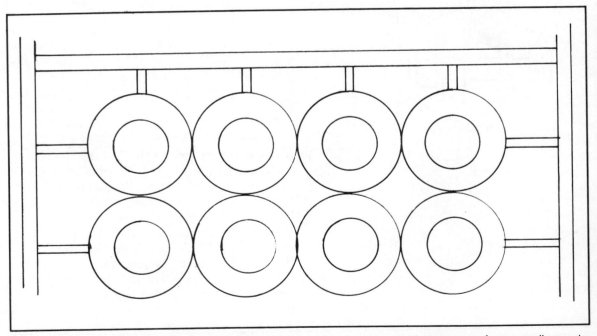

Fig. 7-8. A wall of tires that can be assembled under a climbing frame to screen a swing or trapeze from a sandbox under the frame.

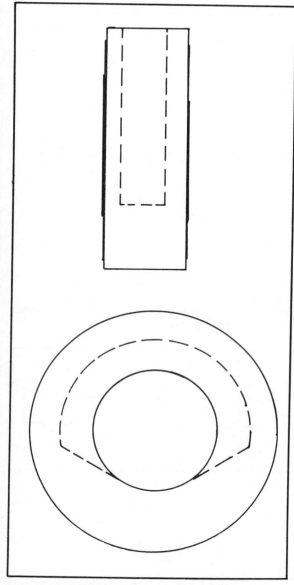

Fig. 7-9. A side view and a front view showing how a tire should be cut to make an inside-out tire swing.

MORE SWINGS, A TRAPEZE, A HAMMOCK, AND A SEESAW BAR

The placement, design, and function of most of the following equipment has been described in previous chapters, so some assembly details will be given here. I will also tie up ends left loose in other places. For example, it was mentioned in an earlier chapter that a swing made from a tire, turned inside out, is one of the safest types of swings for very small children. Figure 7-9 shows a side view and front view of how the tire should be cut to make such a swing. To hang the swing, refer to the knots described with Fig. 5-16. Use two half hitches to tie the rope to the tire and either two half hitches or a clove hitch to tie the rope around the tree limb.

Figure 7-10 is a template you can enlarge and trace on wood to make seats for swings. Such seats should be 6 to 8 inches wide, depending on the age of the child to use it. The length is also variable but should be no less than 12 inches; 16 inches will accommodate most adults.

Figure 7-11 shows two methods of hanging the swing with rope. On the right, two lengths of rope are used, and an overhand knot under the seat prevents the rope from being pulled through the hole. On the left, the rope is passed under the seat, then back up through the other hole. This method is preferable if you are hanging the swing for the first time because it allows you to adjust the height of the swing by untying and retying only one side. It is also easier to level the seat using this method.

Figure 7-12 shows another method of hanging a swing. For the swing described in Fig. 7-11, exterior grade plywood, 3/4 to 1 inch thick, would be ideal, but for this method, a plank about 1.25 inches thick is best. For this method the alternate holes indicated in Fig. 7-10 are drilled, but note from Fig. 7-12 that one hole is drilled only half way through the plank. A U bolt is then inserted through the bottom link of the hanging chain. As the nut is tightened, the other end of the U bolt will be drawn down into the hole drilled half way through the plank.

This assembly method is also used to make the trapeze bar shown in Fig. 7-13. The bar itself should be of a strong pipe. The chains should be attached

be used to form a wall under a climbing frame. Such a wall might prevent a child from stepping into the path of a swing or trapeze built onto the side of the climbing frame. Attach the tires to the posts and climbing frame platform with assembly B of Fig. 7-6 and fasten the tires together with assembly A.

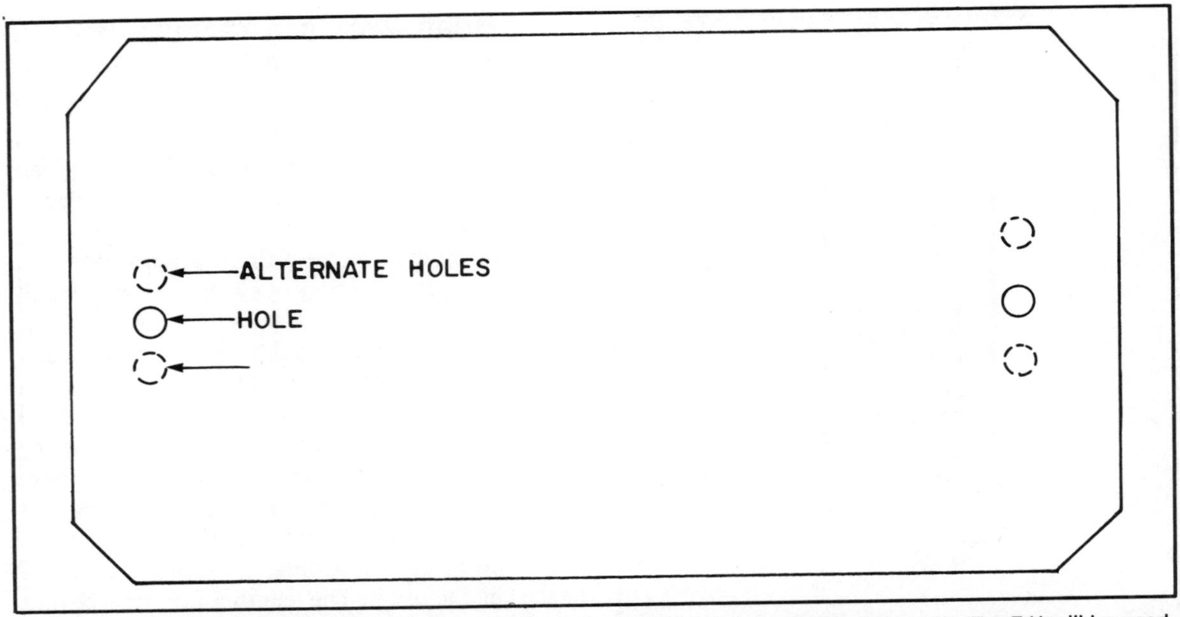

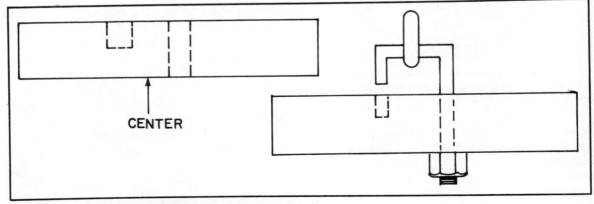

Fig. 7-10. A template for a swing seat. Two holes should be drilled if the hanging method shown in Fig. 7-11 will be used, but the four alternate holes must be drilled for the hanging method shown in Fig. 7-12.

ALTERNATE HOLES

HOLE

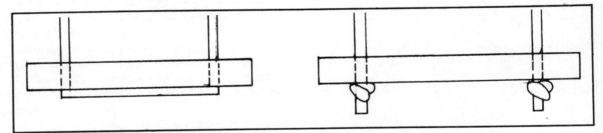

Fig. 7-11. Two ways to hang a swing seat using rope.

CENTER

Fig. 7-12. How to hang a swing seat using chain and a U bolt.

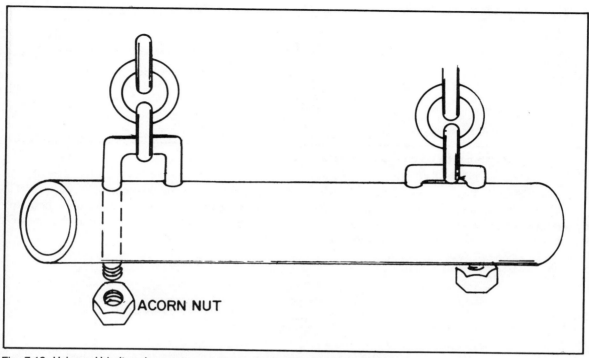

Fig. 7-13. Using a U bolt and an acorn nut to attach hanging chain to a trapeze bar.

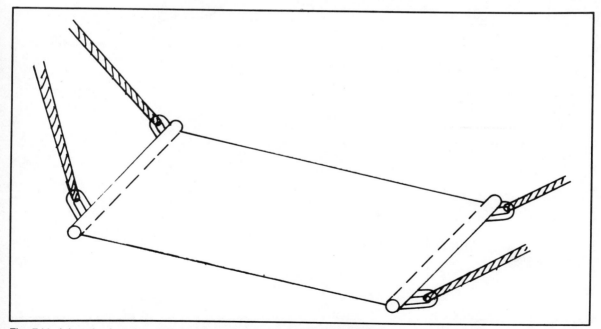

Fig. 7-14. A length of canvas stitched to two trapeze bars to form a hammock.

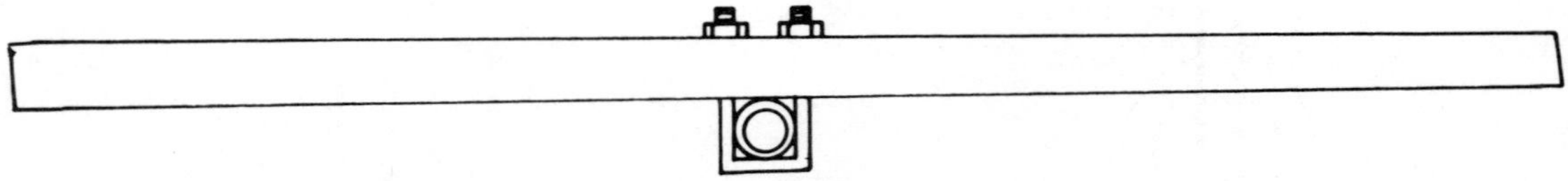

U BOLT

Fig. 7-15. Large U bolts can be used to keep a seesaw in place on its bar.

with shackles to U bolts or eye bolts at the top.

Figure 7-14 shows a hammock that can be made by assembling two trapeze bars, then stitching a length of canvas between them. The hammock can be hung with nylon rope or chain.

Figure 7-15 shows how to use two U bolts to keep a seesaw in place on a bar such as that shown in Fig. 4-6.

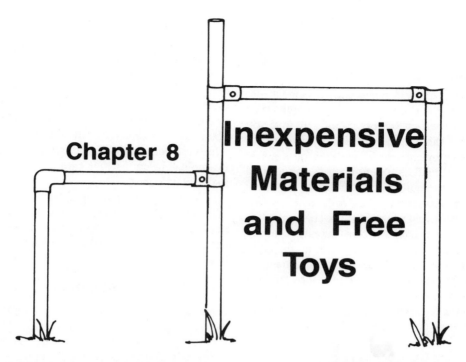

Chapter 8

Inexpensive Materials and Free Toys

A T THE CURRENT PRICE OF GASOLINE, EVEN materials you don't pay for aren't strictly free. There's also the matter of your time, which has to be worth something. Nevertheless, if you don't mind taking the time—better still, if you enjoy taking it, perhaps even making a family outing of it—hunting for materials you pay little or nothing for can be rewarding. The major material categories follow, with suggestions on the best places to look for them and any cautions on using them.

After the materials list, there are eight projects that your kids may be able to make on their own, or with some supervision from you, depending on their ages and skills. These toys can be made from items you already have around the house or that you can easily obtain. If you've just moved into your house and there's no play equipment in the yard, the kids can make these eight to give them something to do until the equipment you make is complete.

TIMBERS AND RAILWAY TIES

The railway companies are the obvious places to

look to when you seek ties. But you may be able to use other heavy timbers if ties aren't available. The best places to look are demolished buildings and houses, private companies, and used materials yards. The company demolishing the house or building may want you to pay for the materials, and the used materials yard will certainly expect payment. You may be able to work off the payment with the former, pulling nails, stacking and cleaning bricks, and so forth. The private company is more likely to donate timber for your play equipment project if it's for a whole neighborhood than if it's for your exclusive use. Occasionally, however, you may be able to find a general contractor who has to burn or haul material from his construction site; he may give you everything you are willing to haul away.

PLYWOOD AND PLANKS

The fences around construction sites are often made of 3/8-inch exterior grade plywood nailed on 2-inch-by-4-inch timbers, both excellent play equipment materials. The wooden planks used in making forms for the pouring of concrete are another excellent material. General contractors and large private builders are the best sources.

SCRAPS AND OFF-CUTS

Some lumberyards and dealers have barrels into which they toss the short pieces left over when they cut pieces for their customers. Some will give you the contents of the barrel, some expect payment for it. If you drive by carpenters working on a house or building or small shopping center, look around the corners of the building site. Chances are you'll see a pile of rubbish containing wood, cement sacks, empty paint cans, and so on. Because the carpenters will have to burn or haul away this rubbish, they are equally willing to have you help with its disposal. The pieces of wood will be of varying lengths, widths, and thicknesses, and some will be suitable only for the barbeque pit or for giving to a three-year-old intent on learning how to pound in nails, but other pieces can be put to other uses.

POLES AND PALLETS

Utility and telephone companies are the best sources of poles. The poles tend to be old and splintery, however, so you have to be wary of how you use them for play equipment. Provided the pole is sound, it can be covered with old tires to protect the children from splinters. In some applications, such as stockade-style sandboxes, the splinters aren't quite so critical.

Pallets are useful for several things. Taken apart, they yield strong, hard boards and timbers. Used as is, they form a handy floor for a cubby or a bay screened off from the rest of the playspace with hedges (Figs. 2-12 and 2-13). Stacked several high, and held together with boards nailed to each pallet, they can quickly bring the vertical dimension of height to the playspace. Similarly, five pallets can be nailed together in a few minutes to form a cubby (Figs. 8-1 and 8-2). Almost any company that sends or receives goods can be a good source of pallets. In San Antonio I used to get them regularly from a firm that sold cleaning supplies to cleaning contractors.

BOXES AND CRATES

Boxes and crates can be disassembled for their plywood and boards, kept whole for stacking or holding planks on climbing frames, or knocked apart and used to screen sandboxes from wind and blowing sand or to screen a trapeze from a sandbox under a climbing frame. The wonderful thing about them is that they come in all sizes, most of which are very useful for one thing or another. For example, big crates that cars come in are ready-made playhouses.

When seeking sources of crates or boxes, think of what might be imported into your area that is heavy or fragile: cars, motorcycles, window glass, car parts, and electrical components. Companies dealing in such items are your best sources.

CABLE REELS

Cable reels are big, strong, heavy, long-lasting, and available in many areas. Individually they can be tables or seesaws, and they can be stacked to form many different types of play equipment (Figs. 8-3 to 8-5). Telephone companies and utility companies are the most obvious sources, but a lot of general contractors also can furnish empty reels.

DRUMS, BARRELS, AND TANKS

Drums and barrels make good storage units. With both ends out they make good tunnels. Tanks make good playhouses. You should never use a drum, barrel, or tank, however, and giving it a thorough cleaning without knowing what it contained before letting the kids climb in. You can sometimes get good, big tanks that held water in old buildings or houses. Drums and barrels are available from companies receiving anything from soap to industrial chemicals to rope. Even if you get a drum or barrel from the local dump, you can often check on its former contents and any safety precautions by telephoning the company the vessel was shipped to; its name will often be stenciled on the side. If you are really desperate for a drum and you find one in the dump with the name of the receiving firm rubbed off, look for a label or some other indication of what the drum

Fig. 8-1. The vertical dimension can be added to your playspace by stacking several pallets on top of each other and securing them with diagonal boards as shown. Pallets are made from tough, wiry wood, so you may have to drill guide holes for the nails.

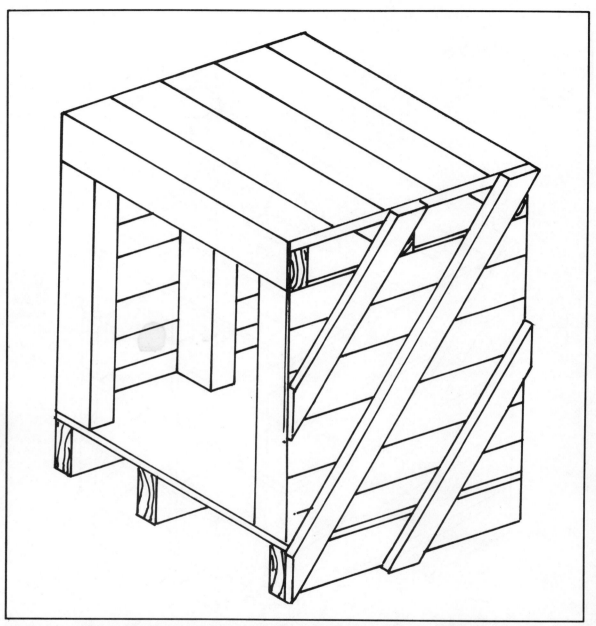

Fig. 8-2. Five pallets can be quickly fastened together with diagonal boards to form a cubby. Adjuncts such as planks and ladders can also be used with this cubby to give the vertical dimension to the playspace and to give the kids something to climb on and jump off.

contained. If that is available, take the drum home and lock it away from the kids. Then take a walk through the yellow pages with your fingers and con-

tact the chemical firms and ask them to advise you on using the drum, including what to use to clean it. If none of the companies can help, take the drum

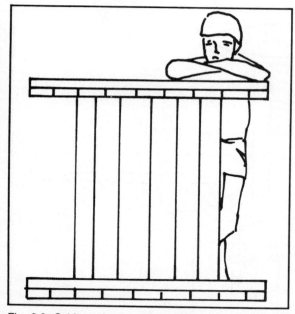

Fig. 8-3. Cable reels make good tables for the yard and playspace. They enable kids to do outdoors many of the same things they enjoy indoors, such as playing chess or checkers, coloring in coloring books, drawing, painting, and having a play lunch with their friends and playmates.

back to where you found it and keep looking.

TIRES

Most service stations and tire companies will happily give you every old tire you will take away; some will even deliver. Your local dump is another good place to look for tires.

CHUTES AND SLIDES

Some companies use chutes to move their products or the raw materials they use in manufacturing their products. Because a broken chute causes so much expensive down time, they usually replace the chutes long before they break. Cleaned up, these chutes, which might be made from wood, plastic, rubber, steel, or a combination of materials, often make excellent slides. If you have contacts in the business or manufacturing circles of your city, ask them about the possibilities of getting an old chute. If you have no such contacts, call your local chamber of commerce or chamber of manufacturers. Some one there can usually give you good leads to follow.

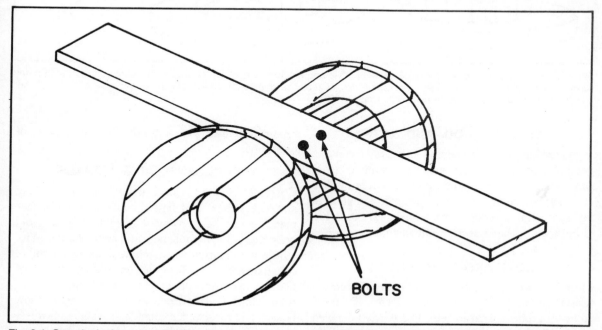

BOLTS

Fig. 8-4. One plank plus one cable reel, plus two nuts, bolts, and washers equals one quickly made and sturdy seesaw.

139

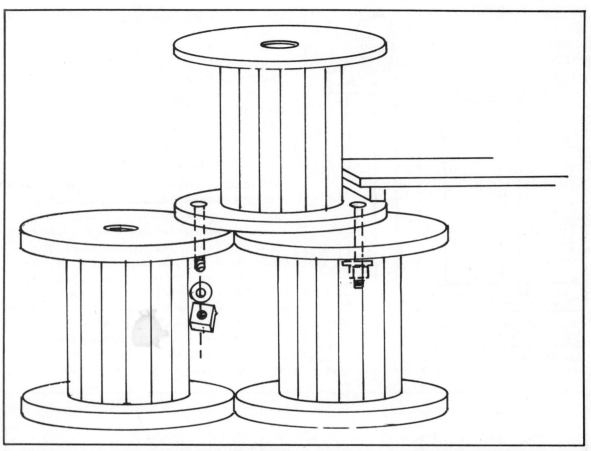

Fig. 8-5. Cable reels can be butted against each other and stacked one on top of another and bolted together in many ways to create climbing towers, bases for plank-slides, high places to jump off, and other sources of merriment. The washer and the nut are already in place on the bolt on the right.

SPRINGS, ROD, AND BARS

If you are handy with a welding torch, you can make good play equipment from steel bits scavenged from the dump. Even if you don't have the equipment to cut and weld steel, you can sometimes put steel to use by cutting it to size with a hacksaw and using U-bolts and other nut and bolt fasteners.

ROPE AND CARGO NETS

Shipping companies and governmental instrumentalities, federal, state, county, and city, are good sources of rope and cargo nets. These may be frayed or even broken in some sections, but you can tie a repair piece into place and save yourself the cost of new rope.

MISCELLANEOUS MATERIALS

Concrete blocks, bricks, paving stones, paving slates, benches, bird baths, cupboards, and other material can be scavenged from junk yards, old buildings being demolished, and some dumps. With a little imagination you can have a playspace full of cars (one steering wheel plus one old barrel), trains (ice cream cartons nailed onto large boxes and barrels), ships (bath tubs, row boats, long shallow boxes), and rockets, airplanes, space ships, corrals—almost anything you and the kids can dream up.

SURPLUS EQUIPMENT SALES

If you think you are good at accumulating junk—always a bit more than you have closets, spare rooms, storerooms, and attics for—consider the plight of the governmental instrumentalities in your town. Governmental bodies at all levels, from federal to local, accumulate extra gear either through over-purchasing or replacement. Sometimes you can get on their mailing lists and visit their surplus equipment yards or warehouses.

These are wonderful sources of old typewriters and adding machines, lockers, boxes, clothing, autos, trucks, ropes, netting, stationery, pots and pans, and kitchen sinks. You name it, and some surplus warehouse probably has it for sale. Some of these items are outside the strict realm of play equipment you construct for yourself, but they still make excellent playing and learning things for your kids. If you can pick up an adding machine for 50 cents, for example, who cares if it winds up in many pieces, ultimately, in the garbage can, if the kids have a good time and learn something (how to loosen screws and nuts and bolts and springs, if nothing else—which is highly unlikely) in the process?

The best way to find out about these sources of surplus equipment is to call the purchasing offi-

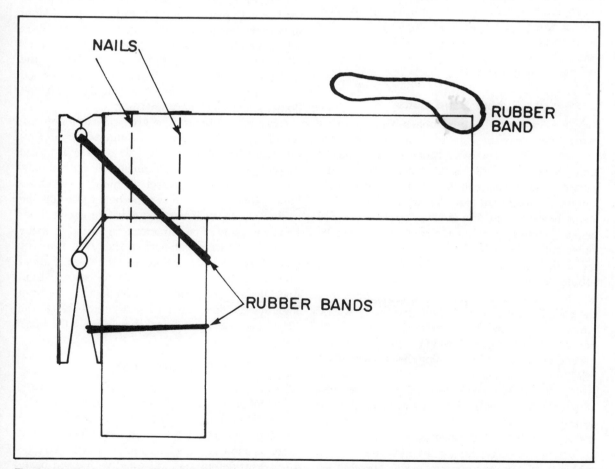

Fig. 8-6. A simple rubber band gun that most kids can make. The clothespin is attached to the handle with two rubber bands. This can be done without dismantling the clothespin. The pin can also be nailed onto the handle with small finishing nails, but this often splits the wood and involves taking it apart, nailing it on, then reassembling it.

cer of the governmental outfit or the educational institution you suspect may be a good source. School boards, universities, and community colleges all have to get rid of surplus gear. If the purchasing officer doesn't handle the surplus, he'll know who does.

EIGHT PROJECTS FOR THE KIDS TO DO BY THEMSELVES

After you establish certain ground rules, such as how to use tools and where they should be put when the kids have finished with them, you may be able to turn the kids loose on these projects. If they ruin a few pieces of wood or bend a few nails in the process, it won't matter, as most of the projects are made from scrap, surplus, or even junk materials you probably accumulate around the house in the process of daily living.

Rubber Band Guns

Figure 8-6 shows a simple rubber band gun that many kids over the age of four can make for themselves. This one has a round barrel salvaged from the end of a dowel, but the barrel can be square, which is easier for little kids to nail onto the handle. Assuming an older kid who enjoys a challenge, however, this gun is made by using a wood rasp to flatten that end of the barrel that has to be nailed onto the handle. Once the barrel is nailed on, the clothespin can be attached as shown with two rubber bands. The pistol is then ready for use.

To load the pistol, a rubber band is looped over the end of the barrel. It is then stretched back far enough for its other end to be held by the clothespin. The shooter then takes aim and squeezes the lower end of the handle, opening the clothespin and releasing the rubber band.

I never allow the rubber band guns to be fired at people or animals. The first transgression is severely dealt with; the gun is broken into pieces before the eyes of the transgressor. If you provide an alternative target before the kids fire the first rubber band, however, you can usually prevent their even sneaking shots at one another. Figure 8-7 shows a good, alternative target you can make from a corrugated cardboard box. The lion is shown on a box, 26 inches by 15 inches, but you can vary the length or height of the lion to suit your box.

Many kids will enjoy ruling off the squares in pencil on the side of a box, then drawing the lion, whose mouth should be cut out. Those triangles around his mouth are meant to be teeth, so they should be painted white if the lion is painted. On the other hand, if your young Picassos or Paul Klees want a lion with purple teeth, green eyes, red mane, chartreuse tail, and pink body, allowing them to create such a colorful creature should keep them occupied for quite some time. The way it has usually worked in my family is this. The lion is drawn on the box with pencil and the mouth cut out by Mom or Dad; the lion is then gone over with a heavy, black felt-tip pen to make him show up. Many days later, after the fever of the first safari has died down, the lion acquires some color. This is often occasioned by a comment like, "Anna (the neighbor girl) isn't home, and I don't have anything to do."

Prevent arguments by giving each hunter different color rubber bands. The hunt starts out simply with each hunter standing about 5 feet from the target and firing away, in unison or individually. After each player has shot all his or her rubber bands, the hunters look in the box and count the rubber bands, awarding one point for each rubber band they find. The game can be varied in many ways. The shooters can back farther away from the box. They can place themselves at angles of about 40 degrees to the box. They can lie on their tummies, fire around corners or through bushes or from high places. They can start with their backs to the target and whirl and fire at the sound of the lion's roar.

Bean Bags

The lion target or something similar can be used with the next project, homemade bean bags. Figure 8-8 shows the two steps in making the bags. A rectangle of cloth is folded once and sewn on two sides as shown on the left. The bag thus formed is turned inside out and half filled with dried beans or very small pebbles. The top ends are then turned inside the bag, and it is sewn shut as shown

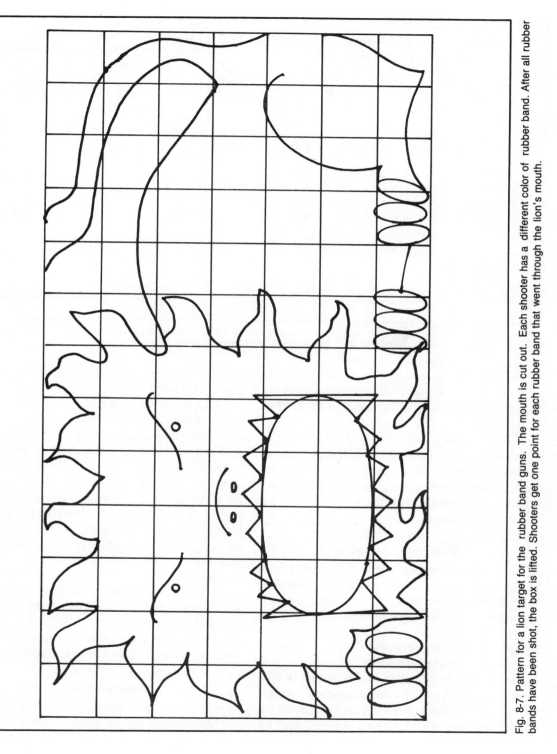

Fig. 8-7. Pattern for a lion target for the rubber band guns. The mouth is cut out. Each shooter has a different color of rubber band. After all rubber bands have been shot, the box is lifted. Shooters get one point for each rubber band that went through the lion's mouth.

Fig. 8-8. Making a bean bag. Left: a rectangle of cloth folded in half and sewn down two edges to form the bag. Right: the bag, turned inside out, half filled with dry beans, tops tucked in, being sewn shut.

on the right; the lines of dashes indicate the edges of cloth inside the bag. Note that the needle and thread will now be going through four thicknesses of fabric.

These bean bags can be tossed at the lion target or something similar. As a variation, they can be dropped into the mouth of the target from heights such as the stack of pallets, tossed with the tosser blindfolded, or tossed with the tosser at difficult angles to the target.

Nine (or More) Pins

You might get shampoo, cleanser, or cooking oil in plastic bottles such as those shown in Fig. 8-9. Save them. When they are thoroughly clean and you have at least six, give them a good coat of paint, all over, to cover the printed directions and anything else on the bottle. Paint on some additional colors; three colors are indicated by the bands with differing lines around the bottles in Fig. 8-9. Numbers can be painted on, cut from adhesive plastic and pressed on, or cut from dark paper and glued on. Match the ball to the size of the bottles—a tennis ball for

smaller bottles, a 5-inch rubber ball or a softball for quart-size bleach bottles, and so on.

This game will take a bit of adjusting, for you may find that the wind knocks over the bottles the first time you set them outside. Put in some sand, dirt, or water to make them stand up until struck by the ball. The kids can actually do this. When they strike the right balance of sand to bottle, they can put some glue on the threads of the bottle and then replace the cap, which will then stay put and keep the pin at its desired weight. Six pins are usually set up in a triangle, with number one in front, numbers two and three in the middle row, and numbers four, five, and six in the third row. Nine pins can be set up diamond fashion, starting out as you do with six pins but adding a fourth row of two pins and a fifth row of one pin. Ten pins and 15 pins are usually set up in triangles with each row having one more pin than the row preceding it.

Wooden Blocks

Blocks in this sense means any piece of wood that can be stacked or set one against another (Fig. 8-10).

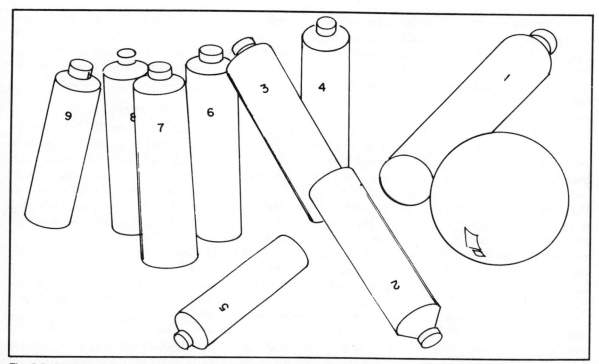

Fig. 8-9. A game of nine pins made by partially filling old plastic bottles with sand, painting them with bright colors, and knocking them down with a ball.

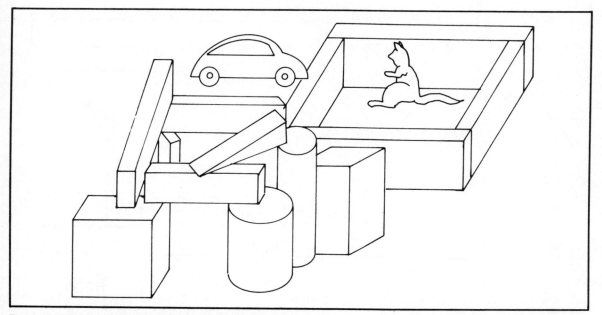

Fig. 8-10. Off-cuts of wood can be used as building blocks.

Save your own off-cuts. Salvage what you can from the rubbish piles where carpenters are working. Rasp off the splinters. Give them to the kids and stand back and enjoy. They'll make pens and zoos for their animals, garages and parking garages for their cars, buildings, houses, and all sorts of fanciful constructions.

When they get tired of the blocks, let them disappear for a while, during which time you give them a coat of paint or stain. When the blocks reappear, they'll be like brand new toys the kids are seeing for the first time. You can use an enamel paint that covers just about everything but that often takes a while to dry, or you can use a water-based paint that dries much faster. If the wood has never been painted, you can give them a quick and relatively inexpensive color treatment by using food colors or Easter egg dyes. Mix a few drops of dye or food color into a bowl of water; make up several colors. Carefully drop the whole block of wood into the mixture and leave it for several minutes. Let the blocks dry on cookie racks. Repeat the process, first strengthening the solution if necessary, until you get the shade you want. Blocks colored this way can be painted later on, if you wish, but you can't very successfully use this method on previously painted blocks.

Paddle Boats

Figure 8-11 shows the basic boat. It can be cut out of any, or almost any, piece of scrap wood you have around the house. Anything more than 1 inch thick gets a bit heavy for the kids using a coping saw, however, so try to start them off with a piece of 1-inch-by-4-inch wood, 1 × 5, or so on. The bathtub often becomes the sailing lake, so the boat shouldn't be too large.

Figure 8-12 shows the fancy version of a paddle used to propel the boat, and Fig. 8-13 shows a simpler version that will still make it chug along acceptably. The dimensions of the paddle must be 1/2 inch smaller, on three sides, than the rectangular cut-out in the end of the boat. Thus, the length (L) of the paddle equals the width (W) of the cut-out

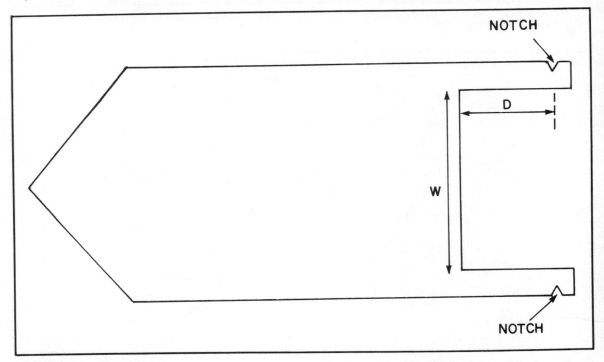

Fig. 8-11. A simple paddle boat.

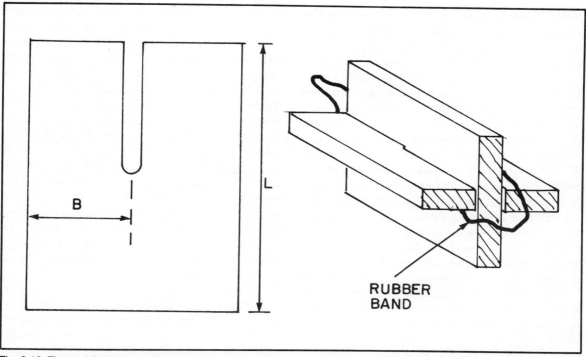

Fig. 8-12. The paddle for the paddle boat. Two parts must be cut according to the pattern on the left. Then they are fitted together as shown at right, and a rubber band is stretched around them.

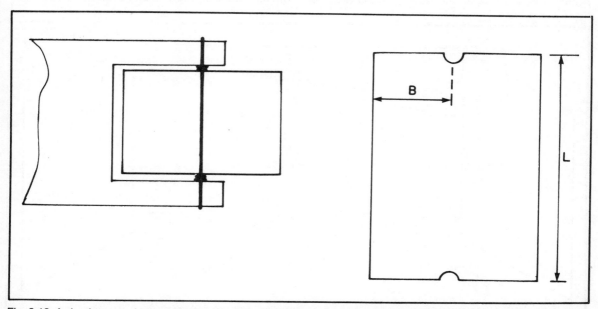

Fig. 8-13. A simpler, one-piece paddle for the paddle boat. Left: the paddle in place in the end of the boat with the rubber band in place and the paddle wound up and ready to propel the boat.

minus 1/2 inch. And, half the width of the paddle, or B in the drawings, equals the depth of the cut-out (D) to the notch minus 1/2 inch. Paddles can be cut from anything that is thin, strong, and rigid, such as plywood or a thick sheet of plasticlike material, such as Formica, left over from remodeling the countertops in the kitchen or bathroom.

After the rubber band is put around the paddle, it is stretched to fit into the notches on the boat. The paddle is twisted many times (at left in Fig. 8-13). Then the boat will usually take off when set free in the water. Sometimes the boat may be a bit too heavy, or the paddle a bit too small; this situation calls for lightening the boat. Get some of that hard, foamlike plastic material used to keep tape recorders and TV sets from shifting around in their cartons during shipment, and glue a piece onto the bottom of the boat. It should then paddle along at a more acceptable clip. This treatment is also necessary for a boat that starts out all right but that acquires a heavy cabin or other appurtenance on deck.

The Magic Marble Window Game

Figure 8-14 shows a simple game you and the kids can construct from the side of a corrugated cardboard box. First cut out a long, thin rectangle. Mark a line on either end about 6 or 9 inches from the edge; hold a board beside this line, then take the handle of a screwdriver or some other hard, rounded object and press it hard along the line. This will flatten the cardboard and enable you to crease it (Fig. 8-14), which will help the game to stand up on the patio or on the family room carpet. Next, cut out the little doors or openings as shown. These are just suggestions, of course, and you can make your 10-point opening as large as your one-pointer if you wish. You can also include a large, "lose-all" opening in the board. If a player's marble goes through this opening, he loses all the points he's gained during that round. If you have different colors of marbles, as from a set of Chinese checkers, you can give each player a different color.

Vary the rules to suit your family. For example, if the kids are big enough and skilled enough to get their marbles through the openings, then "close" won't count; the marble has to be all the way on the other side of the cardboard to score. If the kids are less skilled, then any part of a marble that enters the opening counts the entire number of points in-

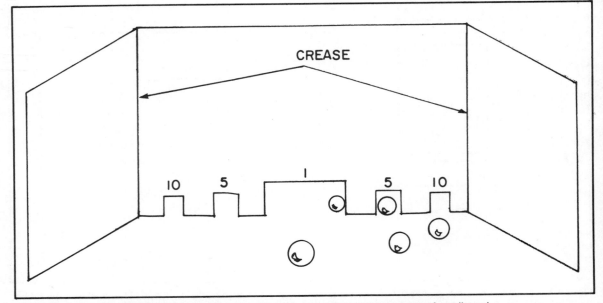

Fig. 8-14. A simple game in which marbles are rolled through holes cut in a sheet of cardboard.

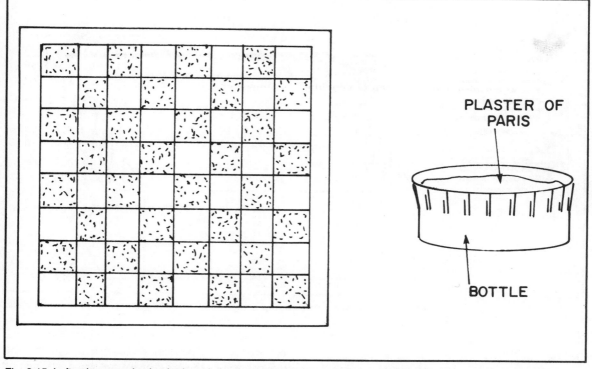

Fig. 8-15. Left: a homemade checkerboard glued on a piece of corrugated cardboard. Right: checkers are made by pouring plaster of Paris into old bottle caps, sanding them smooth, and then painting them.

dicated over the opening. With smaller, less skilled kids, none of their marbles may go all or part of the way through. In such a situation, each player's closest marble can be counted.

Like blocks, this is a game that becomes new again as it acquires new paint jobs. The game can be painted like a pirate's face, for example, with each opening being a missing tooth. Or, it could be painted as several houses, or one big mansion, with each opening being a door. Outlines of bowling pins can be painted around the openings, or the outlines of rockets, astronauts in space suits, and so on.

Homemade Checkers

Figure 8-15 shows the side of a large corrugated cardboard box with a homemade checkerboard on it, with (at the right) the plan for one of the checkers. The checkerboard can be as simple or complicated as your kids' abilities and skills require. At its

simplest, you might rule off the lines with a yardstick and have them color in the squares with crayons. At its most challenging, you give an older kid the job and turn the project over to him or her entirely. The squares might be made from newspaper, brown paper bags, solid-color gift wrapping paper left over from last Christmas, leftover bits of shelf paper, adhesive-backed plastic, or anything else the child chooses. The squares might be glued on or pasted on and covered with a coat or two of clear plastic or varnish.

The checkers are made from old bottle caps filled with plaster of paris. When the filling is dry, the cap should be turned over and rubbed on a piece of sandpaper stretched over a piece of wood. This will make a good, flat surface so that the checker will sit properly on the board. The checkers needn't be the traditional black and red, but they should be painted in two contrasting colors. The colors also

149

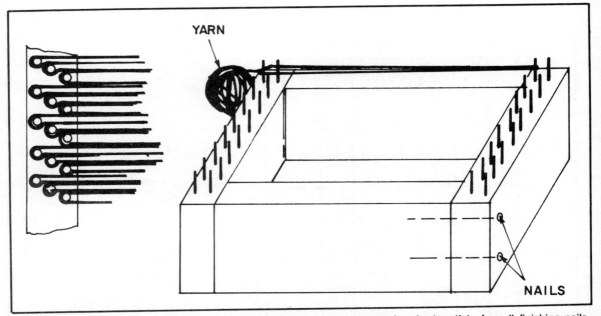

Fig. 8-16. A simple loom most kids can make from four pieces of scrap wood and a handful of small finishing nails.

have to contrast sharply with the checkerboard colors.

Simple Looms

Figure 8-16 shows a loom most kids can make with four pieces of scrap wood and a handful of small finishing nails. The nails can be put on in one, two, or three rows depending on how close together the weaver wants the lengthwise, or warp, strands of yarn. To the left of the loom is shown the top view of nails driven in in three rows, producing an almost solid expanse of yarn when it is threaded on the loom.

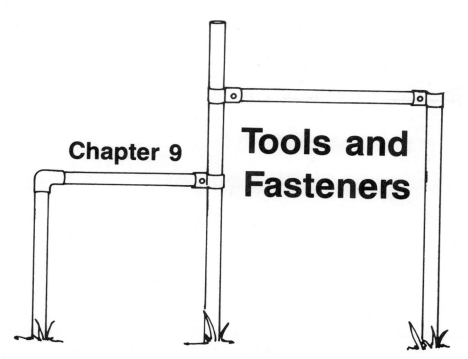

Chapter 9

Tools and Fasteners

M OST AUTHORITIES ON BUILDING PROJECTS start their chapters on tools with two items, handsaws and hammers. This chapter begins with a discussion of where you can get good tools at a fraction of their retail price.

The three best sources are estate sales, garage sales, and second-hand dealers. A tool may be made from good steel or mediocre steel. It may have a handle of good wood, shoddy wood, sturdy plastic, or cheap junk plastic. If you don't know much about tools, you ought to do some window shopping and get some advice from reputable hardware stores before you make any purchases. To a novice, a hammer is a hammer is a hammer, but the pro can show you how the head on the good one is put on much better than on the cheaper model, how the balance is better, and other good points that are really more than just salesman's palaver. When you are getting this good, free advice, get it by brand names. Most salesclerks won't criticize the opposition's product; they'll praise their own. Now, if there are one or two brands no one mentions, they may be the ones to avoid. If that's your suspicion, check it out with a

carpenter or a neighbor who is handy with tools, for their advice is about an unbiased as it comes.

When you know what you are looking for, and you think you can recognize good quality tools even if you don't recognize the brand, watch the papers for estate sales and garage sales. When you find a good buy, take it, provided you try out the tool first if it is electric or has moving parts, like a Yankee screwdriver. You can't get your money back from these sales, so be sure before you buy.

DRILLS

One of your first purchases ought to be an electric drill. These tools have come down in price so that they are in the reach of almost everyone, and they do much more than drill holes. They can stir up paint or ceramic glazes, drive screws, drive saws, grind the paint off walls or wood, and knock the rust off metal, adding a polish in the process.

Figure 9-1 shows a common electric drill. The chuck is removable so that the drill can be used to power other tools. When you twist the chuck one way, it opens to take the drill bit. Twisting the chuck

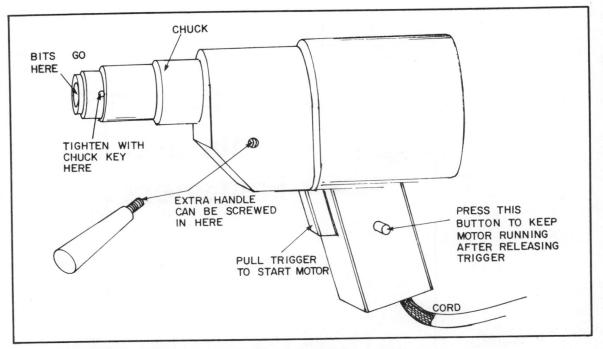

Fig. 9-1. An electric hand drill should be one of the first purchases for your tool box.

in the opposite direction tightens it around the drill bit. Before using it, however, you should insert the chuck key and twist it in all three little holes provided for it. You can now drill holes in wood, plastic, and, if you get a special bit, masonry and concrete. You can drill holes in metal with the same bits you use on wood, if your drill has a slow speed and a fast speed; use the slow for metal, the fast for wood.

A 1/4-inch drill can take bits (Fig. 9-2) that are 1/4 inch in diameter, or smaller, on the end that fits into the chuck. The bit may bore a hole 1/2 inch in diameter. If you want to drill a hole of large

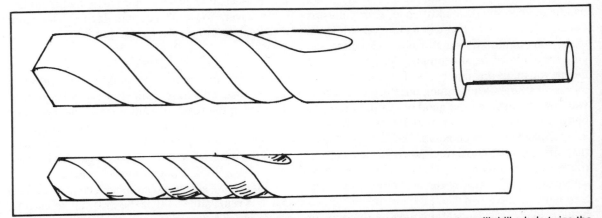

Fig. 9-2. Drill bits for the electric hand drill. Both will fit into the chuck, although the one on top will drill a hole twice the diameter of the other bit.

diameter, however, you are usually better off starting with a smaller size first. This is especially true if you are drilling into something that is hard and smooth or that has a rounded surface, like a post. For example, say you want to drill a hole 3/8 inch in diameter through a post of pine that has been treated to resist rot and insect attacks. If you try to use the 3/8-inch bit with no guide hole, it is likely to skitter all over the place, and you will drill a hole that is off center or higher or lower than you want.

Tap the point of a nail into the center of the spot for the hole; it has to go in only about 1/32 of an inch. Now choose a small bit, 1/16 inch, for example, and put it in the chuck. Put the tip of the bit into the nail hole, but don't press too hard or you might snap the bit in two. Squeeze the trigger and then gently press the bit into the hole as deep as it will bore.

The drill bits are fluted on their sides. When you drill a soft wood like pine, drill shavings will usually climb right out of the hole via the fluted sides of the bit. When you are drilling hardwood,

like oak, or making a deep hole in a soft wood, however, the shavings won't always climb out of the hole as you drill. Sometimes they pack up near the tip of the bit and don't climb the flutes. This creates extra friction at the bit's cutting end, and, when you pull the bit out of the hole, the cutting end may be black and smoking. It doesn't take much of this kind of treatment to dull the bit. So, as the drill goes in every 1/2 inch, pull it all the way out. You will pull the shavings out with the bit, keeping the hole clean and retaining the edge on the tip of the bit.

The harder the wood, the more smaller-size bits you should use before finally using the big one. This ever widening guide hole doesn't have to be drilled to the maximum depth of each successive bit, but it ought to be at least 1 inch deep. When you put the 3/8-inch bit into the guide hole, you'll find it quickly chews its way to the bottom then slows down as it has to bore its entire way through the post. Pull it out every 1/2 to 3/4 inch to clean the hole and cool the bit.

When you buy your first set of drill bits, be sure to get the kind that will make holes in metal as well

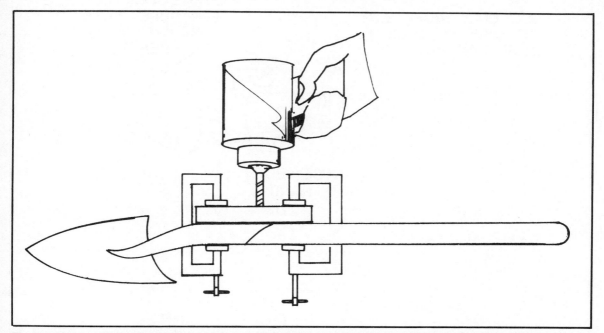

Fig. 9-3. How to drill a hole in a round object, whether it is wood or metal. First, clamp a piece of wood on the top of the round piece. Second, drill a hole in the wood. Third, insert the bit in the hole in the wood and drill through the round piece.

as wood. The safest practice is to buy a brand recommended by a good tradesman. You need a nail hole or something similar to keep the bit from skittering on the surface of the metal, and this is sometimes very difficult to accomplish. Figure 9-3 shows one method of drilling a hole where you want it in metal, that part of a spade or shovel that a new wooden handle fits into, for example. Just remember to change the speed from fast to slow when you get through the wood. It is also a good practice to put a drop of household oil into the hole to lubricate the bit as it chews through the metal.

When drilling through concrete or masonry, don't put in oil or water to ease the bit's burden. Just keep the drill on the lower speed and pull the bit out often to clean the hole and cool the tip. Drill plastic as you drill wood.

Sanding with the Drill

To begin with, you'll be much better off using a rigid disk than the circles of sandpaper that can be used with the flexible, rubber disk that comes with the drill. You are supposed to hold the rubber disc as shown in Fig. 9-4 and keep it at that angle. But several things happen when you pull the trigger. The whirling of the disc pulls the whole drill with it; the sandpaper may bind and tear; and you get a series of circular scratches in the surface you had hoped to sand smooth.

If you want to sand a surface smooth for a coat of varnish or clear plastic to show the beauty of the grain, you are much better off using an orbital sander. These sanders can be rented at reasonable costs if you don't have enough work to justify buying one.

Your drill is best used for sanding rough jobs that will be covered later on. In one of our houses, I wanted to put ceramic tiles on some of the kitchen walls, which were coated with a good quality paint over plaster. We used a rigid disk that cut through the paint in a wonderful manner and covered

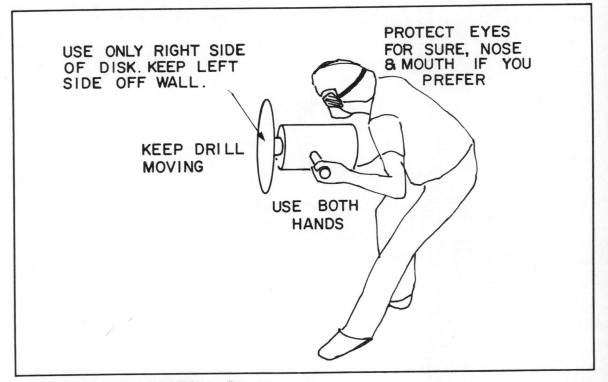

USE ONLY RIGHT SIDE OF DISK. KEEP LEFT SIDE OFF WALL.

PROTECT EYES FOR SURE, NOSE & MOUTH IF YOU PREFER

KEEP DRILL MOVING

USE BOTH HANDS

Fig. 9-4. How to use the hand drill for sanding.

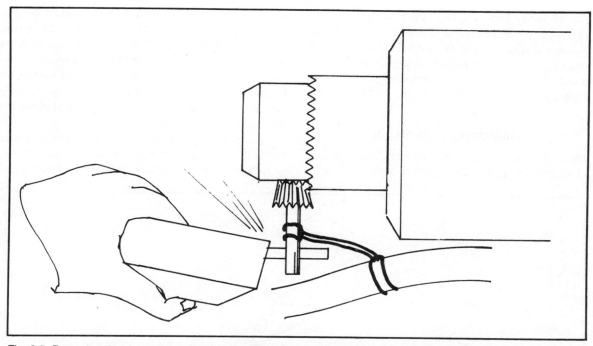

Fig. 9-5. Removing the chuck from a hand drill. With the chuck key fully inserted, rap it sharply with a block of wood; finish removing the chuck by twisting it off with your hand. Chuck keys aren't expensive, but they are easily misplaced. I recommend tying the key to the electrical cord, as shown, with nylon string.

everything in the kitchen with fine dust. The cleanup took some time but was easy, and I had a good surface to take the tile adhesive on the wall. In some places the disk cut indentations shaped like a new moon, but these were filled in with adhesive and covered with tile.

Grinding or Polishing with the Drill

An abrasive wheel and a wire wheel can be put into the chuck for such jobs as grinding a new edge on an old rusty hatchet or knocking the rust off a neglected metal tool. Grinding is often best done with the drill in a stand provided by the manufacturer, but wire brush polishing sometimes has to be done with the drill held in your hands. Be sure to wear goggles for this work and follow other safety precautions.

Another useful function of your drill is polishing the car. You can get sheepskin covers for the sanding pad and buff the surface of the paint until it shines like a mirror. You can also get a high shine on wood floors with this attachment.

Sawing with the Drill

One reason I recommend that your first tool purchase be a drill is because you can get a good electric saw in the bargain. The saw saves you so much time and energy, that your projects can be finished faster and easier and neater.

Some of the best tools of this kind have saw attachments that snap onto the drill after the chuck has been removed. Figure 9-5 shows how to remove the chuck by giving the key a sharp rap with a piece of wood. The chuck is then simply twisted off and put in a safe, handy place.

The saw blade may not go all the way through a 2-inch-by-4-inch piece of lumber, but it is a simple process to turn it over and finish the cut on the other side of the board. Even logs of 4- to 6-inch diameters can be cut this way, but you have to finish the job with a handsaw. With the saw attached, you can hold the drill by hand and take it to the work. Some sets also come with a table that the saw foot slips into, enabling the blade to extend up through a slot. The table should be clamped to a workbench to keep it from moving about (Fig. 9-6).

HAMMERS AND NAILS

Figure 9-7 shows two types of hammer, the curved-claw and straight-claw. The straight-claw is a wrecker's hammer; it is great for prying apart crates and other items, but it mars the surface of the wood when used to pull nails. Because you will probably be using your hammer to build things more often than tear them apart, get the curved-claw hammer. It drives nails just as well as the straight-claw hammer and minimizes damage to the surface of wood when used to pull nails.

Hammers with metal of fiberglass handles are virtually indestructible when exposed to dampness or heat, such as in a chilly garage or a basement

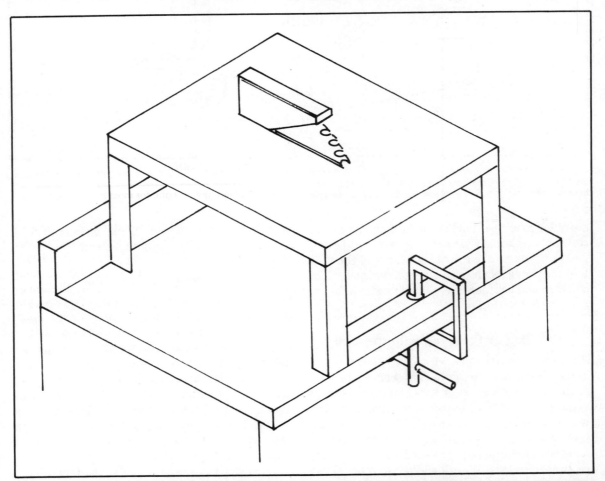

Fig. 9-6. The electric hand drill has been snapped into its saw attachment, which has been locked into place in a metal sawing table. The table should be fastened to the workbench to prevent it from tipping and tilting. A C-clamp has been used to fasten the right rear leg to the bench. Note how the legs have feet to keep them flat on the bench top and to prevent their scoring it. A board has been placed between the front legs, on top of their feet, and secured to the workbench with a C-clamp.

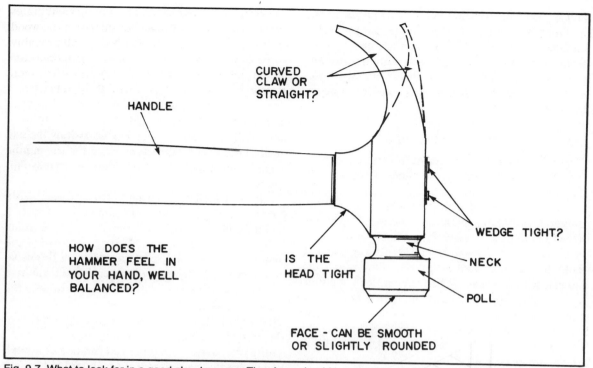

Fig. 9-7. What to look for in a good claw hammer. The claws should be curved, not straight, for most handyperson jobs.

near the furnace. Wood may expand or contract a bit, loosening the head, but many people still prefer wooden handles.

The final general point before discussing buying tips is this: the 16-ounce hammer is the standard, but it is not necessarily the best hammer for your use. I prefer a lighter hammer. It probably takes slightly more effort to drive nails in, but I don't drive nails all day for a living, so that makes little difference to me.

Now, then, you know you want a curved-claw hammer with a sturdy handle. Go to a store and swing several hammers as you would when driving a nail. Note which one feels most comfortable. Try wooden handles and other handles as well. Look at how the head fits on the handle. If it isn't straight, reject that hammer. Look down on the top of the head and see how the handle comes up through the head (on wooden handles, anyway) to be sure there are no gaps between the wood and the metal. One or more metal wedges will be driven into the wood

from the top to spread the wood and make it grip the head firmly. None of the wedges should be protruding; all should be flush with the top of the head. Now have a good look at the claws or the long triangle between them. This triangle should end in a nice point. If it is rounded or square, it won't grip small finishing nails when you want to pull them. Next, run your thumb over the edges of the claws, as though testing them for a sharp edge. In fact, although they shouldn't be sharp enough to cut your thumb, they should have an edge and not be rounded or blunt. For one of these edges is your first weapon in prying up the head of a well-driven nail so that you can then grab it between the claws and pull it all the way out.

A hammer that meets all these tests may have been made in the USA, Asia, Britain, Europe, Australia, or elsewhere. Similarly, hammers that fail the tests may have been made anywhere. When shopping for a secondhand hammer, pass up anything with a loose head. Loose heads can fly off and bruise, cut, or blind you or a child using the hammer. You can get a new handle, but putting it on takes expertise, time, and luck to finish up with a hammer you are really pleased with, not to mention the money for the handle itself. It's worth the wait to get a hammer that pleases you in all respects to begin with.

How to Drive Nails

The following directions for driving nails are for a right-handed person; reverse hands if you are left-handed.

Hold the nail between your left thumb and forefinger. Gently tap it with the head of the hammer. Don't try to bash it, or you'll probably smash your left fingers. For starting the nail in this way, you may hold the hammer about the middle of the handle but no closer to the head. When the nail will stand up on its own, after several of the gentle taps, move your left hand away from it. Move your right hand all the way down the handle; don't "choke" it near the head. Keep your eyes on the nail, especially as the hammer head strikes it. If you don't look at the nail, or if you close your eyes as you are about to strike it, you will tend to hit the nail off center and bend it or knock it right out of the wood. Never try to hit the nail with all your might because that also usually ruins your aim. Just use firm, moderate blows until the nail goes all the way in.

Most hammers are bell-faced, the face is slightly rounded. Professionals using such a hammer can drive a nail flush with the surface of the wood and leave not a mark on the wood. Beginners using either a bell-faced or a plain-faced (flat-faced) hammer will often leave a dent like a half moon on the surface of the wood from the last hammer blow. On play equipment, this may not make any difference at all. On other projects you may want to drive the nail until only 1/8 inch or so is still protruding, then finish driving it in with a nailset. A nailset looks like a steel pencil stub, about 4 inches long. You put the pointed end on the head of the nail, then tap the other end of the nailset with your hammer until the nail has gone flush or slightly below the surface of the wood.

Much has been said in previous chapters about the desirability of driving in nails at an angle for some applications, such as putting ladder rungs on the posts of climbing frames. Nails driven in at an angle almost always form a stronger join than nails driven in at right angles, although this extra strength isn't always absolutely necessary. Sometimes nails will go in at angles, even undesirable angles, whether you want them to or not. With practice, you will be able to draw the nail back to the desired direction by giving the handle a slight pull in the desired direction just as it strikes the nail.

It is difficult to drive nails into hardwood without first drilling a guide hole. That's why I recommend an electric drill so strongly. Drill the guide hole at least 1 inch deep. Make it 1/2 to 3/4 the diameter of the nail. Start the nail with the usual gentle taps and keep tapping gently until the nail reaches the bottom of the guide hole. Now is the time to strike harder blows, for by now enough of the nail will be in the wood that it will likely go in the rest of the way without bending.

If you have an old table you can use as a work bench, try this experiment. Put a board in the center of the table and drive a nail in the board. Next, lay the board on the table so that it is directly over a table leg; drive in another nail. You'll probably notice that the second nail goes in much easier than the first. Anytime the force of your blow can go from the hammer through the nail and down into something solid, it is easier to drive the nail. Because you can't always take the old table to the job, you have to rig means of ensuring a solid object to absorb the force of the blow. When you are nailing wire onto a board between two fence posts, for example, you can prop a log or post against the board on the side opposite to the one you are nailing into. Other ideas for this kind of support are discussed in Chapter 3 along with Fig. 3-4.

How to Pull Nails

There are two objectives when pulling nails: to get the nail out and to minimize damage to the wood. Both objectives can be best met if you keep the nail straight. If it bends while you pull it out, the hole in the wood might be twice as big at the surface as it began. Nails that bend during the pulling also are harder to get out. Figures 9-8 and 9-9 show the best way to get a nail out without bending it. The illustration shows only a single piece of wood being used under the hammer while pulling a long nail, but there is nothing to keep you from starting with one piece and adding more as you need to.

If the nail goes through two pieces of wood, and if it has a head on it, you can usually get enough of the head to surface for a good grip with the claws by prying the boards apart about 1/4 inch. Then tap the boards back together, taking care not to hit the nail. The boards usually go back together leaving the nail head high above the surface. If this doesn't work, get an old screwdriver and tap its flattened edge under the nail head to raise it enough to grip it with the claws. As a last resort, cut away some of the wood around the nail head so that you can get a grip on it.

Finishing nails have heads so small that they usually stay put when you try to pry apart two boards held by the same nail. The easiest thing to do is pry the boards completely apart, which will pull the nail completely through the top board; that hole can be filled with putty or plastic wood or some other filler, if necessary, and the nail can now be pulled from the second board.

Pulling Nails without a Hammer

Europeans pull nails with a tool that looks as if it were made for pinching (Fig. 9-9). Note how the shape of the tool is rounded so that it can be rocked back to pull out the nail with minimum damage to the wood surface. You can pull nails the same way with a pliers. If the nails are small enough, you can pull them out by brute force and a little twist. If the nails are harder to budge, put blocks of wood under the pliers, just as you do with the claw hammer, to keep the nail straight as it comes out. If the nails bend slightly at or near the head, they come out fairly easily by this method.

The thicker, stronger nails that don't bend when grabbed by the hammer have to be drawn out with a slight variation on the basic theme. Start out in

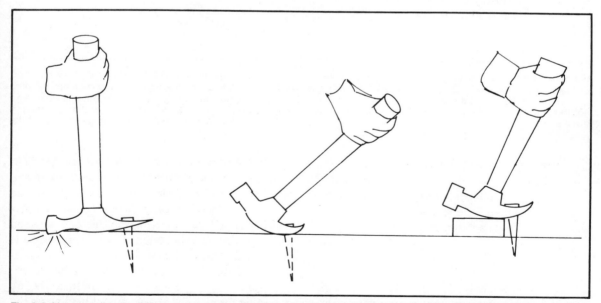

Fig. 9-8. How to pull nails with a hammer. Left: when you pull a nail with a straight-clawed hammer, the poll of the hammer has to dig into the wood as you pull back on the handle. That's why you should choose a curved-claw hammer. Middle: when you pull back on the handle of a curved-claw hammer, its rounded design enables you to pull out the nail with minimum damage to the wood surface. Right: placing a piece of wood under the hammerhead enables you to pull the nail out easier by keeping the nail from bending excessively.

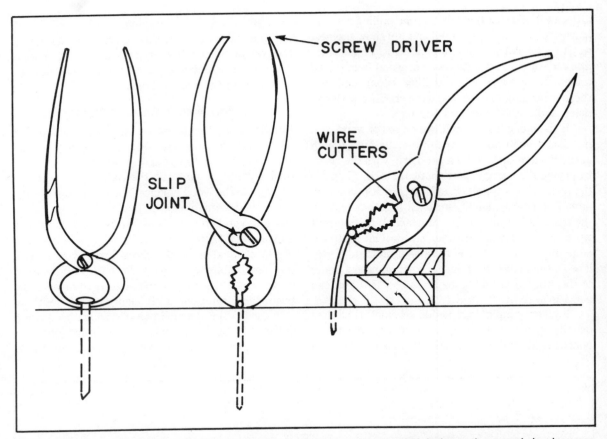

Fig. 9-9. Right: a European-style nail-pulling tool. Note the similarity of its rounded design to the curved-claw hammer. Center: pulling a nail with slip-joint pliers. Right: blocks of wood under the pliers increase leverage and keep nail bending to a minimum. Note that the pliers can cut wire and drive large screws (provided you get pliers designed to do so and not the sort with plastic-coated handles). In the position shown, the pliers' jaws will meet if taken off the nail head. If the handles are slipped apart as far as the slot labeled "slip joint" will allow, the fine teeth will no longer meet, but the jaws can be put around a larger nut or bolt head.

the usual way, but as you pull more and more nail out, and you have to add the second and third blocks of wood, place the blocks farther and farther away from the nail hole. The nail will bend slightly and enlarge the hole as it comes out, but it will come.

NESTED SAWS

The set of saws shown in Fig. 9-10 has a handle, shaped like a pistol grip, that is common to three or more saw blades. The handle might be wood or plastic. After fitting a blade into the handle, tighten a wing nut to keep the blade in place. The three

standard blades are a crosscut saw blade, a key-hole saw, and a hacksaw blade. You might also get a pruning saw (for cutting small living limbs and branches off trees) and a blade that looks like a second hacksaw blade but thicker; this one is called a plumber's saw. It is designed to cut through nails embedded in wood, leaving a kerf, the slit formed by the passage of the saw blade though the material, wide enough for a wood saw to continue the job of cutting through the board without binding on the sides of the nail.

Many countries and manufacturers seem to have competed in producing the cheapest, poorest quality set of nested saws, but if you look at enough sets you'll find one that will do. Even the good ones may look or feel flimsy, however, but that might not be a disadvantage. My pruning saw blade got hung up in the process of going through a gummy branch; it had to be pulled out, and it emerged with a bend of about 70 degrees in it. I straightened it out with my fingers, put it back in the kerf, and continued. It worked all right. All this is not to suggest that the blades in the nested saw set will do your jobs as well as saws with blades rigidly set in their handles. The nested set equips you with several saws for the price of one with a rigid blade, and you can do most jobs with it as well, if not quite as fast.

THE FOUR-IN-ONE WOOD RASP

A rasp looks like a file, but if you look at it sideways you'll see the little triangular projections that constitute its business side. A rasp can quickly reduce the diameter of a new handle for an old shovel blade or take the sharp edges off pieces of wood your kids will step down on hard when climbing homemade ladders. Figure 9-11 shows several views of the four-in-one rasp. The teeth are raised on both the flat side and the half-round side, giving you two rough cutting edges and two smoother cutting edges. Experimentation will teach you when to use the flat side, when the rounded. The smooth, slightly rounded ends of the rasp are preferable in the beginner's

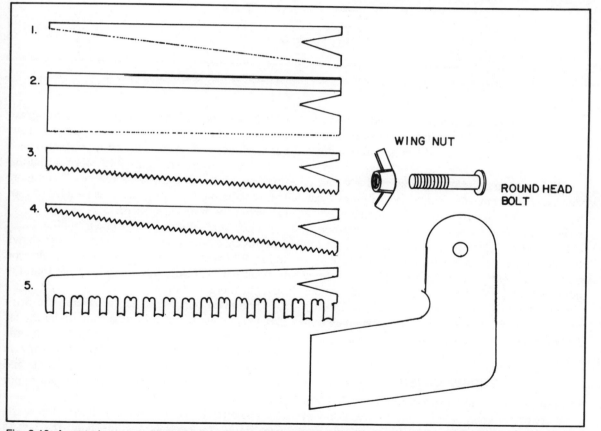

Fig. 9-10. A nested saw set. All the blades will fit into the handle, one at a time. The roundhead bolt is then inserted and a wing nut tightened on the other side to hold the blade in place. Not all sets have the blades shown here, so shop around. The blades are (1) a hacksaw blade for cutting metal; (2) a backsaw blade, with a stiff, rigid back and fine teeth; (3) a crosscut saw blade, with bigger teeth; (4) a keyhole or compass saw blade, which can be used for cutting curves and circles; (5) a pruning saw blade for trimming small limbs and branches on living trees.

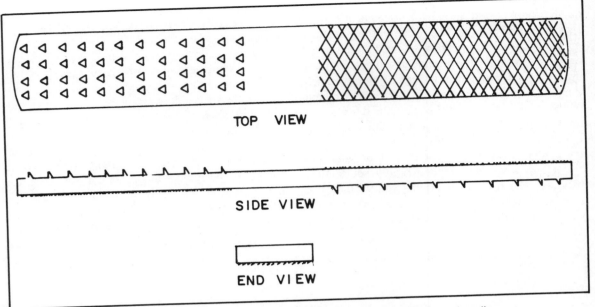

TOP VIEW

SIDE VIEW

END VIEW

Fig. 9-11. The four-in-one wood rasp. The teeth are tiny raised triangles that take off wood easily.

tool box to the type with a pointed end (called the tang) that is designed to go into a wooden handle, because without the handle the tang makes a good hand puncher.

With a rasp to take off rough edges, sharp edges, and splinters, with an electric drill-saw to cut the wood to size and to drill the holes for the bolts or the guide holes for nails or screws, a hammer to nail the pieces together, and a nested saw set for the minor cuts not made with the electric saw, you are now equipped to build most of the projects in preceding chapters. Some other tools may make parts of the job go easier or faster although only two or three might be considered indispensible in the beginner's tool box—screwdrivers, a pliers, and a wrench.

SCREWDRIVERS

Screwdrivers come in all sizes and shapes, but you can start with a good old-fashioned straight model with a tip about 1/4 inch wide. It will enable you to drive most of the screws you need for the play equipment in this book. You can and should add screwdrivers of different sizes and shapes later on.

Get at least one with a narrower tip, for making adjustments on certain tools, tightening parts on sewing machines, and so on. Eventually you'll also need a Phillips screwdriver. Figure 9-12 shows a Phillips-tip screwdriver and cross-slot screw; you'll commonly find them on the door or window handles of your car or on the rear-view mirror.

They don't always seem to be available, but if you can get a 3-headed screwdriver like that shown in Fig. 9-12 you'll get a screwdriver that enables you to twist with considerably more leverage than the straight models allow.

The main purpose of screwdrivers is to drive screws, of course, but they also come in handy for prying up embedded nail heads, prying apart boards nailed together, prying off soda bottle caps in emergencies, scraping off old, flaking paint, and scoring wood for a saw cut when you forgot to put a pencil in your pocket.

How to drive a screw. To drive a screw, the first thing you need is a guide hole; the last, a screwdriver. You can buy special drill bits that drill holes in a single operation to accommodate the threaded root of the screw, its body, and its head.

Driving a screw into such a hole enables you to drive the head down into the wood, leaving a nice flush surface. This is called countersinking the screw. But, I've never used such a drill bit, in spite of their reasonable price. I simply choose a drill bit that is about 3/4 the diameter of the screw and use it for the guide hole. If I want to countersink the screw head (Fig. 9-13), I either carve away enough wood with a pocket knife or use a 3/8-inch drill bit to chew out a depression in the surface to accommodate the screw head.

When the guide hole is prepared, the screw should be prepared. It'll go in easier if the threads are rubbed on something slippery. Some people use soap; others claim this promotes rot. I've used soap without having problems, but I've also used parafin wax, which does as good a job and repels, rather than absorbs, moisture.

The first few times you drive a screw you'll find that the screwdriver keeps slipping out of the slot in the head of the screw. You can make better time if you lightly hold the screwdriver in place with your free hand. Make the first few turns very carefully to ensure that the screw goes straight into the hole. If it gets started at an angle, you'll be tempted to go ahead and drive it all the way in, but you'll run into strife as the screw by-passes the guide hole and tries to break its own new pathway.

Once the screw is started on a straight and true path down the guide hole, you can bear down harder on the screwdriver. It's usually comfortable to hold the screwdriver as you would a dinner knife,

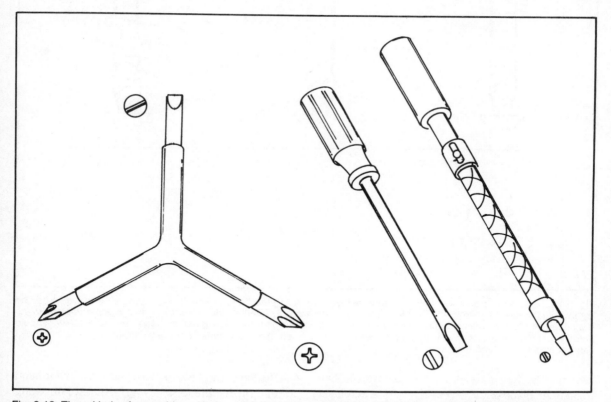

Fig. 9-12. Three kinds of screwdrivers. Left: a triple-header, containing two Phillips head screwdriving ends and one for driving slotted screws. The type of screw head each will drive is shown beside it. Center: an ordinary blade-type screw driver. Right: a Yankee-type screwdriver. Pushing on the handle makes the shaft revolve along the X-shaped lines, twisting the blade and driving in the screw. The triple-header and the blade screwdrivers are drawn about half size, but the Yankee type is shown at about a 20 percent reduction.

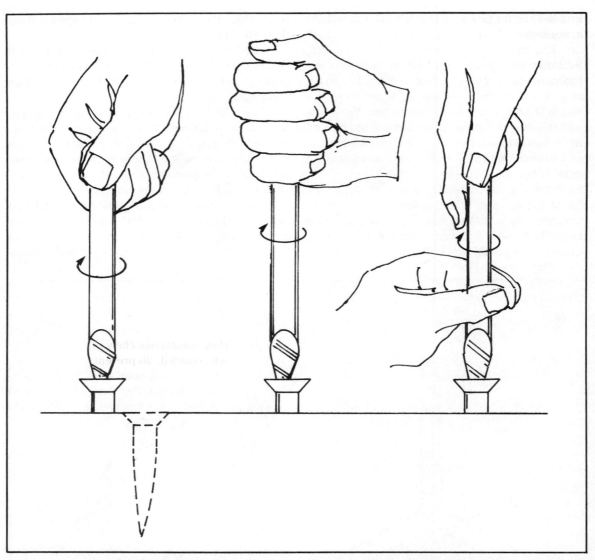

Fig. 9-13. How to drive a screw. Left and right: two ways of using the "dinner knife" grip on the screwdriver. You can lightly hold the blade in place with the other hand, as shown at right. Center: the "ice pick" grip can sometimes be used. It enables you to use different muscles in your wrist and forearm, and it gives good leverage. Flathead screws should be fully countersunk, as shown with dotted lines at the left. If left above the surface of the wood, the edges of the head can become foot-cutting instruments.

twisting the screw about 1/4 turn before you have to take the blade of the screwdriver out and reinsert it. It is sometimes possible to change your grip on the screwdriver handle (Fig. 9-13), holding it as you would if you wanted to chip ice. If you are holding the screwdriver vertically, a little practice will enable you to leave the blade in place and swivel your hand around the handle for a new grip, instead of taking out and reinserting the blade each time. Driving a screw this way requires different muscles in your wrist and forearm, so when you have many screws to drive, you can alternate between the dinner knife grip and the ice pick grip and give all your muscles a workout.

The triple-headed screwdriver shown in Fig. 9-12 may be a misnomer, because we refer to the business end of the driver as a blade rather than a head. The triple-whatever has one flat blade and two Phillips screwdrivers on it. You usually have to start the screws in their guide holes in the manner described above with a straight screwdriver, then switch to the triple-header, which will enable you to twist the screw harder. It is especially valuable for driving screws into hardwood.

If you are countersinking the screw, drive it in until the head is flush with or slightly below the surface of the wood. If you are using round- or ovalheaded screws, drive them in until the head stops the inward movement of the screw. It is possible in softwood to drive a screw all the way into its guide hole. Then give it several extra twists. But this is not only unnecessary, it is undesirable because it can lead to the loosening of the screw later on.

Driving screws into hardwood is more frequently a problem than worrying about a screw's loosening in softer wood. If you are at all worried, switch to a different fastener, like nuts and bolts, if possible. If you have to stick with screws you can fill the guide hole with glue before driving in the screw. A white glue is excellent for this; you can also use plastic wood and other fillers. If you use a filler that comes as a powder you add water to, however, read the directions carefully. If the directions say you have to paint nail heads with an enamel paint before using the filler on nail holes, don't use it to fill guide holes for screws, for it will make them rust and hasten the loosening process.

PLIERS

Figure 9-9 shows the different things you can do with slip-joint pliers. For this reason it is a good idea to carefully inspect any pliers before paying the full retail price to ensure you are getting all the tool possible for your money. The screwdriver blade at the end of the handle, for example, is bigger than the blades most householders buy, and the way you would hold the pliers when driving screws is much like the way you would hold the triple-headed screwdriver, which gives you considerably more leverage when driving the screws. Many pliers have plastic-coated handles, which means you won't get the screwdriver blade.

Most pliers, whatever the shape, have blades for cutting wire just behind their notched jaws. If the nut and bolt loosen on the slip-joint pliers, the blades will bend the wire at a right angle instead of cutting right through.

The slip joint slips to two different positions. Closed, it enables the pliers to grab small things, like finishing nails. Slipped to the other position, it enables the jaws to open wider and get around bigger objects, like bottle tops too stubborn to be opened by hand.

Pliers can also be used to twist ends of wire together to make longer pieces or to tighten a loop around something. They can be used to pull nails and staples. They can be used to tighten nuts and bolts, but they sometimes chew off the edges and make the nut rounded. To prevent as much of this as possible, slip the joint open and try to grasp the nut with the finest teeth rather than the bigger teeth in the curved parts of the pliers' jaws. If you can use the pliers to hold the nut or bolt stationary while tightening or loosening at the other end, you can usually avoid rounding the nuts. This is sometimes possible if you grab the squared part of a carriage bolt just under the half-rounded head.

There are many other sorts of pliers, but you can add them as your pocketbook allows. One of our favorites is a real grabber. It has long jaws set at an angle of about 60 degrees off the handles. It also has a slip joint, which enables it to open to about 1.75 inches. It opens even bigger jars and bottles than the mechanics's pliers described above. We also like a needle-nosed pliers to reach through small openings and grab wires, and blunt-nosed pliers for working with heavier wire on grape arbors, trellises, and fences.

A GOOD WRENCH

A wrench such as that shown in Fig. 9-14 will ad-

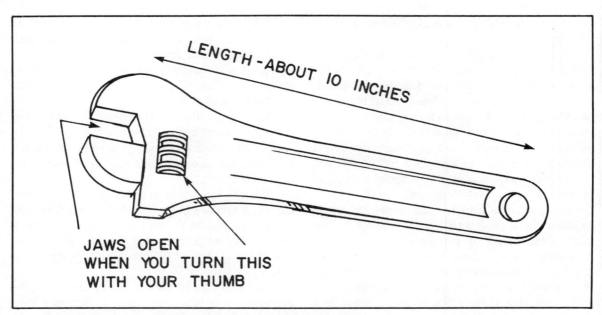

LENGTH - ABOUT 10 INCHES

JAWS OPEN
WHEN YOU TURN THIS
WITH YOUR THUMB

Fig. 9-14. The first kind of wrench you should buy for your tool box.

just to any size nut, from the tiniest up to 1 1/8 inch, just be twisting the threads with your thumb. This is probably a little larger than you'll need for the nuts and bolts used to fasten together the parts of climbing frames, swings, and trapezes. When it comes to loosening nuts, however, the longer the handle, the greater the leverage, so it is best to have a larger wrench than you think you need.

ADDITIONAL TOOLS

By "later on" I mean after you've bought the materials for your play equipment and you have money to spare to complete your tool box. You have to establish your own priorities for getting the things that follow. If you want to put fancy curlicues on a playhouse, for example, you may want to get the jigsaw or electric saber saw first. If you want to make some picture frames, a miter box and rigid-backed backsaw would be your first choice.

Coping Saws, Jigsaws, and Saber Saws

A coping saw is shown in Fig. 9-15. It's a great saw for adults and kids alike, for it cuts around curves and circles with the greatest of ease. You can buy the blades in hardware stores or dime stores. If you twist the handle one way, it tightens the blade; twist it the other, and it loosens the blade. You can turn the blade 90 degrees (as you can a hacksaw) to continue a long cut when the coping saw's metal frame would stop you otherwise.

Coping saws are sometimes called jigsaws, and electric jigsaws are sometimes called saber saws. The electric jigsaw shown in Fig. 9-15 consists of an electric motor that jigs a 3-inch blade up and down several thousand times a second. The foot rests flush on the surface of the board, sheet of plastic, or piece of metal to be cut. Thus, the blade is in and under the board, never on top. Therefore, as long as you keep your hands on top, you won't cut off a finger or gash your hand.

You must change the blade according to the material you wish to cut—wood, metal, or plastic. You can cut straight lines or fanciful scrolls. To change blades, simply loosen two screws; the old blade will drop out, and you insert the new one and tighten the screws.

The possibilities for the jigsaw are almost endless: gingerbread for playhouses, rocking chair seats between profiles of swans, hobbyhorse heads,

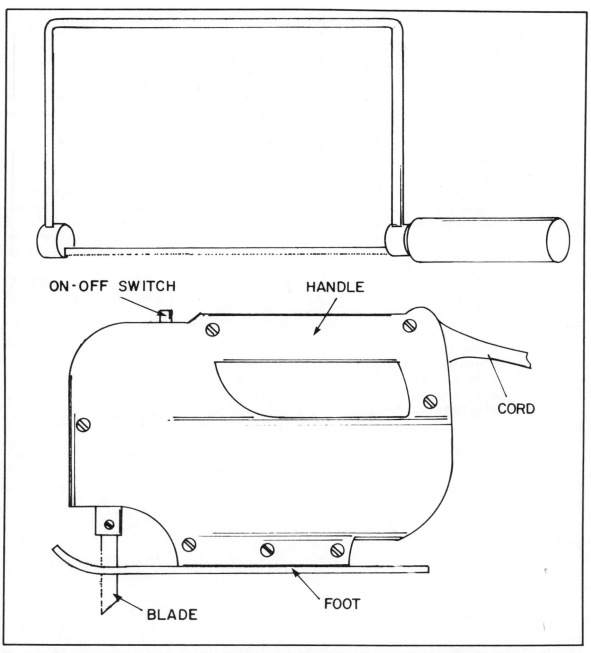

ON-OFF SWITCH

HANDLE

CORD

BLADE

FOOT

Fig. 9-15. Top: a coping saw. This saw has a thin blade that can be used for cutting curves and curlicues in softwoods. The blades are available in many shops and are easily replaced. The blade is loosened by twisting the handle. With the blade still in the wood, the handle can be twisted to loosen the blade and the saw frame can be set at right angles to the blade; the handle is then twisted in the opposite direction to tighten the blade in its new position. Hacksaw blades can also be set at right angles to their frames. Bottom: An electric jigsaw. This saw is more versatile than the coping saw and will do the same kind of curves and curlicues. It will also cut through frozen meats.

jigsaw puzzles, fancy arches for indoors, and fancy window shutters for outside.

If you have a key-hole saw blade in your nested saw set, you already have one blade that will cut around curves (Fig. 9-10), but it isn't nearly so fast or versatile as the electric jigsaw. Nor does the electric jigsaw have to start with a hole drilled in the stock. Draw a line where you want to make a cut then hold the saw so that the tip of the blade is on the line. Gently turn the ON button or pull the trigger, depending on which model you have; the saw blade will work its way through the stock, and you then make the cut as usual. This takes a steady hand, so it is best to get some practice first in holding the saw and starting cuts with the foot flat on the stock.

The trick in using this tool, if there is a trick at all, is in keeping the foot flat. Start out by resting the foot on the stock with the blade not quite touching the pencil mark where you want to make a cut. Turn on the machine. Gently push it up to the mark; the blade will eat into the stock. Now, gently push the jigsaw along the pencil mark. Don't hurry it. Let the saw do most of the pulling.

One last accolade to this versatile tool: you can cut right through frozen meats, bones and all, as long as you don't thaw them first.

A Bench Hook and Miter Box

A drawing of the bench hook (Fig. 9-16) will get its purpose across more easily than 1,000 words here. A bench hook can be made in minutes, and you'll soon think it's worth its weight in precious metal for holding pieces of wood still while you make careful cuts in them.

The miter box (Fig. 9-17) can be used to cut pieces of wood at angles of 90 degrees and 45

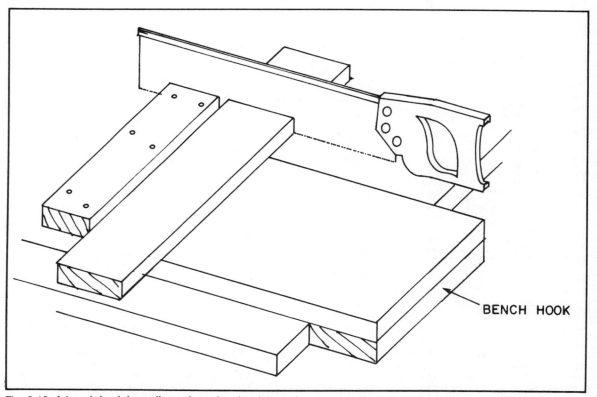

Fig. 9-16. A bench hook is easily made and makes it easy for you to hold wood steady for fine cuts with the backsaw.

168

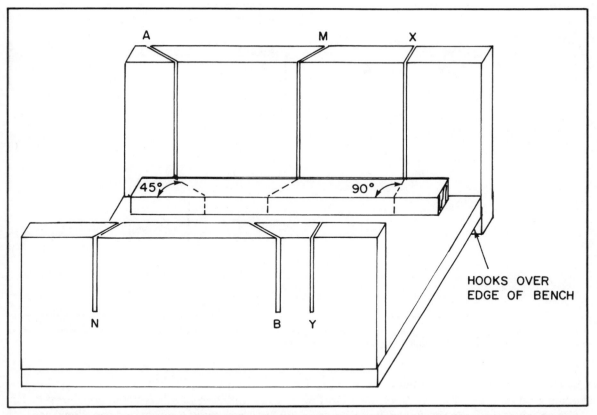

Fig. 9-17. A wooden miter box. Putting the backsaw blade through slots X and Y enables you to cut a neat, accurate, and square edge on a board. Slots A and B give you a 45-degree angle, as do slots M and N. This is a handy tool for constructing picture frames and other projects requiring nicely fitted corners.

degrees. They are fairly inexpensive, even new, but if not used carefully their kerfs widen. Thus, if you are cutting something like picture frames, it's best to do it while your miter box is new. Note that one side of the miter box is slightly longer than the other. This is so you can hook it over the side of the workbench, as you do the bench hook.

For more money you can get a steel miter box, which enables you to cut angles ranging all the way up to about 170 degrees. The backsaw comes as part of the steel miter box, in most sets.

Backsaws

A backsaw is a saw with a short, straight blade, fine teeth, and a piece of steel wrapped over the top of the blade to hold it rigid while you use it. It is pic-

tured with the bench hook in Fig. 9-16. Its fine teeth enable you to make neat cuts in picture frames, window trim stock, and other applications where appearance is important.

Chisels

Here's a case where I advise against the general rule of buying good, secondhand tools—unless you really know what you are doing. There are several different kinds of chisels, not all of them suitable for wood. With some of them you must use a wooden mallet or plastic-faced hammer, which means the purchase of yet another tool.

If you shop at a hardware store that carries good quality merchandise, you'll be able to get a set of chisels you can use with your claw hammer. Tap the

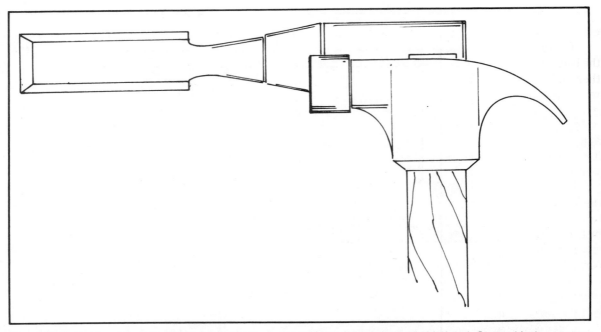

Fig. 9-18. Using the side of the hammerhead to tap a wood chisel with an unbreakable head. Some chisels are more delicate and require a wooden mallet or plastic-faced hammer.

chisels with the side of the hammer (Fig. 9-18). I bought a set of three chisels, with blades from 1 to 1/2 inch wide, made by the Fuller Tool Company of Whitestone, New York. The handles are said to be unbreakable. That may be stretching a point slightly, but I have used the chisels with a claw hammer with no ill effects to the handles.

When you shop for chisels, get professional advice from the salesclerk and be sure you can get your money back or a replacement set of chisels if the handles don't hold up. Unless you are going to use wood turning equipment, avoid the long-handled chisels you hold by hand against a piece of wood spinning in a wood turning machine to turn out curved table and chair legs.

Chisel blades are easily sharpened by hand if you work slowly and carefully as shown in Fig. 9-19. The same techniques are used to sharpen the blades of planes. It is well worth your time to keep these tools sharp, for they are much more enjoyable and satisfying to use when they make good clean cuts and don't hang up in the wood.

Planes

A block plane and a jack plane are shown in Fig. 9-20. A jack plane is larger, and you should use both hands when using it. The block plane can be held in one hand. When you use the plane, move it in the direction of the grain. It should make a nice, smooth, clean shaving that comes off in curls, which will delight the kids. If the plane chips the surface of the wood, or bucks and revolts as you try to push it along the surface, you are probably going against the grain. Try planing in the opposite direction, and you'll probably find that you get smoother cuts and that you can draw the plane back for the next cut by barely lifting it off the surface of the wood.

A plane is handy to use if you can easily adjust the blade to make shallow or deep cuts. On block planes, this adjustment is made by twisting a small knob that sticks out slightly from the back of the plane. If you hold the plane on the side and watch the blade as you give this knob several turns both ways, you should be able to see the blade moving back and forth. This is the best kind of plane to buy, even if another sort is cheaper.

The cheaper model has a coin-shaped wheel at the back. Turn this wheel and the blade loosens. You then pull out or push in the blade and retighten the wheel. As you retighten the wheel, you sometimes move the blade away from the position you carefully put it in by hand, so you have to start all over again. This doesn't always happen, of course, but it can make the extra money for the other model well worth it.

The jack plane works much the same way as the block plane. You can adjust the depth of cut by turning a little wheel (Fig. 9-20), and you can adjust the angle of the blade by moving the lever on top. You can check whether the blade is sticking out parallel to the sole of the plane by holding it upside down and looking at it against a light.

If you are buying a new plane, have the salesclerk show you how to remove the blade. If you buy a used plane, you may have to do a bit of fiddling and figure it out for yourself. At any rate, you should keep the blades retracted when not in use, and keep them sharp. Sharpen the blades with the same method shown for chisels in Fig. 9-19.

Handsaws

There are two types of common handsaws, crosscut and rip saw. Figure 9-21 shows the difference. The teeth of the crosscut are like little daggers, and the teeth of the ripsaw are like little chisels. Ripsaws are used for turning a wide board into narrower

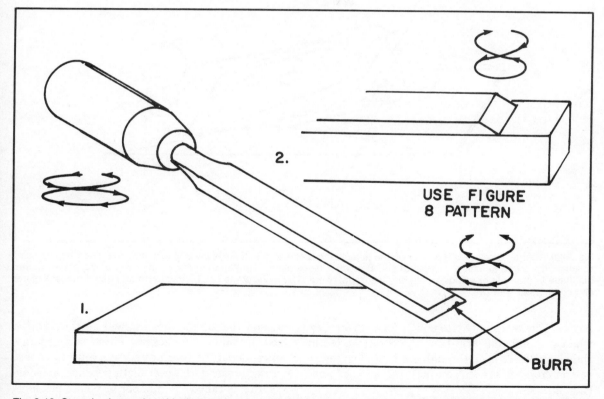

2.

USE FIGURE
8 PATTERN

1.

BURR

Fig. 9-19. Steps in sharpening chisels and blades of planes. One: using a broad, figure-8 pattern, sharpen the bevel side of the chisel. After a while a burr will form on the flat side. Two: turn the chisel over and rub the flat side in a broad, figure-8 pattern to remove the burr and to complete the sharpening process. The sharpening stone has a medium and a coarse side. Use the coarse side then the medium side. While sharpening chisels and plane blades, keep the stone lubricated with a light oil, such as sewing machine oil or a penetrating oil.

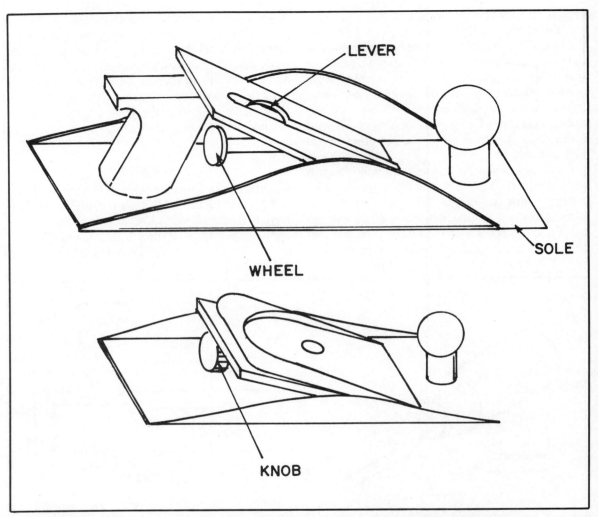

Fig. 9-20. Top: a jack plane. The lever on top adjusts the blade so that it stays parallel with the sole. The wheel is used to adjust the blade to alter the depth of cut. Bottom: a block plane. Turning the knob at the back of the plane causes the blade to protrude or withdraw, altering the depth of cut. The block plane can be used with one hand; the jack plane should be used with two.

boards. The teeth only bite on the forward stroke; when you pull your arm back the chisellike teeth slide harmlessly back through the kerf. The teeth on the crosscut saw cut on both the forward and back strokes.

As most of your cutting will be across the grain, your first choice should be the crosscut saw. Experts say you shouldn't use it for making rip cuts, but it will do so. The more teeth per inch, the finer the

cut, and the slower the saw will go through the wood. If you have a backsaw, either as a separate tool or as part of your nested set, you can choose a crosscut saw with fewer teeth per inch. Incidentally, this is called the number of points per inch. As Fig. 9-21 shows, an 8-point saw actually has eight points but only seven full teeth to the inch. My advice is to select your saw by sight, not description, of the number of points; get one that adds to

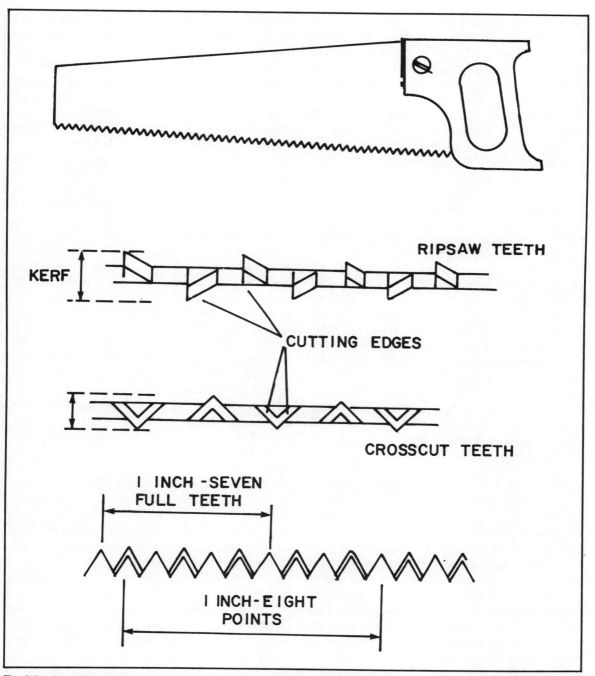

KERF

RIPSAW TEETH

CUTTING EDGES

CROSSCUT TEETH

I INCH - SEVEN
FULL TEETH

I INCH - EIGHT
POINTS

Fig. 9-21. A handsaw. A magnified drawing in the center shows the difference between the teeth of a rip saw and a crosscut saw. Rip saw teeth are like small chisels; they cut only on the forward stroke. Crosscut saw teeth are small triangles sharpened on both sides that extend away from the saw blade. They cut on both forward and back strokes. Bottom: an 8-point saw has eight points and seven full teeth to the inch.

and doesn't repeat your tool collection. Pay the extra money and get one recommended by a carpenter. To the layperson's eye there is no difference between a cheap saw and a quality one, so don't buy one off the discount store's rack without checking its reputation first.

Nothing looks easier than cutting with a saw, and nothing is so frustrating as when it skitters on the edge of the board instead of cutting into it or when it cuts only 1/16 inch deep and then jumps out again or when it lets you draw it back 4 inches and then stops dead. The way to start the cut is to put the saw teeth on the board and draw the saw toward you, slowly. Don't start any farther down than half the blade, and you'll find it easier if you use the 6 inches of teeth nearest the saw handle. Draw the handle toward you several times till you get a notch deep enough to hold the saw blade and keep it from jumping out and scoring the board where you don't want to saw. Then you can bear down a little harder, letting the saw do most of the work, and you'll be through the boards very quickly. You can pull and push with great force, but I speak with bitter experience in telling you that unpleasant things can happen. If the blade hangs, the handle will have to go somewhere; it can skew to the side, causing nearby teeth to gash your hand, arm, or leg. It's not easily done, but you can also snap the blade.

I advise marking the boards to be cut with a ball point pen, unless their surface is so rough the pen won't mark them. The pen doesn't go blunt, as a pencil does, nor does its point snap off and require sharpening. Even if you get a good sharp line, saw to the outside of it (Fig. 9-22). Most of the designs in this book don't require precision sawing but if you are cutting out a cabinet or a set of book shelves, you'll want the boards to be as close as possible to the exact measure. If the board is slightly long, put a sheet of rough sandpaper on a block of wood and take off the offending length. (This is why I recommend the electric saw/drill set before the handsaw; with the electric saw in the table you can saw the width of the saw blade off the end of the board.) If you cut a board slightly short, you can usually make it do by building up the end with a sliver of wood and glue, hold it in place, and drill guide holes for the nails or screws that will hold it where you want it.

Here are a few sawing tips, most of which are common sense. Raise the board to be sawed high enough so that the saw blade doesn't strike the floor or ground on your down stroke. Don't leave the saw lying on the ground, unless it is desert ground on a bright sunny day. Don't pile hammers, planes, screwdrivers, chisels, or any other implement on the saw blade as it lies on the table or workbench. If you are notching a piece of wood, don't twist the saw blade to knock the waste out of the notch or off the corner; hold the piece of waste as you make the final saw cuts very gently and let the waste piece come loose in your hand. Similarly, if you are sawing the end off a board, hold the waste end as you reach the final stages of the cut, especially if the waste is going to be big enough to start bending earthward as you finish the cut. If you just keep on sawing, intent on allowing the waste to simply drop off, it will take with it a long splinter from the bottom side of the board as it falls. If your boards aren't new, inspect them carefully for nails, especially the sneaky saw-breaking sort that have broken off inside the wood, leaving no head showing. Avoid sawing through knots. It's hard to get a handsaw through a knot, and sawing through a tight knot sometimes loosens it, turning a blemish into a defect.

Finally, I advise against trying to sharpen a saw by yourself. You need good equipment, patience, skill, and time. Have your handsaw sharpened professionally. With electric saws, dealers often have a blade exchange service. You give them your old, dull blade and a few dollars, and they give you a sharpened blade that a customer before you traded in dull.

When you are finished with the saw, rub the blade with an oily rag, leaving enough oil on it to prevent rust, and either hang it on the wall or put it in the tool box to protect it.

Hacksaws

A proper hacksaw allows you to cut through metals

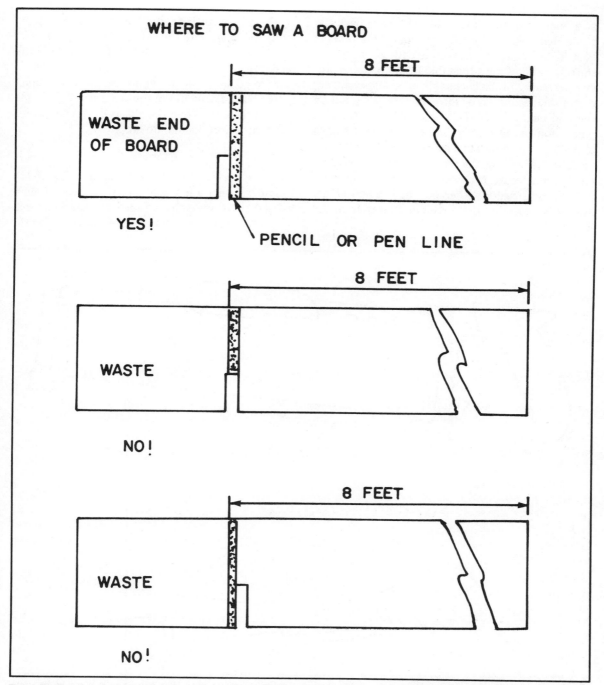

Fig. 9-22. One correct way and two wrong ways to saw a board. The saw blade should always go on the waste end of the board, never down the middle of the pencil or pen mark and never on the good side of the mark. Ball point pens are best for marking boards for cuts because their points don't go blunt and widen. Pencils are second best; felt-tip pens, third.

at a faster rate than that allowed by the hacksaw blade that comes with the nested saw kit. This is because you can hold the handle with one hand and the other end of the adjustable frame with the other. The blades of the hacksaw can be interchanged, or new blades put in, by loosening the wing nut on the end near the handle. Pins hold the blades in place. You can also turn the blade at right angles to the frame to make deep cuts (Fig. 9-23). A "hard" blade is one in which the whole thing has been hardened by tempering; in a flexible blade, only the teeth have been hardened. When putting in a new blade, always be sure that the teeth point away from the handle.

If you are cutting something round, like a pipe, guide the blade with the side of the thumb on your free hand until the cut is deep enough to hold the blade; then use both hands to complete the cut. If you are going to cut through something flat, don't lay the blade flat on it. Put the blade at a slight angle to start the cut. When the slot is deep enough for you to use both hands, do so.

Clamps

The first clamps to get are C-clamps (Fig. 9-24). Clamp together a few pieces of waste wood before using them on wood that will go into a finished product so that you can get the feel of how they work.

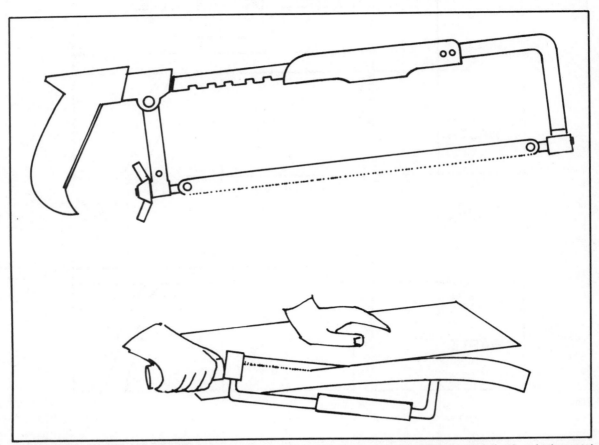

Fig. 9-23. A hacksaw with an adjustable frame. The blade is held in place with pins. With the blade in place in the metal it has been cutting, you can loosen the blade and turn the frame to a position at right angles with the blade, then retighten the blade. This enables you to make long cuts, as shown at bottom, in materials that would otherwise block the motion of the frame.

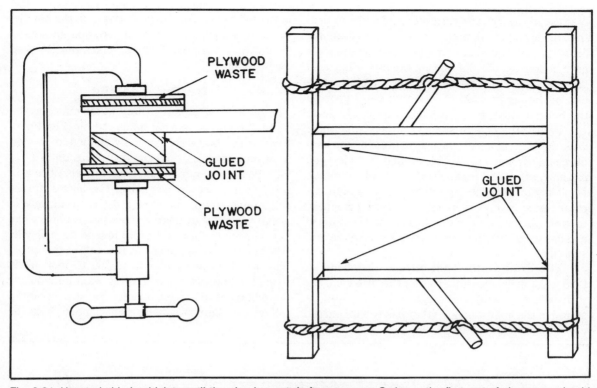

Fig. 9-24. How to hold glued joints until the glue has set. Left: a common C-clamp, the first sort of clamp you should get for your tool box. The clamping ends will mar the wood they are tightened against, but you can protect the surface of the wood by using bits of waste wood as shown. Right: drawn to a much smaller scale is a good means of holding larger structures, like drawers, while glue sets. This is a top view, except for the boards with ropes looped around them. Always place the boards so that they hold rigid, not flex like diving boards. Loop rope around both boards, then twist the rope with a small stick as shown in the center. When the rope is tight enough, you can rest the stick against the glued structure to prevent the ropes from untwisting.

With softwoods, you'll notice how the clamp makes a dent with both its clamping surfaces. Sometimes these dents won't matter, for the dented side of the wood will be nailed onto something so that it can't show. If a dent would matter, don't put the clamp directly onto the surface of the wood; protect it with a small piece of waste or an off cut of plywood.

Spring clamps are like oversized clothespins; they are okay for light work. But a C-clamp is also okay for light work, so if you don't have an unlimited tool budget, you can pass up the spring clamp. There are some other special purpose clamps that I recommend only if you want to do woodwork as a business or a hobby. These include the bar clamp, which can be used to glue together boards des-

tined to become table tops; corner clamps, for gluing the corners of picture frames; and hand clamps, which can be adjusted to many angles.

More Drills

I've already sung the praises of the electric drill. But there are times when you want only one or two holes, or where there may not be a convenient source of electricity. That's when a hand drill is nice to have. The hand drill (Fig. 9-25) has a chuck that takes bits, like the electric drill. You can use the same bits that the electric drill takes, although less expensive carbon drill bits are sufficient; they also save your high-speed bits for use exclusively in the electric drill. Once the jaws of the chuck have firm-

177

ly grasped the bit, you turn the big handle to drill the hole in the wood, metal, or plastic. You can use drills up to 1/4 inch in diameter. The best models have hollow handles for storing the bits. They also have two gears, one on the top and one on the bottom of the big gear. Models with a small gear on the bottom only often develop a wiggly big gear.

To drill the hole, make a dent or a small hole with the point of a nail. Be sure to hold the top handle steady. If you let it wobble around in circles, you can snap off the bit in the wood or plastic or metal. Don't try to turn the big handle with smooth circular turns; if you use more of a starting-stopping motion, putting most of the pressure in the upward and downward strokes, you'll be able to hold the drill steadier.

The Push Drill. The push drill shown in Fig. 9-25 won't drill holes much larger than 1/8 inch, but it drills them easily and quickly. The bits can be stored in the hollow handle; they easily slip into the jaws of the drill. As you push down on the handle, the drill body spins on the crisscrossed lines carved into it diamond-fashion, like the Yankee screwdriver.

The Brace and Bit

The bit, of course, is the thing which cuts into the wood. The brace is what holds the bit (Fig. 9-26). Bits for the brace are specially shaped at the top to fit into its chuck. You can drill holes up to 1 1/2 inch in diameter in wood. You can also drive in screws with a screwdriver blade. The bigger bits are called auger bits, and they must be used only in wood. You can start them without the customary nail hole punched in first, but I recommend the nail hole. Although the sharp point at the end of the auger bit will drill its own guiding hole, you are more likely to get the hole exactly where you want it if you use the nail point to make a hole for the sharp point to fall into. Assuming you are right-handed, hold the

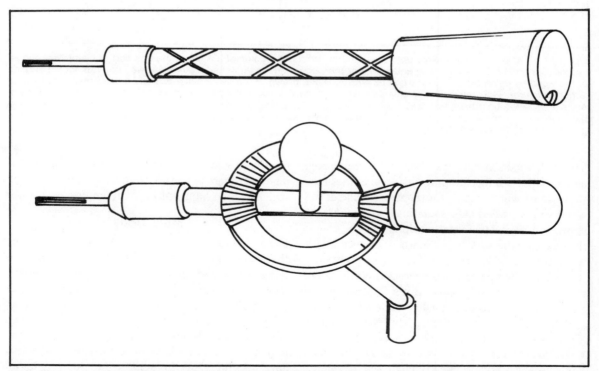

Fig. 9-25. Top: a push drill. Bits can be stored in the handle; they come out through the notch on top. The bits snap into the drill at the bottom. Bottom: a hand drill, with small gears at top and bottom of the larger, turning gear.

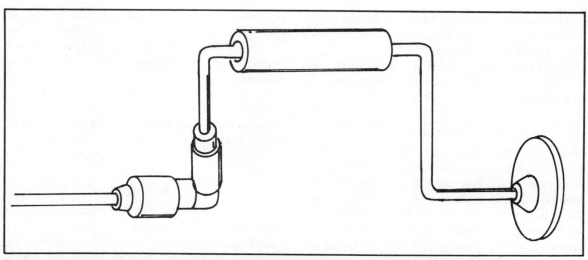

Fig. 9-26. A brace and bit. The auger bit shown has a point that can drill its own guide hole, although I recommend tapping in a nail point first to form a hole for the point to drop into. Bits for the brace are specially made at the top to fit into it.

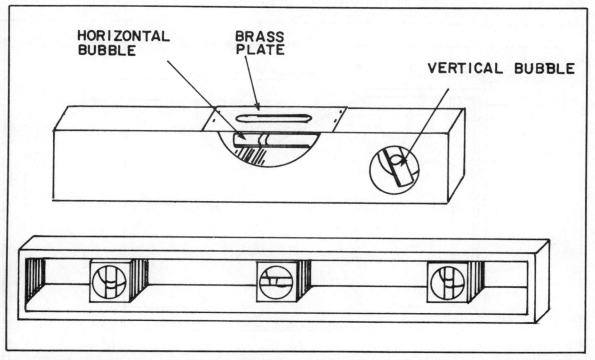

Fig. 9-27. Top: a carpenter's level. The horizontal bubble can be seen from the side or from the top, through the large hole in the brass plate. The level is made from wood. An indentation is carved on the side, parallel with the brass plate, for your finger tips. Bottom: a bricklayer's level. Not drawn to scale, this kind of level is a little more than twice as long as the carpenter's level. It is made of metal, and it will sit on several bricks at once. Note that it has one horizontal bubble, in the center, and two vertical bubbles.

knob on top with your left. Lean over and put some, but not all, of your weight on the brace; turn the handle with your right hand.

There are several ranges of braces, and the best doesn't usually cost appreciably more than the cheapest. I recommend the best quality.

Levels

Figure 9-27 shows two types of levels, a carpenter's level and a bricklayer's level. If you don't knock your level around, it'll last more than a lifetime. Little can go wrong with them, so I recommend buying them at estate sales or secondhand dealers; they aren't likely to be on the tables at garage sales, but if you're lucky enough to find one there, buy it.

Note that both levels have a vertical as well as a horizontal bubble. This allows you to check walls, corners, and posts for such things as swings. A post will be vertical, not leaning to one side or the oth-

er, if the bubble is in the center of the tube when the level is held flat against the post. Hold the level on several sides of the post, especially if it isn't perfectly round (for example, poles cut from pine trees with only the bark knocked off). Similarly, a horizontal board or member is level when the bubble is in the center of the tube. If the board or member isn't level, the bubble will go to the high side, indicating that the other end of the board must be raised to make the board horizontal.

Squares

A combination square (Fig. 9-28) will enable you to draw lines of 90 degrees and 45 degrees. It has a ruler that serves as a straightedge, and it even has a level in it. I recommend it, if you get a good reputable brand, such as Stanley. I had a cheap, unbranded model once, in which the ruler wiggled, so I was never sure my 90-degree angles weren't in fact

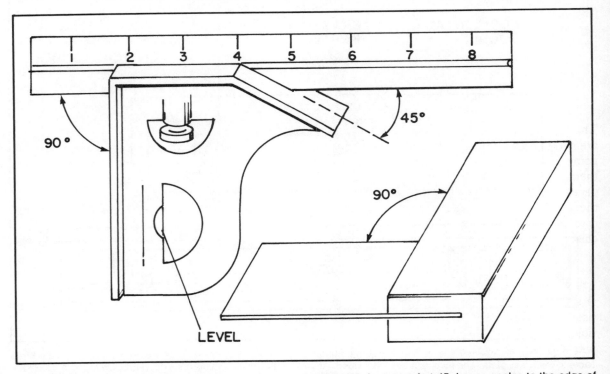

Fig. 9-28. Top: a combination square can be used to draw lines at 90-degree and at 45-degree angles to the edge of a board. A level and a 12-inch ruler are parts of this square. Bottom: a try square, used for drawing lines at 90-degree angles to the edge of a board.

180

88 or 102. On most play equipment designs, such a variation won't matter, but on drawers and book shelves, it matters a great deal.

The try square is a thin piece of metal set into a wooden handle at a 90-degree angle. By laying the handle against the edge of the board (Fig. 9-28), you can draw a line using the metal piece as a straightedge. A saw cut made along that line will guarantee a square corner (assuming the saw blade follows the line without variation).

Rasps and Files

I've already recommended a four-in-one wood rasp for your first purchase. It leaves the wood somewhat wooly in appearance, but that can be smoothed out with sandpaper, if smoothness is necessary. You can buy other wood files with finer cuts (Fig. 9-29), but I recommend them only if you are going into wood-work in earnest.

I do recommend, however, that your tool box eventually have a metal file for sharpening hoes and hatchets, sharpening blunted nail points, removing burrs from the surface of metal used in play equipment, and other applications where metal must be smoothed off or made smaller in one part.

Special Hammers

The plastic-faced hammer and the wooden mallet are necessary with certain wood chisels. If you are going to get serious about woodwork, you'll need them. However, if you plan to confine yourself to general handy-person projects, you can save yourself the price of a mallet or plastic-faced hammer by carefully selecting your chisels. See the section on chisels for more details.

Awls

A scratch awl looks like an ice pick, and it can be used as one. You can hold it in your hand and bore holes in heavy leather or canvas, or you can hit it with a hammer and make holes in wood. Guide holes for screws can be made in this way.

A brad awl looks like the scratch awl until you examine the tip, which isn't pointed but flattened out like a screwdriver blade. You can twist it back and forth and make wider, deeper holes in wood than with the scratch awl. Used with care, it won't split the wood.

TOOL SAFETY

Many tool safety ideas are really just good common sense. In general, if you confine your uses of tools to the functions they were designed for, you won't go wrong. Occasionally you can extend the use, cutting frozen meat with an electric jigsaw, for example, if you carefully think through what you are going to do beforehand.

ELECTRIC TOOLS

Don't use electric tools on a patio if the rain has left puddles on it.

If you accidentally cut through all or part of a cord, repair it properly before using it again.

Inspect your tools frequently for loose screws or other parts that may have loosened. A good time to do this is when you put a drop of oil on the bearings.

Unplug the tool before making any adjustments. This is especially important with tools with trigger-type on-off switches. If these are nudged with a wrist, forearm, or elbow, you can have a bad injury before you know it. Similarly, when you have removed the chuck from your drill and you want to snap it into the saw attachment, you can partially snap it in and get it to whirling dangerously if you accidentally pull the trigger, which would be a natural thing to do with many models because of their pistol grip.

Always look to where the tool is going to go or drill. For example, don't curl your fingers around the edge and over to the underside of a board when you are holding it in preparation of drilling a hole into it. To keep the drill bit from going through the board and into your fingers, keep them on the top side and place the board so that the drill bit will exit the board either into the air or into a waste board.

I advise using your electric saw in a table if possible. This enables you to hold both sides of a board, the good end and the waste, as the saw blade

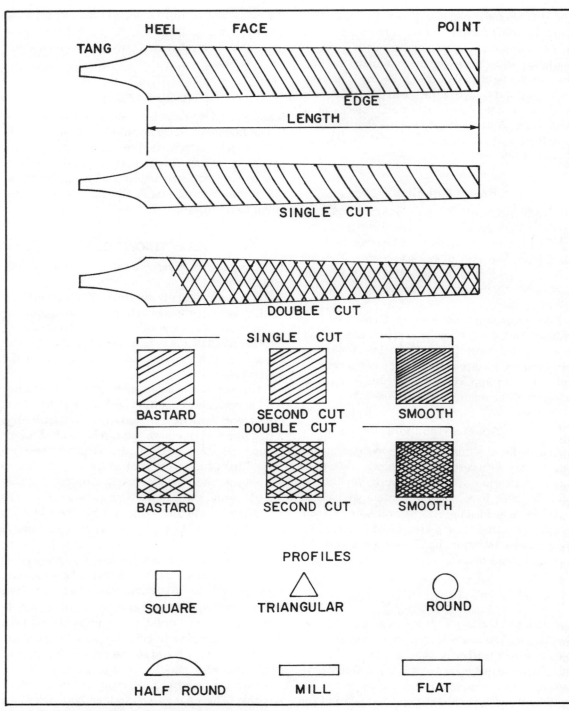

Fig. 9-29. The parts, cuts, and profiles of rasps and files.

cuts through it. All the fingers and thumbs of both hands are top side, where they belong, and holding onto the board on both sides prevents long, board-weakening splinters. If you have to take the saw to the work, put a spare saw horse, a concrete block, a box, or something else under the waste end of a board to support it during the last stages of cutting; this will enable you to keep both your hands on the saw.

Always protect your eyes when using electric sawing equipment. You can drill holes without worrying about shavings flying into your eyes, but don't use the drill as a sander without protecting your eyes. Nor should you ever use the grinding wheel or the wire brush attachment without eye protection.

Respirators, which fit over your mouth and nose, are sometimes necessary when you are sanding something that makes a lot of dust.

HAND TOOLS

Claw hammers are great for driving in nails and pulling them out again, but they weren't designed to break up big rocks, to shape or knock corners off old concrete, or to be used with anything else that's hard. Misuse of the claw hammer can lead to the steel chipping off and flying into your face or eyes. You can use the hammer to drive wooden dowels into place or to drive in wooden stakes or tent pegs. It'll tend to bash up the wood quite a bit, so unless the thing you are driving is expendable or replaceable, go as gently as you can. Never use a hammer with a loose head, and never leave your hammer lying around in dirt. Don't stack it with other tools so that it will bend saws or blunt the edges of chisels, saws, or planes. Don't toss it to a workmate or toss it into the tool box.

Screwdrivers and chisels make great paint scrapers, if used carefully and if you keep every part of your body out of the path of the tool. A friend of mine now has very limited vision in one eye because she failed to keep her head out of the path of a chisel she was using to scrap paint off a door frame. Chisels should be kept in a plastic or leather sheath when out of use, and neither they nor screw drivers should be thrown around.

Handsaws must not be left lying so that someone can walk or run (in the case of children) by and brush against the sharp teeth. Many right-handed persons hole a board to be sawn with their left hands, holding up their left thumb to guide the saw blade on its first few cuts. If that is your practice, be sure to watch the thumbs of children when you teach them how to use the saw.

Pliers pose a danger when used to cut wire. Somehow or other, the loose and fleshy skin between your thumb and forefinger can get pinched between the jaws of the pliers as you give the final squeeze to get through the wire. Holding the wire carefully, an inch or so from the pliers, will prevent this.

NAILS, SCREWS, NUTS, AND BOLTS

Nails are the fastest, cheapest fastener to use in building play equipment. They don't have the same holding power as screws or nuts and bolts, but if driven in at angles they do an adequate job. Now that more and more nails are being sold in prepackaged plastic bags off serve-yourself racks, you must know something about them to get the best nail for your purpose.

Nails are cut from lengths of steel wire. For some reason the packagers refer to some of their product as wire nails but leave that description off other packages. A "common" nail is that used for building the frames of houses. As Fig. 9-30 shows, the common nail is thicker than the box nail, which is thicker than the finishing (or finish) nail. The thinner the shank, the less likely the nail will split the wood. That is why box nails are used to make boxes and finishing nails are used to nail on the trim wood on door and window frames, where splits would be ugly and would present a time-consuming job to fill and cover. Finishing nails are usually driven below the surface of the wood, and the hole on top is filled with wood putty or another filler.

Nails with two heads are called by several names, duplex, scaffold, and double-headed. Unlike common nails, which are meant to be driven in and to stay in place, duplex nails are designed to be driven in, to hold, and to be drawn out again. They are used in constructing scaffolds and in nailing togeth-

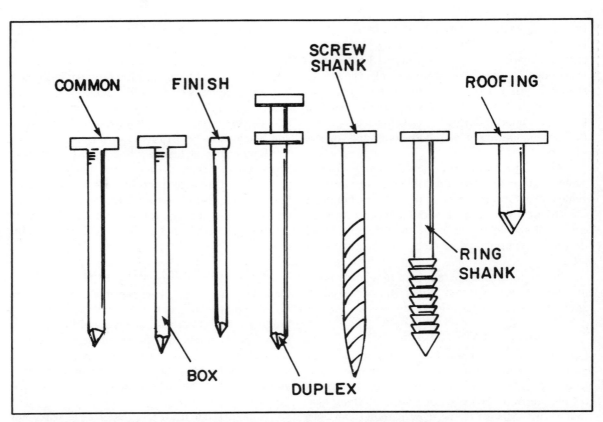

Fig. 9-30. Seven types of nails you can find on the nail rack in your local hardware store.

er the forms that concrete is poured into. If you aren't building scaffolds or forms, don't buy these nails. If you don't use them, your children might, and the extra length of shaft and the extra head sticking out from play equipment is a danger.

Screw shank nails look like screws with nail heads on them. They twist as they go into the wood, and they would have to twist coming out again. This gives them greater holding power than common nails.

Ring shank nails are designed to nail down plywood. The series of rings around the shank acts like a series of barbs to prevent the nail from loosening. Some ring shank nails may look blue because of a coating designed to resist rust. These nails are used with gypsum sheetrock wall material. The joints between the sheets and the nail holes are filled in with a water-based paste, so the nails

mustn't rust through the ruin the appearance of the interior wall.

Relatively short nails with fat shanks and wide, flat heads are roofing nails. They are designed to hold down tar paper, sheets of asphalted roofing material, or asphalted roofing shingles. The broad heads hold the material and keep it from flapping and tearing in the wind. They are made from copper, aluminum, or galvanized steel.

When deciding which nails to use for play equipment, choose nails that are about three times the thickness of the wood they must hold. If for some reason you need to use shorter nails, go to a hardware store that still sells nails by weight and ask for nails with cement on them. The cement looks like big patches of dirt speckled all over the shank of the nail, but it acts a lot like the flutes on the screw shank nail and gives it greater than ordinary holding power. I used cement nails to build a packing crate for shipping some furniture to Australia; they held so well that they tore up some of the plywood when I tried to dismantle the crate to use the wood for other purposes.

On the nail packages you may see a number and the small letter d, like 4d, 5d, and 8d. This is a holdover from our nonphonetic past, for d stands for penny. An 8d nail is an 8-penny nail, which is 2.5 inches long. A 2-penny nail is 1 inch long; for each penny thereafter, add 1/4 inch: a 3d nail is 1.25 inches long, a 4d nail is 1.5 inches long, a 5d nail is 1.75 inches long, and so on, up to the 9d size; it then jumps. Table 9-1 shows the penny size, length, and approximate number of nails to the pound you can expect when buying them that way, which is most economical way to buy them.

Screws take more time to put into wood, but they have several important advantages. They hold better; they're easier to get out when you need to dismantle or alter something; and you don't bang them in with noise, as you do when driving nails. If you want to finish a weekend project in the spare bedroom or the carport or patio just outside the kids' window after they've gone to bed, this relative noiselessness is an important consideration. Drill the guide holes while the kids are awake.

Screws may be made of steel, brass, or aluminum. The steel might be hardened, unhardened, blued to prevent rust, or stainless. In other words, there are many different types of screws, and you should match the screw to its purpose. Blued and stainless steel are good for outdoor play equipment that is exposed to rain and humidity, but you can spare yourself that expense and use ordinary unhardened screws for jobs that will stay indoors.

Use common sense in choosing the size of screw for your job. For example, when the screw is fully driven into place, it shouldn't stick out on the other side. Different types of screws and the parts of a screw are shown in Fig. 9-31. When choosing a screw to go through one board into the end of another, the body of the screw should be no thicker than 1/4 the thickness of the end board. Choose a longer, thinner screw for this purpose, and save the thicker screws for applications where the thickness

Table 9-1. Nail Sizes and Types.

Penny Size	Length (inches)	Approximate Number to the Pound
2d	1	876
3d	1.25	568
4d	1.5	316
5d	1.75	271
6d	2	181
7d	2.25	161
8d	2.5	106
9d	2.75	96
10d	3	69
12d	3.25	63
16d	3.5	49
20d	4	31
30d	4.5	24
40d	5	18
50d	5.5	14
60d	6	11

of the wood won't be a consideration. Remember that the threaded root of the screw, not the body, is what forms the best holding bond. Therefore, although the body can stay in the top board, all or most of the root should go into the bottom board to hold the two firmly together. This also usually means that more than 1/4 inch of threads must go into the bottom board. If that doesn't seem possible there are three other choices. You can use the short screws in combination with glue; together they will hold many materials, and they are especially good when you are building things from chipboard. Change your design slightly so that you can use a longer screw. This may involve gluing a long strip of wood, like quarter-round, onto a thinner piece so that it can take the extra length of screw threads. Figure 4-28 shows this being done to help hold a table top to a rung on a climbing frame. Change the design a bit more and use nuts and bolts instead of screws.

Screw heads come in three basic shapes: round, flat, and oval. Flathead screws should always be countersunk, for their edges become sharp cutting instruments when left above the surface of play equipment. Roundhead screws are best for things you plan to take apart at some later date. The heads

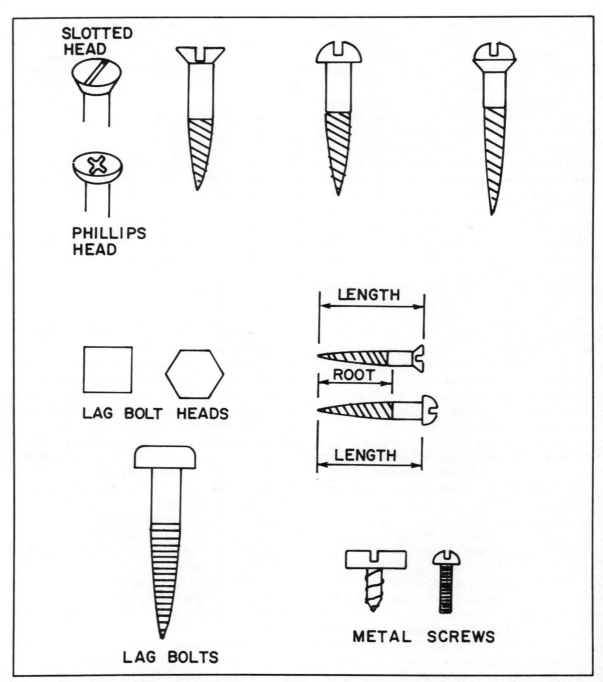

Fig. 9-31. Top: two types of screw head are shown at the left of three wood screws—flat head, round head, and oval head. Lower left: lag bolts have square or hexagonal shaped heads. They are driven in with a wrench. Center: the parts of a wood screw. Only the part that actually goes into the wood is counted in determining the length. Lower right: two types of metal screw. The one on the right looks much like a roundhead wood screw, but it isn't pointed.

are smooth and don't pose a danger to small, bare feet. They are a good choice for the rungs on a simple ladder if you plan to move the rungs greater distances apart as the children grow. Ovalhead screws are also easy to get out when dismantling something, and they go down farther into the wood than round heads. Therefore, they make a good compromise between round and flat heads.

The length of the screw is that part that will actually go into the wood. All of a flathead screw is counted in its length, but the length of a round-head screw excludes its head. The diameter of a screw is designated by a number, with 1 for the smallest, 18 for the largest. Therefore, a number 8 2-inch screw will be fatter than a number 6 2-inch screw.

The least expensive way to buy screws is by the box of 100 or 200 screws. They won't spoil on your workshop shelf. When you buy by the little plastic packet, you often have to buy so many packets for a play equipment project that the box would have been cheaper in the first place.

Lag bolts (Fig. 9-31) are sometimes incorrectly called lag screws. Their heads are shaped like squares or hexagons. They are longer, heavier, and stronger than ordinary screws, so they are ideal for holding together frames for climbing platforms and towers and swings. Drill a guide hole in which to start the lag bolt; the depth of this hole depends in part on the type of wood. In softwood I recommend that the guide hole be drilled only about half the length of the lag bolt. Because the bolt is driven in with a wrench, you can put considerable leverage on it and drive it all the way without having a long guide hole. The fibers of the wood will twist and tighten around the threads of the lag bolt, forming a really secure bond. In hardwood the guide hole ought to be just shorter than the length of the lag bolt; the pointed tip can bore into undrilled wood, but the rest of the bolt needs to fit into a space.

You may use two kinds of bolts in building play equipment, stove bolts and carriage bolts. Stove bolts have heads like screws, round or flat, with slots to hold a screwdriver. The head of the flathead mod-

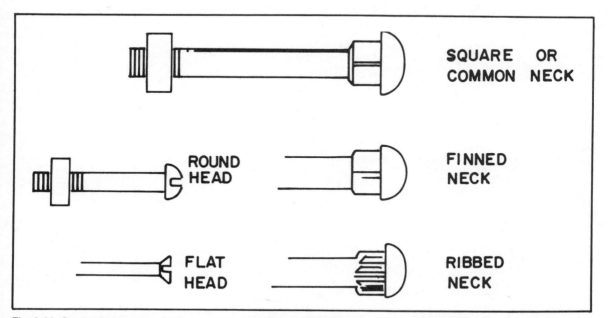

Fig. 9-32. Carriage bolts come in three head styles—square, finned, and ribbed. All three styles are designed to bite into and hold the wood they fit into. Stove bolts may have threads on all or only part of their bodies. They are commonly used on structures that are intended to be taken apart or changed, for they can be tightened and loosened at both ends with a screwdriver blade in the slot and a small wrench or pliers on the nut.

el should be countersunk, but the bottom of the round head can be left flush with the surface of the wood. The threads on stove bolts run almost the full length of the body. You should put a common flat washer over the bolt before tightening the nut.

Carriage bolts have a round head with no slot. Just under the head, the bolt may be square, finned, or ribbed (Fig. 9-32). The bolt usually has threads only on the lower section. The heads are designed to hold the material into which the bolt is driven, to hold the bolt and keep it from turning when you tighten the nut on the other end. All three types hold well in wood-to-wood applications.

Drill the hole for the carriage bolt as wide as the diameter of the shank of the bolt. Drive the bolt all the way through this hole with a hammer; that is what the rounded head on the bolt is for. Put a common flat washer on the threaded end before tightening the nut. When you tighten the nut, you'll find the bolt is drawn farther into the wood on the other end. This is all right in most cases. If you are worried about drawing too much bolt through (for example, when you want only a little threaded end showing on the other side, for safety reasons), you can keep the head from crunching into the wood by using a washer on that end as well as the nut end. Carriage bolts come in diameters ranging from 1/4 inch to 1 inch and in lengths ranging from 3/4 inch to 20 inches.

A third type of bolt you may see usually has a head shaped like a square or a hexagon. These are machine bolts, designed to be tightened with wrenches on the head as well as on the nut. The shape of the nut usually corresponds to the shape head. You may also see some machine bolts with round or flat heads. Machine bolts are usually used in metal-to-metal applications, although they can be pressed into service for play equipment if you already have them or if the hardware store is out of carriage bolts.

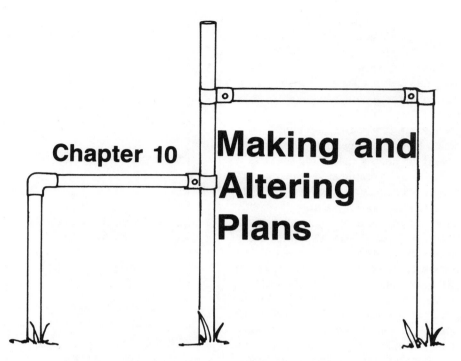

Chapter 10

Making and Altering Plans

YOU MAY HAVE GOOD REASONS FOR ALTERING this book's plans or for drawing your own from the beginning. You may have access to some free or cheap materials that specific projects don't call for but which you figure will do for some play equipment. There may be a location in your yard where you want to put a piece of equipment, but the equipment as I've presented it wouldn't quite fit. Finally, there's the important matter of making the equipment fit your kids. I recently met a seven-year-old Dutch boy who was as big as my son who was nearly 10 years old. This chapter contains some charts and comments about the average-size child and how high off the ground some pieces of play equipment need to be to cater to him or her. But first, let's look at some general planning and design principles and a case study of a project done the wrong way.

TIPS FOR PREPARING GOOD, STRONG EQUIPMENT

■ Keep the design simple. The fewer fancy

joints and special effects your equipment has, the better it will probably be and the easier it will be to build. In some cases it pays to use a design, or a detail of a design, that may appear to be a bit clumsy or awkward if it makes the job easier and doesn't make the structure weak.

■ Don't test gravity; stacking structural members is better than hanging them. The frame for a swing or trapeze may have two upright posts and a crossbar. The crossbar can be bolted onto the faces or it can sit on top and be fastened on with steel strap. The latter method is often the better.

■ Use different colors to indicate different sizes of board, different materials, the location of shelves and other features. With kids around the house, you will probably have different color felt-tip pens. To give you a vivid illustration of how colors can help you understand a drawing, get a fistful of pens and turn back to Fig. 4-9. Color the monkey bars red and the three outer framing members, which are fastened to the posts with lag bolts, yellow. Color the three inner framing members, which are nailed to the outer members, green. Now

189

take a purple pen and trace the line of dashes; you may have to go just outside the monkey bars to make this purple line show up against the red. By now it should be much easier to see the relationships between the framing members. Colors are even more helpful in three-dimensional perspective drawings.

■ Make enough drawings of a planned piece of equipment. One drawing may suffice for something like four boards nailed together for a sandbox. The more complicated the project becomes, however, the more drawings you ought to prepare. You may need not only a front view, side view, top view, and perspective but also drawings of details from those several views. This is especially important where several structural members or other materials come together in several planes; a good example is a corner of a cubby or a climbing frame.

■ Saw as you go; don't try to precut everything. The more complicated the project, the more important this rule. Again, four boards for a sandbox can be precut and then nailed together, but the framing members for a climbing frame should be cut only after the posts are firmly in place with their concrete dried and after the pieces of wood for the framing members have been measured against the posts themselves. Your plan may call for an 8-foot distance between two posts, but if the actual distance is 8-feet, 4 inches, you won't be able to stretch a precut 8-foot board to fit the space.

■ Measuring boards against the structure is preferable to measuring them with a rule or tape measure. This is most important when you have to make cuts at angles other than 90 degrees. For example, consider the board marked D in Fig. 4-27. A step-by-step description of cutting and nailing on another board is in the text accompanying Fig. 3-18. When working alone with long boards, you may have to tack one or both ends in place in order to free your hands to make the cutting marks.

■ If you can't sink a post deeply, sink is widely. Figure 10-1 shows how you can alter the bottom of a post to make it hold steady and firm in a broad, shallow bed of concrete. We've used the method successfully on fence posts set only 12 inches deep over boulders under our topsoil.

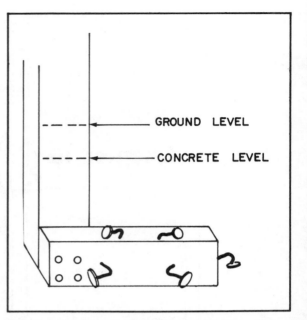

Fig. 10-1. Sinking a post in shallow topsoil. If your lot has hidden boulders, you may not be able to sink your posts in 3 feet of concrete. So, instead, of going deep, go wide and shallow. Get a spare piece of 2-inch-by-4-inch wood and cut it 18 to 20 inches long. Get some old nails and drive them in about 1/3 of their length. Then use the claws of your hammer to bend them over as shown. Then nail the 2 × 4 securely into the post, set it in place, and pour the concrete. The bent nails will help hold the concrete to the 2 × 4. If you have some chicken wire or other galvanized fencing material, it can also be nailed to the 2 × 4 and stretched out over the boulder. The concrete should not come all the way to ground level. The wood will tend to shrink away from the concrete, so about 6 inches of topsoil should be heaped up around the post to allow rain to run off and not drain down into the space between the wood and the concrete.

■ Use triangles in the design for rigidity and strength. Figure 10-2 shows how a rectangle can be distorted into a parallelogram and how triangles stay triangles, no matter how much you push them around. (Incidentally, this makes a good teaching device with classes of children doing simple woodwork projects. Don't let any of them put more than one nail in the corners of the rectangle, however, or you'll have them claiming they've foiled your system.)

Sometimes the triangle-for-rigidity can be formed by the way you drive in nails or screws. If you make a box or a desk drawer, for example (Fig.

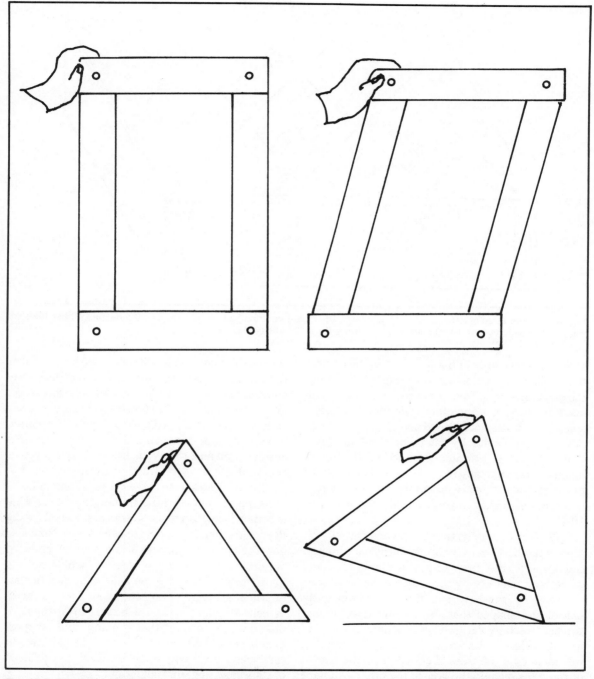

Fig. 10-2. Proof that triangles are rigid and that rectangles are not. If you make a rectangle and a triangle as shown, with one nail in each corner, you'll be able to distort the rectangle into a parallelogram, but the triangle won't change shape. This is a good experiment to conduct with children.

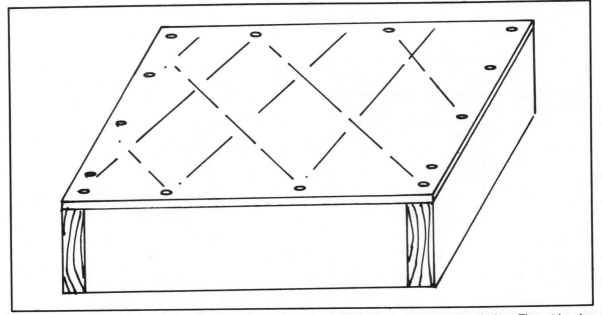

Fig. 10-3. The bottom of a box or drawer. Note how the nails form triangles, as indicated by the dashes. These triangles will prevent distortion of the rectangular box into a three-dimensional parallelogram.

10-3), the placement of the fasteners in the corners forms triangles that dissect the rectangle and keep the structure rigid. In other cases you have to add another board or some other rigid member (like a steel rod or a strap of steel) to make a triangle. Suppose you have built a free-standing climbing frame that threatens to lean in one direction. If you nail long boards diagonally from the bottom of one post to the top of another, you will make the structure much more rigid, and you can halt the lean (Fig. 10-4).

■ Think laterally; the straight and narrow isn't always the best route. In other words, consider all the choices; the first way you think of doing something may not be the only, or the best, way.

Suppose you have four trees so conveniently placed and shaped that you can build an almost perfectly rectangular tree house among them. Figure 10-5 shows two ways of putting the framing members onto the trees. One will have the trunks of the trees outside the house; the other will have the trunks exactly in the internal corners. One maximizes the volume to be enclosed; the other doesn't

necessarily minimize it, but it does lead to a smaller volume. Practically, this means that one design requires fewer square feet of lumber or plywood sheet to cover the floor. If you already have spare or scrap lumber or plywood you plan to use in the tree house, it will pay you to measure it first, then choose a design to ensure that your scrap or spare pieces won't fall short of the framing members.

Figure 10-6 shows two ways of nailing in flooring supports between the framing members. One is better if you plan to use sheets of plywood for the floor; the other, if you plan to use boards. Note also how the smaller supports in the plan for plywood are offset. That makes it easier to nail them into place, for you can drive the nails in perpendicularly, still at an angle toward the ground for strength. Whichever plan you choose, be sure to lay the floor material on top of the framing and support members, not between them, where the kids' weight combined with gravity would increase the likelihood of its weakening and falling out.

■ Don't start nailing until you've considered all the angles. When most people drive nails while

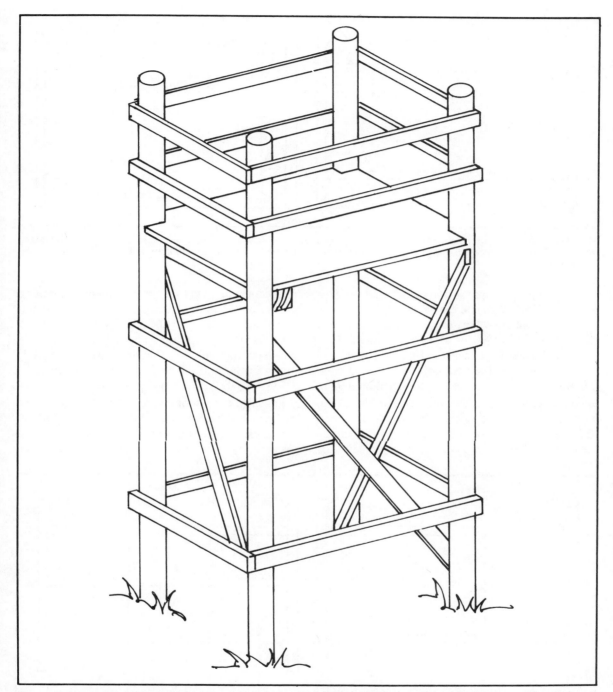

Fig. 10-4. Supporting a free-standing climbing frame. Long boards have been nailed from the top of one post diagonally to the bottom of a post next to it. Note how the post, the diagonal bracing piece, and the ground form a triangle. This is the way to prevent a climbing frame from leaning.

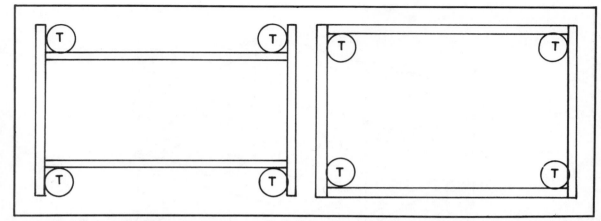

Fig. 10-5. Two ways of framing for the floor of a tree house. The circles with T in them are trees. Left: this method keeps the tree trunks outside the tree house. Right: this method makes the largest tree house floor, but it puts the trees inside the house.

standing up, the tips of the nails tend to arch downward as they go into the wood. Similarly, when they drive nails into horizontal boards, the tips of the nails tend to arch back toward the nailer as they go into the wood. These tendencies can have a serious effect on the strength of the structure. Therefore, plan the direction the nail should go in and indicate it with dashes on your drawings. When it comes to constructing the project, you may have to drill guide holes to ensure that the nails go in the desired direction. If you don't drill guide holes, be

sure to keep in mind the final placement of the thing you are building. For example, if you are constructing a ladder on a workbench or a patio, keep in mind that the ladder will be placed upright for use and drive the nails in at angles that will make it strong in the upright, not horizontal, position.

Figure 10-7 shows this problem and principle graphically. Let's suppose you have three pieces of lumber for a ladder, two for the uprights, one for the rungs. You measure the piece for the rungs and discover that it is just a little short; you can't cut

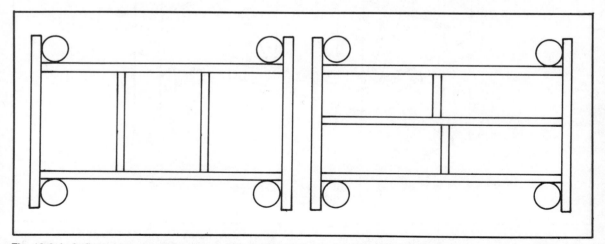

Fig. 10-6. Left: floor support members placed in position between the floor frame for the tree house. This would support a large sheet of plywood. Right: floor support members placed in position for a floor to be made from planks.

194

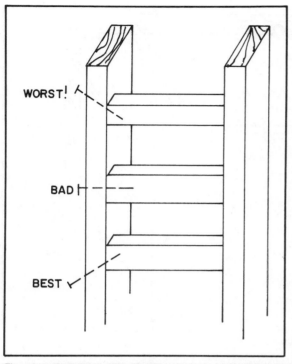

WORST!

BAD

BEST

Fig. 10-7. Three ways of nailing rungs to place between the uprights for a ladder. Position of nails is indicated by dashes. When stepped on, the top rung will probably slide right down off the pointed end of the nail; the middle rung will probably sag; the bottom rung will stay in place.

enough rungs and nail them on the edges of the uprights. However, if you cut them 2 to 3 inches shorter and fit them between the uprights, as shown, you'll have enough rungs to complete the ladder.

The three rungs show three different angles for driving in the nails. The top rung will come off with little use because as the kids put their weight on it, they'll tend to push it right off the pointed ends of the nails. The middle rung is better; what often happens with this sort of angle is that the rung will sag 1/2 inch or so but bend the nails in the process; the fibers of the wood then begin to compress on the tops of the bent nails, and the rung sags no further. The bottom rung is the best proposition. Given normal wear and tear, it will neither come off nor sag.

To get all the nails driven in at the desired angle

on your next ladder, mark the angles they are to go in with pencil or pen on the outside of the uprights. Sometimes you have to position yourself at strange and uncomfortable angles to drive the nails in at their proper angles. When this is so, a predrilled guide hole will make the job easier.

HOW NOT TO PLAN AND BUILD

The worst thing you can do is take short cuts because you are in a hurry. The second worst is to design and build something without thinking of what you will, or can, add to it. I've made many mistakes in various projects. I have combined some of these mistakes into one how-not-to-do-it set of instructions for monkey bars with a climbing frame added on.

Figure 10-8 shows the monkey bars. They look pretty neat. But the 4-inch-by-4-inch posts on the right end are set a bit close together to be used by large kids. Figure 10-9 shows the same set of monkey bars with the climbing frame added. The ladder rungs on the monkey bar posts have been omitted from this drawing only for the sake of simplicity. The project turned out all right in the end, and they enjoyed it. But it got so unnecessarily complicated as it went along that I almost said, "Never again."

Note that the guard rails around the top of the climbing frame are nailed to the three new 4 × 4 posts and to one 2 × 4 that had to be fastened to one of the 4 × 4 posts forming the monkey bars.

Figure 10-10 shows how this was accomplished. (Drawing A corresponds with 1, B with 2, and C with 3; all are drawn from a perspective above but to two sides of the corner.) Drawings 1 and A show the first problem. The side rail of the monkey bars is attached to the wrong side of the 4 × 4 post. So I had to nail on a piece marked P underneath the side rail. I then nailed on pieces S and Q to support the floor sheet of the climbing frame. This necessitated cutting a notch in S to bring its top surface up level with the top surface of Q (which is a little easier to see in Fig. 10-11).

I decided not to notch framing member T and to put it on the outside of the 4 × 4 posts (Fig. 10-11). I could have done this with S as well, but

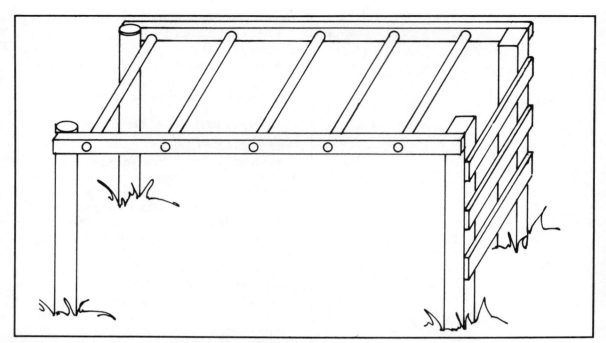

Fig. 10-8. Monkey bars to which a climbing frame will be added.

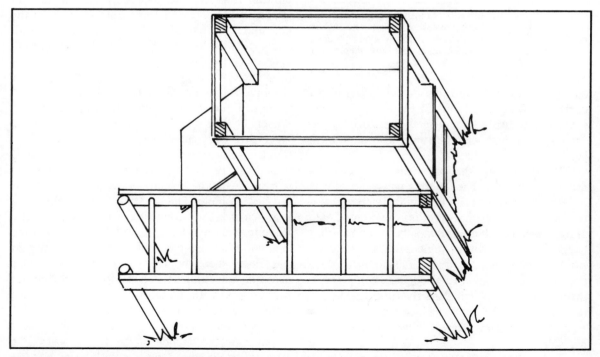

Fig. 10-9. The monkey bars with the climbing frame completed and a sandbox placed underneath.

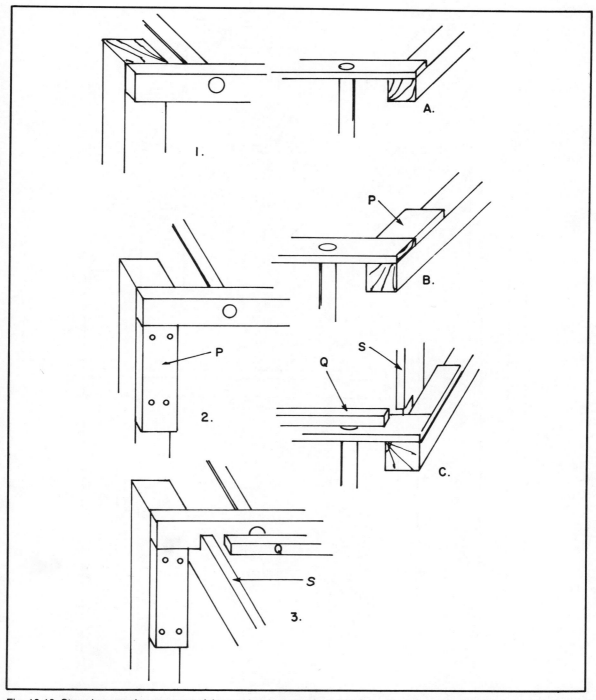

Fig. 10-10. Steps in preparing one post of the monkey bars to take a 2-inch-by-4-inch board for a safety or guardrail post, and the addition of pieces Q and S for the floor frame.

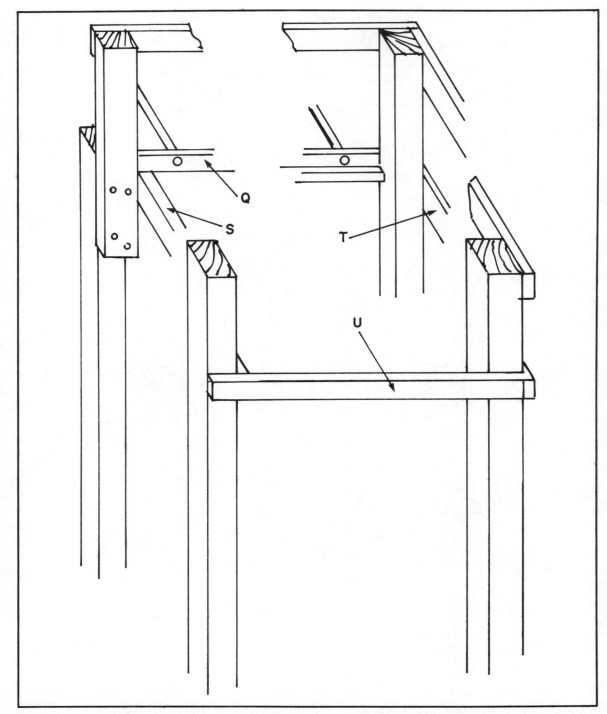

Fig. 10-11. The 2-inch-by-4-inch guardrail post in place, with two guardrails and all four floor framing pieces.

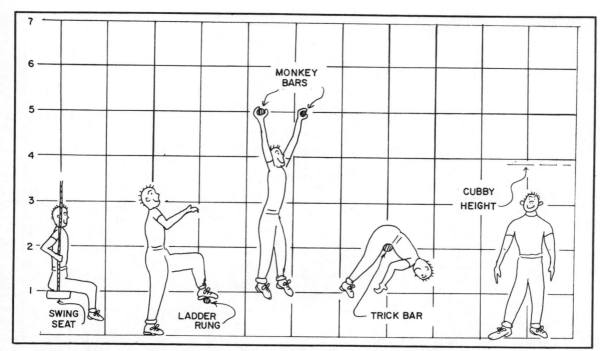

Fig. 10-12. Height, in feet, of five pieces of equipment for the average three-year-old child.

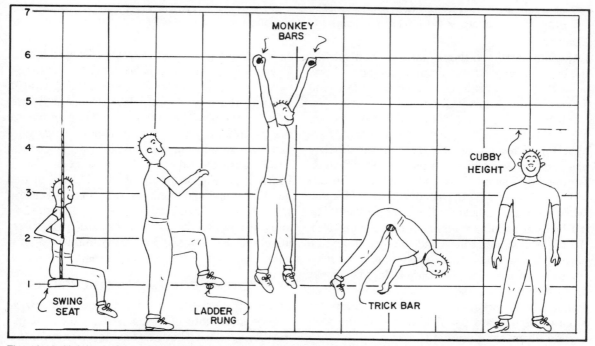

Fig. 10-13. Height, in feet, of five pieces of equipment for the average six-year-old child.

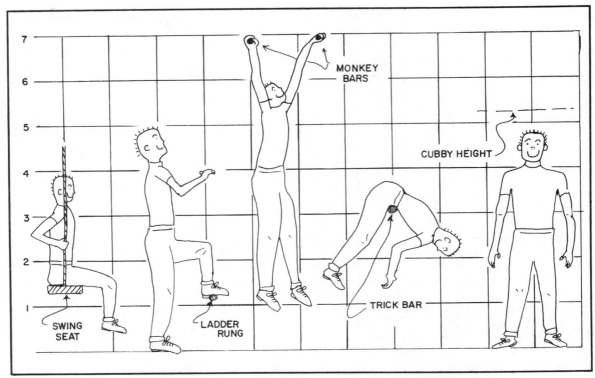

Fig. 10-14. Height, in feet, of five pieces of equipment for the average nine-year-old child.

I was in a hurry and the notched method seemed the best way at the time. Framing member U was not a problem in itself, as it could be nailed on in a simple, straightforward manner.

If you compare this design with those in Fig. 4-2, 4-9, 4-10, and 4-24, you'll see how I should have built this project. For one thing, I should have planned and used four 4 × 4 posts of equal length. For another, I should have used the top of the side rail of the monkey bars instead of board Q for that side of the frame to hold the floor. For another thing, if I had put framing member S on the outside of the posts, I wouldn't have had to notch it, and I'd have had plenty of 4 × 4 to fasten it to. Another complication arose because board Q doesn't actually touch member T. I had to measure carefully and squint around corners to try to make the top surfaces of each board parallel; otherwise the floor wouldn't have sat quite flat.

Figure 10-11 shows the 2 × 4 piece fastened on with four lag bolts with hexagonal-shaped heads. These bolts had to be 4 inches long, for I felt they had to go all the way through board P (Fig. 10-10) and into the 4 × 4 post. Because board P was nailed to the post, I had to be careful about where the lag bolts were placed so that they would avoid nails and go only through wood.

Because the floor sheet was to sit on top of board Q instead of on top of the side rail of the monkey bars, I had to cut the sheet very precisely. It had to slide down between the 2 × 4 on the left and the 4 × 4 on the right. As I mentioned earlier, it worked, but I was almost ready to throw up my hands and quit before it was finished.

PLANNING EQUIPMENT DIMENSIONS

Figures 10-12, 10-13, and 10-14 show charts with suggested heights of swing seats, ladder rungs, monkey bars, trick bars, and cubby ceilings for the average three year old, six year old, and nine year old. Use the charts as a guide only. Your kids may be bigger than average. They may also be smaller than average, but err on the too-big side, not vice versa, for even smaller than average kids grow and outgrow equipment that was designed too small.

To get the best dimensions for your kids, keep in mind their genes. Are they likely to spurt up like bean poles? Do they come from shorter, sturdier stock? Are they likely to be early bloomers, as big at 10 as other kids are at 12 years old? Examine the things they use now. For example, if there is a stool or chair they really like and are really comfortable on, measure its height and add 4 inches for foot clearance to find a good height for a swing seat. The chart shows a swing seat about 16 inches off the ground for a nine year old, but your nine year old may require one 14 or 18 inches high.

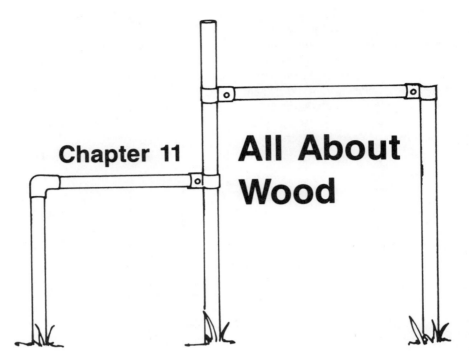

Chapter 11

All About Wood

F OR THE HANDYMAN OR HANDYWOMAN, WOOD is the easiest material to work with in producing play equipment. It isn't necessarily the best for all things. Monkey bars made from pipes of various dimensions, for example, are better than those made of wood. But, wood is available almost everywhere. It is easy to cut into various shapes and sizes. It takes paints and stains fairly well. Some of it resists rot naturally, and all of it can be treated to resist rot and deterioration.

Metal, on the other hand, is harder to cut and has to be welded together to form most of the kinds of joints that nails and screws make possible in wood. It doesn't take paint as easily, although it can be galvanized to resist rust and deterioration. Metal is also more expensive than wood.

Although wood is the best material for play equipment, you can't just walk into the supplier's store and order "everything necessary for a climbing frame," and walk out again, secure in the knowledge that you got the best for the lowest price. In point of fact, you will probably walk out with, literally, the best material at the highest price, when you

should be walking out with second or third best at a price that leaves a few dollars for your next building project.

So, how do you do it? How do you know what to ask for, what to select when given choices, and how to know if the cheaper material with defects would still do the job? Worse still, when you go into the discount stores that serve the home builder and handyperson and that have uninformed clerks who can't help customers, how can you make intelligent purchases at the attractive prices these outlets offer (Fig. 11-1).

The simple answer is that sooner or later you have to ask someone. I've built projects in Texas, New York City, Milwaukee, Little Rock, South Australia and Tasmania. In every case, I've based my choices of lumber on two factors: a basic understanding of the strengths, weaknesses, advantages, disadvantages, and origins of lumber, and information furnished by a salesperson whom I trusted, having first established that I knew a few basic facts myself. Here are some of those basic facts.

Fig. 11-1. Discount stores serving the handyman or handywoman often have attractive prices, but little or no technical information from staff. It is essential that you learn something about wood before buying from such a store.

TREE GROWTH

Think of the tree trunk as a rope or cable, only not twisted quite so much. Further, think of the outer strands of the rope or cable as tiny pipes or conduits; in the tree they are the pipelines that carry the sap, which carries the food and water and building materials up and down the tree, from the roots to the crown. If you cut the cable in half lengthwise, you will be able to see how long and straight some of the strands are. If you cut the tree trunk in half lengthwise, you will see also how long and straight some of the little pipes and conduits are, some dark

and some light. Similarly, if you cut the cable, or if you simply hold the end of it and look directly at the end, as though trying to see if there's a hole down the center, you will see that it is made up of strands and that these strands touch each other and form about three large concentric rings, with smaller concentric rings inside each of them. If you look down on a tree stump, you will see one large circle, with concentric circles inside it.

Each spring of the tree's life it had a growth spurt. With the onset of warmth and spring rains, the three rapidly built up a thick layer of soft, large cells, expanding its diameter in the process. As the weather became even warmer, the growth rate slowed, and the tree produced smaller cells, more tightly packed together, just outside the softer spring cells. Thus, the spring wood is lighter, the summer wood darker, and together they make up the annual rings that you can count on the stump to determine the age of the tree (Fig. 11-2). If we cut a board from the length of the trunk, we can see the long lines of summer wood alternating with long lines of springwood, and these make up the grain of the wood.

Continuing with our analogy of conduits and pipes on the outside of a large cable, it will come as no surprise that the wood closest to the bark of the tree through which the sap comes and goes, is known as sapwood. Figure 11-2 shows that the wood at the center of the tree is known as heartwood; it is darker than sapwood. Depending on the species of tree, the transformation of sapwood to heartwood takes from 9 to 36 years.

The sap actually travels in the cambium layer, just between the bark and the sapwood. The cambium layer will become sapwood, so, as its arteries harden, the tree forms another type of cell just between the cambium and the older sapwood. These cells are pithy, and they help the flow of materials between the cambium and the hardening sapwood. In many types of wood, these pithy tubes, which run perpendicular to the tubes in the cambium, become invisible, but they are easily seen in oak, where they look like lines of tiny holes. These are called the medullary rays (Fig. 11-3). They may make the piece of oak lumber look as if an insect has eaten tiny bites here and there, but they don't affect the strength of the lumber; they are simply part of it.

The condition of the grain varies according to the species of tree. "Fine grained" or "close grained" woods are those like maple and birch, which are made up of small cells tightly packed together. "Coarse grained" or "open grained" woods, such as oak, walnut, and mahogany, have cells that are large, open, and porous. If you are a furniture maker, you'll have to fill the grain of such woods with a wood filler before you can get a good finish on them, but the openness or closeness of the grain doesn't make any difference in play equipment.

The grain in some woods is long and straight (Fig. 11-4). Boards from such woods may look as though a draftsman drew long, almost parallel lines down the length of the board. You can imagine how straight and tall the tree must have been to produce boards with such grain. On the other hand, imagine a tree that isn't straight. If it twists or lends on its way toward the heavens, boards cut from its trunk will display a grain with waves and whorls and patterns. In furniture or in floors, these patterns can be immensely attractive. For building play equipment, however, choose the straighter grains, for they will be stronger.

HARDWOOD AND SOFTWOOD

Hardwood comes from trees with broad leaves, which drop before the winter. Softwood comes from trees with leaves like needles, such as the pines', or with flattened, somewhat fleshy leaves, such as the junipers', which are evergreen. Hardwood usually is so hard that you can't put a nail into it without a guide hole, but there are exceptions. The yellow pine, a softwood, is harder than the butternut, a hardwood.

Softwood is probably more common than hardwood; that is, there'll be more of it in your local lumber yard or supply house because softwoods are used in every part of house building: frames, siding, floors, paneling, and trim. Hardwood, on the other hand, is used only for specialized applications, such as doorsills and floors or for paneling or trim. But don't let this discourage you from using hardwoods for your play equipment. If you are building a cubby or a climbing frame or a frame for a swing or trapeze, you can put it together with nuts and bolts, thus avoiding the bent nails and broken drill bits. What's more, you might be able to get hardwood at a very attractive price from a mill.

HOW LOGS ARE CUT INTO BOARDS

When trees are felled and trimmed of their branches, they are taken to the mills to be cut into boards while they are still green and full of moisture. This is because the boards will dry out

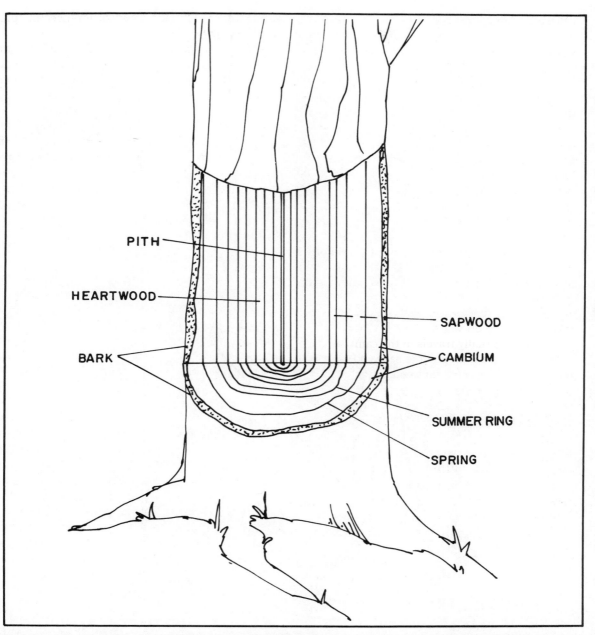

Fig. 11-2. A cut-away view of how a tree grows. Note that the heartwood is darker than the sapwood. There will be many more summer rings and spring rings than shown in this illustration, but note that each spring ring will be bounded by two dark summer rings. A summer ring with spring ring just inside it equals one annual ring. There are no fall or winter rings in the annual ring. The cambium layer is just inside the bark, on the surface of the sapwood. The pipelines of sap travel in the cambium layer. The annual rings are rings on a stump only, for if you can imagine a long board cut from this tree trunk, you can see from the section marked heartwood that the board would have long lines of alternating spring wood and summer wood, dark lines alternating with light lines, running the length of the board. These lines are called the grain of the wood.

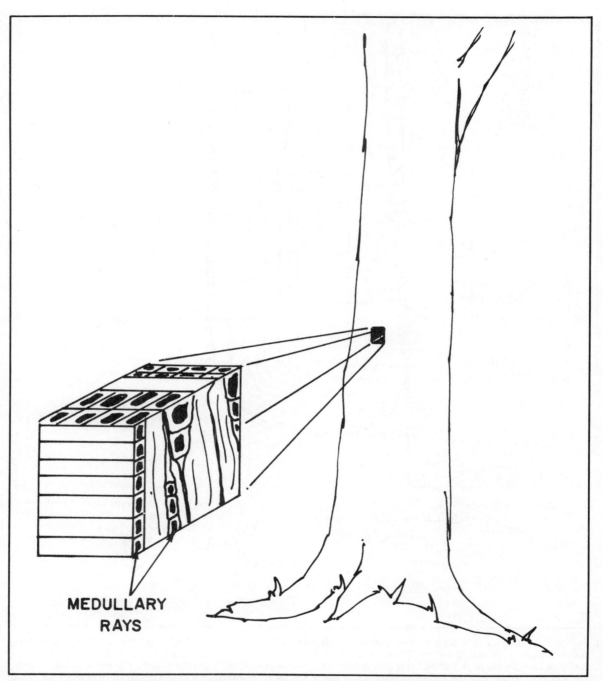

MEDULLARY
RAYS

Fig. 11-3. A highly magnified section of the cambium layer. Note that most of the tubes, or tiny pipelines for sap, run vertically. The little tubes that run horizontally are called medullary rays. They help with the flow of materials between the cambium and the hardening sapwood. In oak boards, these rays are very visible, having the appearance of tiny circles chomped out by insects. They don't affect the strength of the wood.

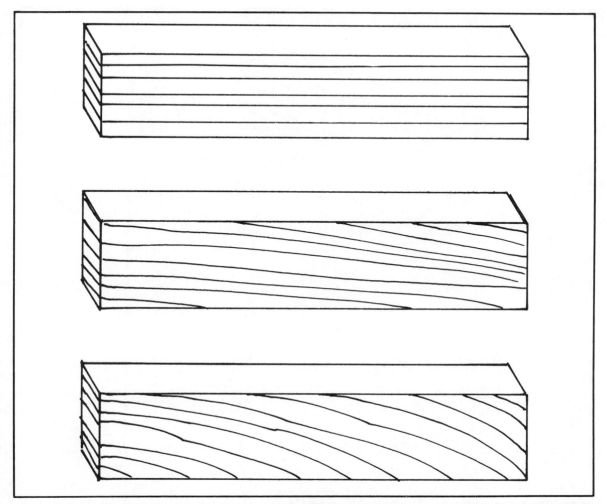

Fig. 11-4. Some different patterns of grain. Top: long, straight grain usually means a long, straight, strong board. Middle: although not quite so strong as the top board, this one is still usable, for some of its lines of grain extend from one end to the other. Bottom: none of the lines of grain extend the entire length of the board, making this board inherently weak. This is called cross grain.

and season faster than logs, decreasing the time the company has to hold the merchandise before putting it on the market, and because green logs don't blunt the sawmill's saw blades as fast as old, dry, well-seasoned logs.

The green logs are cut down their entire lengths according to two generally used methods, slash cutting or rift cutting, which is also referred to as quartercutting or quartersawing. Slash cutting (Fig. 11-5) a log has exactly the same effect as using an

egg slicer on a whole boiled egg. You get pieces of uniform thickness, fast. For this reason slash-cut lumber is cheaper than rift-cut lumber. Rift cutting starts out by cutting the log into quarters; then each quarter is cut into boards (Fig. 11-6). All those increased cutting steps mean more time on the equipment, more costs, and higher prices to you.

If hardwood is being slash cut, the mills say they are plain sawing the wood. But if they are slash cutting softwood, they call it flat-grain sawing.

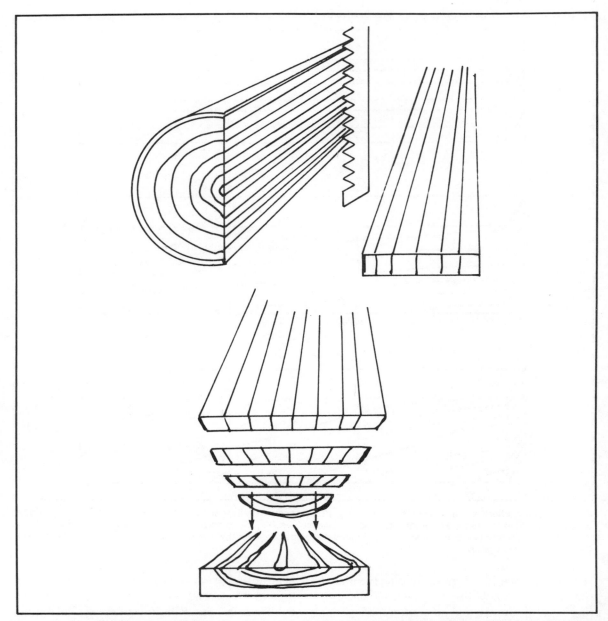

Fig. 11-5. A log that is being slash-cut in the lumber mill. A board from near the center of the log lies to the right of the saw blade. Note how the lines of grain run up and down on the end of the board as it lies flat. This particular board has actually been rift-cut, but only because it came from the center of the log. The other boards already cut from half the log are shown below, with a magnified section of the first board on the bottom. Note how the lines of the grain go from the vertical in the middle boards to the horizontal in the first board that was cut. The lines of grain along the length of a slash-cut board will often appear to have flowed out and flattened on the surface of the board. Compare the bottom board with the one lying by the saw blade and with the boards in Fig. 11-6. Cutting boards this way is cheaper than sawing the log into quarters first. Slash-cut boards are called "plain sawn" if cut from hardwood, but "flat-grain sawn" is cut from softwood logs.

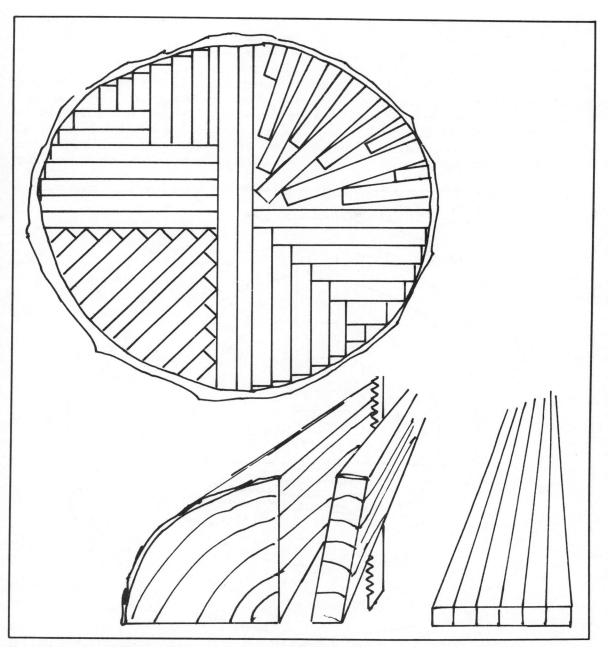

Fig. 11-6. Top: four methods of dividing up the four quarters of a log when the rift cutting pattern is used. From 12:00 to 3:00, radial quarter sawing. From 3:00 to 6:00, alternate quarter sawing. From 6:00 to 9:00, common quarter sawing. From 9:00 to 12:00, triple-cut quarter sawing. This will illustrate why rift-cut lumber is more expensive than slash-cut lumber. Bottom: an illustration of a board being cut from a quarter of a log, with a previously cut board lying beside it. Note that the lines of grain run vertically on the end of the board when it is lying flat. Compare it with the bottommost board in Fig. 11-5, which was slash-cut. Rift-cut boards are called ''edge grain lumber'' if coming from softwood, but ''quartersawn lumber'' if coming from hardwood logs.

Therefore, "flat-grain sawn" and "plain sawn" mean the same type of cutting for different kinds of wood.

If the log is specially cut to provide edge grain (thinner dark lines, as opposed to wider, spread-out lines of grain) along both faces, it is called rift cut (Fig. 11-6). Conversely, if you lay a slash-cut board flat, the dark lines of the grain will look as though they flowed out as wide as possible (Fig. 11-5). If you slash cut an entire log, several boards from the center of the log will actually be rift cut. Again, the

industry has used two terms for the same thing: "edge grain lumber" for boards rift-cut from softwood and "quartersawn lumber" for boards rift cut from hardwood logs.

The most important thing for you to remember from all of this is that a slash-cut board is more likely to cup (Fig. 11-7) than a rift-cut board. So, in choosing the boards, look at the ends before you pull them out of the racks. If the lines of the grain run vertically from the top face to the bottom face, along

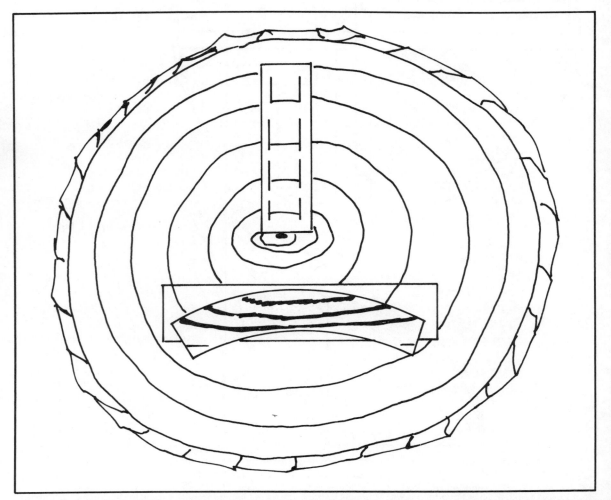

Fig. 11-7. A somewhat simplified illustration of how boards shrink and warp during the drying process. The original size and shape of the boards is shown as a solid rectangle. The board at the top, cut by the rift-cut method, will shrink as shown by the lines of dashes, but it will retain its rectangular shape in profile. The board at the bottom, however, cut by the slash-cut method, cup warps as it dries and shrinks.

the entire length of the board, it is a good one. Incidentally, the boards will shrink in width and thickness but little, if at all, in length.

HOW BOARDS ARE DRIED

When the boards are stacked with spacer boards [called stickers] between them, allowing the air to circulate freely between them, it is called air drying. This can take up to 7 years for hardwoods, 1 year for softwoods. So, the lumber companies have constructed super large ovens, or kilns, in which they can stack the boards the same way, with spacer boards between them, and carefully control the temperature and humidity. This controls the rate of seasoning and makes for a more uniform product, especially if the natural climatic conditions are variable.

I'll leave it to you to figure out which method, air or kiln drying, is the cheaper, all other factors being equal. Consider this additional possibility. If you can enable the supplier to bypass both methods and to sell his product immediately, without having to hold it at all, you'll be providing him with some cost savings he'll be glad to pass back to you. If you can locate a sawmill near enough to your house and if you can season the boards yourself in the rafters of your garage or some other dry place, consider buying green boards and using them in your play equipment.

All lumber is heavy, but green lumber is heavier, with its load of natural moisture. If you don't own a truck, you may have to borrow or rent one. Or, you may have to pay the mill to deliver the lumber. At any rate, consider and inquire into transportation costs before leaping to the conclusion that buying in bulk from the producer will save you money.

Most sawmills are relatively small, informal operations. They sell what is available, rather than importing logs from great distances. The quality will depend on the quality of the raw materials and how the mills treat the logs on the site. Some mills may be able to furnish only rough-sawn boards; others may also plane the boards smooth on the site. Some mills sell their boards at random-width, random-length, and, if you can choose the ones you

want, you can measure and buy boards that will serve your play equipment purposes. Some mills also may have a supply of last season's boards, which will be air dried.

You need to answer several questions before you decide to buy from your local mill.

■ What kind of wood does it handle? Are the available species strong enough for your play equipment? (See the last section, Types of Wood, in this chapter.)

■ Does the mill sell the sizes you need? Remember that the sizes available might still fit your needs, even if they are different from the materials lists in this book. Say the materials list calls for a 4-inch-by-4-inch post, but the mill has none. It might have a 6 × 4 piece of timber, which will still meet your needs.

■ Is there a minimum order you have to put in, or can you buy a few boards at a time?

■ How far in advance do you have to order? Can you get the boards at any time?

■ Can the mill plane the boards smooth if you want smooth lumber, and, more importantly, will it do so on your small order?

■ Will the mill deliver and, if so, how much will it cost?

Assuming you get satisfactory answers to all these questions, your next step will be to look around the mill with a tape measure and a square. Check the boards for squareness. You might find some that look like parallelograms, with 110-degree angles in some corners, 70-degree angles in the others. Don't reject such a board, but be aware that it might be hard to work with if you plan to use it for, an upright corner pole for a playhouse (Fig. 11-8).

Squat down in front of several piles of board and squint down their edges. How straight are they? If bowed, cupped, or twisted, can they still be used? A twisted board can still be used on the outside wall of a playhouse. You just have to have a straight frame on which to nail it.

Take a hard look at the grain in several pieces. Is it straight and parallel to the edges of the board?

Fig. 11-8. Buying big pieces of wood from a local mill. Although this big piece looks like a parallelogram in cross section, the handyman is already figuring out how he can use it as a corner post for a playhouse.

How many knots or other defects do you see? How serious are they?

Next, take your tape measure and check the width and thickness of several boards that appear to be about the same. Variations of 1/4 inch are acceptable for most purposes.

While checking all these things, make mental or written notes about the appearance of the wood itself. See if the ends of the boards that may be split or of irregular thickness can still be used for some purpose. Usually, you have to cut off at least one end of a board. If the mill operators don't mind, bring along the kids who'll be using the play equipment and get their ideas. Some kids have very strong opinions, and you may have to sell them on the idea of using some of the rough-cut lumber. You might also have to point out that the mill can plane smooth the large piece you intend to use for a balance beam. Hold up a board and peep through the knothole at one of the kids. Making a game of a seeming disadvantage can do wonders to win a kid over to your point of view.

If you and the kids are happy with all the answers you get from your conversations with the mill operators and your visit around the wood piles, go ahead and order some wood and save yourself some money.

DRYING GREEN WOOD

If you buy a quantity of green wood for a project like a playhouse or a large tree house, the rafters in your garage probably won't hold it all until it has shrunk enough for use. Solve this problem by stickering the wood in a pile.

Before building the stickered pile, however, you need to know about the drying process itself and how much drying is desirable. Thicker pieces, 4-inch-by-4-inch or bigger, will almost certainly warp and twist themselves into an unusable state if you air dry them. Therefore, it is best to use them right away. For example, if you are going to make a playhouse, using four upright corner posts with boards nailed on the outside for the walls, put these posts in green. Bolt on any green 2-inch-by-4-inch boards necessary for the frame, and nail on the wall

boards as soon thereafter as possible. This will probably mean buying the wall boards first and air drying them, then getting the posts and framing wood several weeks later and putting the whole structure up at once.

Figure 11-9 shows how to stack wood in a stickered pile. The flatter surface you can start with, the easier the job. If you can spare the floor, or part of the floor, of your garage, carport, or patio, you should use it for drying the wall boards. If you have to use part of your yard, choose the flattest, but not necessarily the levelest, spot you can find. The higher off the ground you can get the pile, the faster it'll dry, although heights beyond 18 inches don't really gain much in speed. Instead of choosing something flat, like beams or wooden crates, choose something with a round profile on which to put the first layer of green boards. This minimizes the surface contact of the boards and the supporting structures, thus maximizing the air contact with the green boards.

The stickers are long boards, about an inch thick, that are used to hold the green boards apart to allow the air to freely circulate among them. Let's say you have several 44-gallon drums on which to build the stack. Roll them together and chock them with bricks to keep them from rolling (Fig. 11-9). Put a layer of green boards on the drums, placing them no closer than 1 inch. If you can leave 6 or 8 inches between the two boards nearest the center, you'll create a flue that helps the air to move through the pile (Fig. 11-10). Now lay a sticker perpendicular to the green boards directly in line with the vertical diameter of each drum. Put the next layer of green boards on the stickers, then two more stickers, then a third layer of green boards, and so on until all the boards are on the pile. Take care to leave at least an inch between each green board. Naturally, the more space you can leave, the more air there will be to carry away the moisture evaporating from the green wood.

If your stickered pile is under the garage or carport roof, you need do nothing more than let the wood dry. However, if it is in the yard, or near an open side of the carport where the rain might blow on it, you should put a roof on the pile. Figure 11-9

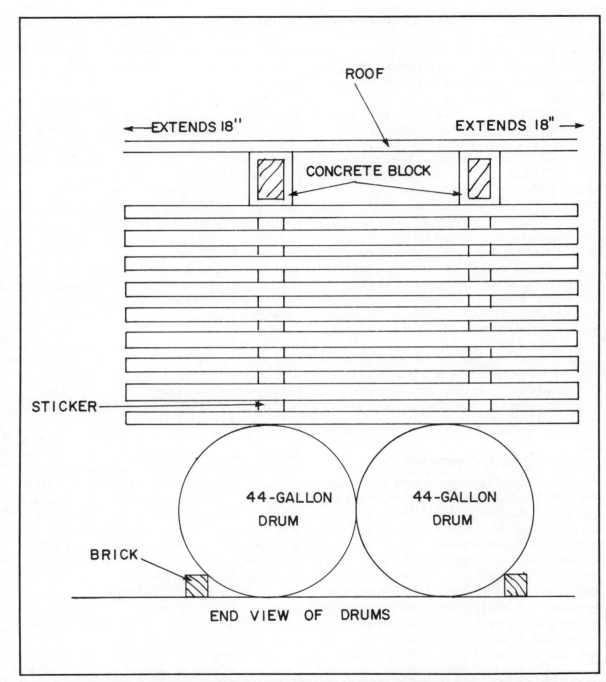

Fig. 11-9. A stickered pile of green boards stacked on two 44-gallon drums. Bricks on either side of the drums keep them from rolling. The stickers, about one inch thick and 2 inches wide, are placed directly over the vertical axis of each drum. The roof should extend 18 inches over the stack on all four sides. Note that the stickers are placed perpendicular to the green boards being air dried.

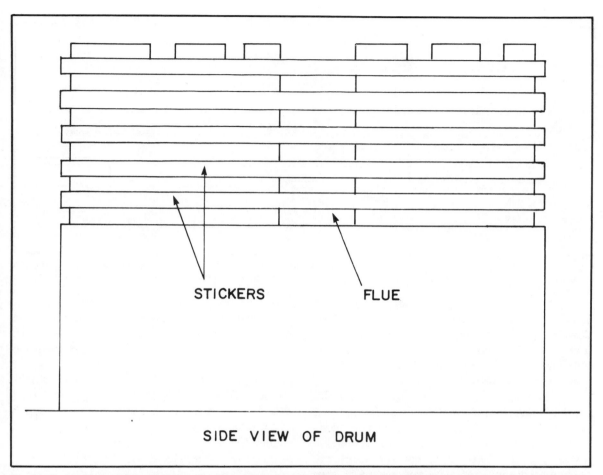

STICKERS   FLUE

SIDE VIEW OF DRUM

Fig. 11-10. A side view of the stickered pile. Although the roof has been omitted from this drawing, it is important to remember to raise the roof at least 12 inches higher than the top layer of green boards, so that the flue will operate properly, create an upward current to draw out the moist air being evaporated from the wood.

shows concrete blocks used for roof supports, but you can use anything that is available. The roof can be roofing metal, plywood, or even wallboard with a sheet of plastic tied on securely to protect the wallboard itself as it protects the stickered pile. The roof should overhang the pile by 18 inches on both ends and along the sides.

The supports for the stickered pile should be no further apart than 4 feet. The whole pile has to be flat, but it doesn't have to be level. In fact, if you build it out in the yard, a slight slope will enable the rain water to drain off. I've stressed keeping the boards apart for maximum air circulation, but I

should also stress now that the stickers have to be vertically placed over the supports to hold the green boards straight.

Figure 11-11 shows an improperly stickered pile. The stickers aren't directly over the pile supports. This allows the green boards to sag and warp. The pile supports aren't of equal height, and the boards aren't supported near their ends. All these factors allow the boards to sag and bend, which will create permanent warps in the boards as they dry.

The green boards will dry until the moisture they contain is equal to the moisture in the surrounding air. Hot, dry summer weather will air dry

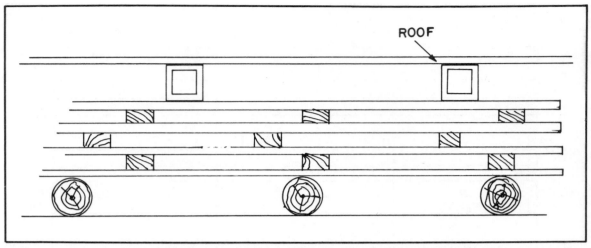

Fig. 11-11. A badly stickered pile. the first layer of green boards isn't level. The stickers are improperly placed, and the concrete blocks supporting the roof are improperly placed. The sags, bends, and warps being created in the green boards will become permanent.

wood boards in 6 to 10 weeks. Wet weather slows down the process and can double or triple the time. You can tell if the drying has stopped, reached its maximum, by checking the shrinkage. Check a slash-cut board (one with the lines of grain that appear to have spread out and flowed) when you first bring it home from the mill. Measure its thickness and width and keep a record of the measurements. Remember that the length will not vary enough to matter as the board dries, but the width and thickness will shrink. Measure your test board every few weeks. Look for about 1/16-inch shrinkage for every 2 inches of width. In other word, an 8-inch-wide board needs to shrink about 1/4 inch to be dry, a 4-inch-wide board, 1/8 inch, and so on.

If you nail your wall boards on the playhouse before they are completely dry, several bad things might happen, depending on how wet they still are and, therefore, on how much further they will shrink. If you butt the boards against each other lengthwise, they will shrink away from each other, creating cracks between the boards. The shrinkage may also cause the nails to pop out. The worst thing, perhaps, is splitting. Figure 11-12 shows a wall made with green boards that were overlapped to shed rain. Nails were driven through both boards, which has the effect of putting two nails through each board,

one near the top edge and one near the bottom edge. As the board shrank between the two nails, something had to give. The nails held, so the wood split.

This problem could have been avoided if nails had been driven near the top edges only. This would allow the board to shrink toward the nail as much as it wanted. Each new board could overlap the nail holding the board below it, giving the wall the appearance of being held on with invisible fasteners.

BUILDING WITH USED WOOD

Perhaps "used" wood is the wrong terminology. What I mean is wood removed from another structure, such as an old barn or shed or chicken house. This wood is always well seasoned, so it has done all the warping and twisting it is going to do. The only thing you need beware of is hidden nails.

If you dismantle the structure yourself, you can be careful to pull out the nails from the boards you intend to use. It is a good practice to keep a piece of chalk in your pocket to mark any nails that break off flush with the surface of the board, for such nails play havoc with saw blades. Incidentally, you should enter an agreement to dismantle a building in return for the lumber only with extreme caution. For one thing, the building might contain so much rot-

216

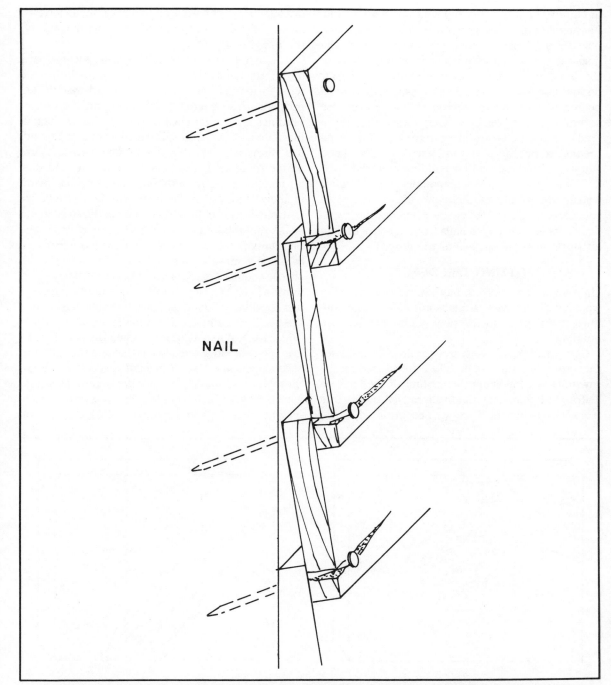

NAIL

Fig. 11-12. One of the perils of using green wood. As the boards shrank in width, they couldn't pull the nails closer together, so they split. If each board had had only one nail in it, it could have shrunk toward the nail, and splitting would have been avoided.

217

ten lumber that the material isn't worth your time. For another, the wood might be sound as necessary, but the structure so well put together that the dismantling takes too much of your time. Inspect the building carefully, sticking the point of your pocketknife blade into the boards, especially painted boards, to check for rottenness. Pry off or pry loose several boards to see how easily they come off the studs. If the nails are in so tight that the wood breaks around them, you can wind up with a good supply of kindling and no building material.

Getting wood that someone else has taken off a structure is quite another story, of course, and all you need be careful of is the price and, as mentioned above, the hidden nails that may have broken off flush with the surface of the boards.

SPOTTING THE DEFECTS

Unless you can afford to buy the very best quality wood, you will have to accept some defects and minimize their effect in the play equipment you are building.

Avoid all boards with cross grain (Fig. 11-4), for they are inherently weak. They are caused by the sawmill's not following the contour of the bark on a straight log, or they might be caused by the tree trunk's twisting as it grew. The grain in an in-dividual board can wave and whorl a bit, so long as most of the lines of the grain run from one end of the board to the other.

A knot is part of a branch that has become part of the tree trunk. The root section of the branch is what forms the knot. If it is cut lengthwise in the process of the board's being cut from the log, it becomes an elongated cross section that is shaped like a long triangle. This is called a spike knot, and it is always a defects (Fig. 11-13). Therefore, a board with a spike knot is to be avoided unless, and this is an important consideration because such a board is likely to be cheap, the board can be trimmed so that you don't use the part containing the spike knot.

A round knot is formed by cutting a cross section through the branch root. If it's so loose that you can easily move it, it's a defect, and you should choose another board (Fig. 11-13). If the knot doesn't move when you press it with your thumb or finger, it is considered a blemish, rather than a defect, and the board containing it is usable for most purposes (Fig. 11-14). When it comes to using the board, however, you should avoid sawing through the knot for several reasons. First it is hard to get a handsaw through some knots. Second, the half of an otherwise tight knot in the end of board you saw through may become loose and fall out. Third, the knot of

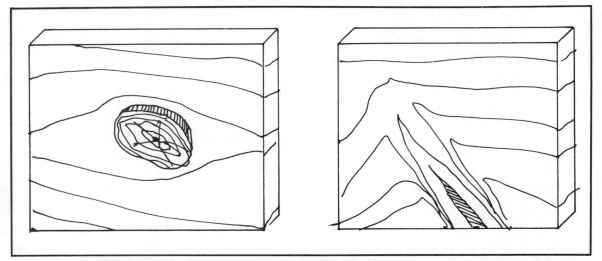

Fig. 11-13. Two defects to watch out for. Right: a spike knot. Left: a round, loose knot: this one has even started to fall out toward the front of the board.

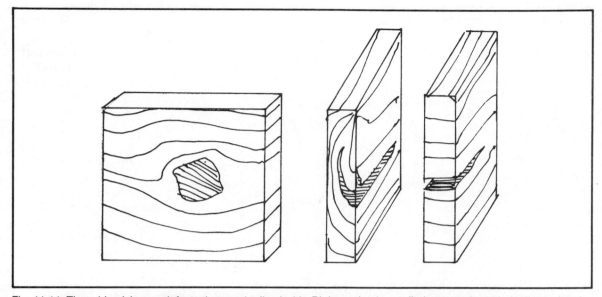

Fig. 11-14. Three blemishes or defects that can be lived with. Right: a check, a split that runs through the lines of grain. Middle: a shake, a separation between the lines of grain. Left: a tight knot, one that you can't budge with your thumb or finger.

half knot leaves that much less clear wood to drive nails or screws through.

A pitch pocket might contain liquid or solid pitch; reject the board containing it. You usually find them in pine, spruce, Douglas fir, and tamarack or Western larch.

A split (Fig. 11-14) goes all the way through a board, all the way through the lines making up the grain. This defect is also known as a check. It usually develops during the drying process. A checked or split board might still be usable if the splits are small, can be cut off, or placed where nails go on either side of the split to hold it firmly in place.

A shake (Fig. 11-14) differs from a split in two ways. First, it doesn't go all the way through the lines of the grain; it is a separation between two of these lines. Second, it doesn't always go all the way through the board. Like split boards, those with shakes can be used if the defect is small, can be nailed around or cut out, or even placed face down so that the defect isn't visible.

A bark pocket is formed when the tree grows over, completely or almost completely, a patch of bark. Individual boards containing bark pockets that go all the way through are defective, like those with

loose knots, and should be rejected. In other boards, so little of the bark pocket remains that you can easily remove it. If the board is still sufficiently thick to retain its strength, you can buy the board.

Blue stain is more a blemish than a defect. It can be painted over, and the wood retains all its strength. It is caused by a certain mold fungus.

Decay is caused by various types of fungus that feed on the fibers of the wood until it becomes soft and spongy. This seriously affects the strength of the wood, even when the wood seems to still be sound. Avoid such wood, even if the dealer is trying to sell it to you at a price you can't refuse. Even if you spend five cents on it, it will probably be five cents wasted, and if the wood fails on the play equipment, the medical bills will almost certainly wipe out any savings, real or imaginary, you had on the wood.

Warping comes in four general guises: bow, crook, twist, and cup. Cup warping has already been described (Fig. 11-7). The other forms are illustrated in Fig. 11-15. Your dealer may or may not give you a discount on warped boards because carpenters can often use them almost as well as straight boards by straightening them out as they nail them onto sound

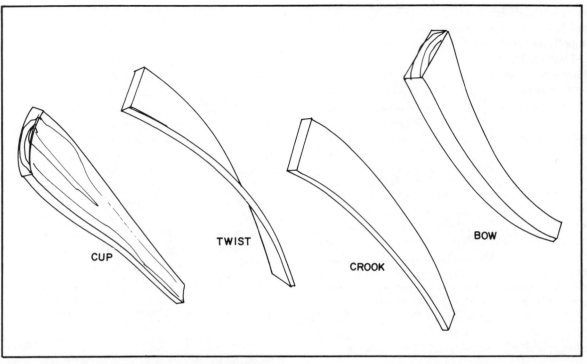

Fig. 11-15. The four most common forms of warping.

and square frames. If you aren't going to get a discount on the warped lumber, you might as well insist on straight boards and let the professionals make use of the warped boards.

"Wane" is a general term that is applied to any corner or edge of a board that is less than its full thickness or width. You may find it on many of the boards in the discount houses' racks. Whether the board is usable depends on the amount of wane and where you plan to use the board. Minor wane can be tolerated in boards to be nailed on the sides of a play house, for example, for the strength of the structure depends on the frame more than on the wall covering.

While on the general subject of looking at individual boards, let's broaden it slightly to poles and to square, heavy pieces that you will need for corner posts of cubbies or climbing frames or for the posts to hold such things as balance beams. Figure 11-3 showed that sapwood is lighter than heartwood, so you'll easily be able to tell which is which. Heart-

wood is generally the stronger, but sapwood absorbs chemicals more readily if you want to treat the wood to resist insects and rot. For this reason, poles with the bark removed but the sapwood intact can be a good buy. Square parts containing some sapwood are also good. You can treat them with creosote, a mixture of kerosene and sump oil from your car, or a commercial preparation, which will usually contain chrome, copper, and arsenic or a flour-ansenate-phenol compound.

LUMBER SIZES

In earlier chapters I've mentioned that a 4-inch-by-4-inch post won't measure 4 inches square when you put your ruler on it, if you've bought from a retailer representing the end of the production line. Only green lumber measures, or slightly exceeds, what are known as the nominal sizes. As the lumber is seasoned, it shrinks; then the mill shaves some of the surface off in the process of planing the boards smooth. So, the finished 4 × 4 post winds up smooth, easier to handle without work gloves, and just over 3.5 inches square. The process of smoothing out the surfaces is called dressing. Table 11-1 will enable you to compare the nominal size and the dressed dimensions, in inches, of some common sizes of boards.

Most softwood is cut to even-numbered lengths, but hardwood is sometimes cut to both even- and odd-numbered lengths.

LUMBER GRADES

The simple answer under this heading is that lumber is graded in a very confusing manner because many industry associations and governmental bodies have gotten into the act. Our general advice is not to worry about the grade; common sense will tell you that the best quality, prettiest material will carry the highest price tag. You should look at the various grades of lumber in the supplier's racks and choose lesser quality wood that looks as if it will still do the job. Don't bother trying to decifer industry stamps that tell you the mill the wood came from, moisture content, and other less relevant facts.

It is useful to know, however, that grade A will be the highest quality in the racks; therefore, grade D won't be quite so pretty and will be lower priced. In fact, grades A-D all refer to lumber that will take a beautiful finish, with A being practically blemish-free and C and D requiring painting to cover their blemishes.

Number 1 Common lumber is really a bit

Table 11-1. Nominal Dressed Dimensions of Some Common Board Sizes.

Nominal Size	Dressed Dimensions
1 × 6	25/32 × 5 5/8
1 × 8	25/32 × 7 1/2
1 × 10	25/32 × 9 1/2
2 × 2	1 5/8 × 1 5/8
2 × 4	1 5/8 × 3 5/8
2 × 6	1 5/8 × 5 5/8
2 × 8	1 5/8 × 7 1/2
2 × 10	1 5/8 × 9 1/2
2 × 12	1 5/8 × 11 1/2
4 × 4	3 5/8 × 3 5/8

aristocratic. It is high class enough to be used in constructing watertight crates. It is tight knotted, and it contains only a few defects.

Number 2 Common contains a few defects, but nothing so serious as a knothole.

Number 3 Common contains an occasional knothole, as well as a few other serious defects. This is the grade you'll probably use for many of your projects if you want to get the best value for money. The grade is in the price range that will enable you to pay the lowest price for the boards that will serve your purposes.

Number 4 Common lumber and Number 5 Common should be passed up from the beginning. Number 4 will contain many knotholes, shakes, checks, and even decay; Number 5 is even worse.

Other terms you may encounter are construction grade, utility, framing quality, economy, and yard grade. These tend to mean different things in different parts of the country, hence our earlier advice to use your eyes rather than your memory in selecting individual boards. The only exception is factory or shop lumber. These terms almost always mean good, sound pieces that are going to be cut up into smaller-sized pieces. Therefore, if you are shopping for big strong pieces, you can sometimes get shop pieces for the same price as smaller (and, therefore, not-so-strong) dressed pieces.

THE MEANING OF BOARD FEET

Few things are as frustrating as trying to do your shopping by phone and having a lumber supplier tell you that the price per board foot differs for pine, fir, and so on. The concept of "board measure" or "board feet" is really sensible when you keep in mind that the supplier is handling a three-dimensional product. Every piece he sells will have thickness, not just length and width.

A board foot is 144 cubic inches. Think of a board 1 inch thick, 12 inches long, and 12 inches wide. There you have a theoretical board foot. Remember that the number of board feet you pay for is based on the nominal, not the actual or dressed, size of the boards.

The easiest formula for determining the

number of board feet in a given board is this: thickness in inches × width in inches × length in feet divided by 12. Here's an example. You need a 2-inch-by-4-inch board, 12 feet long (Fig. 11-16).

$$\frac{2 \times 4 \times 12}{12} = 8 \text{ board feet}$$

CHOOSING PLYWOOD

Throughout this book I have emphasized that you must get exterior grade plywood for play equipment to be used outside. The glue used to make this type of plywood is completely waterproof. If you try to save a few dollars by using an interior grade, you'll probably find that the plies will separate after

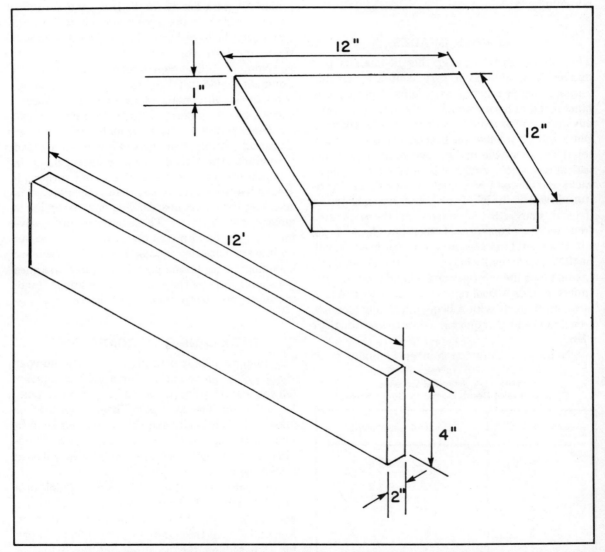

Fig. 11-16. Right: an illustration of 1 board foot. The board foot is an abstraction, for in reality the 1 inch of thickness, after the rough surface of a board has been planed smooth, will be much closer to 3/4 inch. Left: an illustration of a board containing 8 board feet.

several months. The only thing to do if that happens is to show the kids how plywood is made—by gluing several thin sheets of wood together with their grains running perpendicular to each other.

Like lumber, plywood is graded A through D, with A being the best grade, and D having some surface flaws such as knotholes, pitch pockets, splits, and some surface discoloration. But, plywood is graded with two letters, A-A or A-C, for example, to indicate the quality of both sides of the sheet. Grade A-C is very popular for interior projects, such as storage cabinets, but there is no reason that B-C or C-C won't do for many of your play equipment projects.

TYPES OF WOOD

Ash. Found east of the Rockies. It is strong, tough, hard, and elastic. It has a close, straight grain and is a long-lasting wood. It is used for making farm implements, hammer handles, baseball bats, oars and boat thwarts, and other items that need to hold up to wear.

Balsa. Imported from Ecuador. You probably know it from kits for old-fashioned airplane kits, for it is one of the lightest of all woods. It is also very soft. It is good for heat and sound insulation. But, it is simply not strong enough for most play equipment applications.

Basswood. Found east of the Mississippi, except along the coasts. This is a soft, brittle, lightweight lumber that takes nails well and doesn't twist or warp. It is, therefore unsuitable for most play equipment constructions, although it might be used in such things as drawers or shelves in play houses.

Beech. Found in the states east of the Mississippi and in southeastern Canada. This is a hard, durable wood provided it stays indoors, for it shrinks and checks when exposed to rain and weather.

Birch. Another wood found in much of eastern North America. It is a hard, durable, tough, strong, stiff wood that takes a beautiful coat of paint. It is popular in the furniture-making trade as an imitation of mahogany. If used outside, however, it has to be protected.

Butternut. Found from Florida to southern Canada, as far west as Minnesota. It is coarse grained and strong, with a color like walnut. An easy wood to work with, it is made into toys, boats, furniture, and interior trim. Paint or preserve for use in play equipment.

Cedar, Red. A tree found in a band running east from Colorado, but stopping north of Florida. This is the popular cedar-chest wood, with the natural oil and odor that make it excellent for mothproof chests and closets. It is light, soft, and easily worked. It finishes so beautifully under a clear coat that it would be a shame to cover it with paint. Best used indoors.

Cedar, White. Found on the eastern coast of the United States and around the Great Lakes. A terrific wood for outdoor applications because it holds up so well when exposed to water. Use it for poles in cubbies, climbing frames, and for such things as foundations for balance beams.

Cypress. A tree that loves water; found along streams and rivers from Maryland to Texas and along the Mississippi valley to Illinois. When cut into boards, cypress makes long-lasting water troughs for stock or even for photographic darkrooms. If available locally, it is a good prospect for outdoor play equipment.

Fir, Douglas. British Columbia and the Pacific coast. A strong, easily worked wood with a straight grain. It is cut into pieces of all sizes and dimensions for building purposes, and it is also made into plywood. Excellent for play equipment but protect it with paint or stain. Posts cut from the heartwood can be used in the ground without treatment, although treatment for rot and insect resistance would, of course, extend their life.

Fir, White. Also a northwestern tree. Used for many of the same purposes in building as Douglas fir, white fir is not quite so durable outdoors. It shouldn't be used for posts, and it must be painted or stained to make it last.

Elm. Found in most states east of Colorado. A hard, tough, heavy wood that is durable enough to be made into wagon wheels and cross ties for railways. It is a good wood to use in play equipment.

It rots easily if not protected, however, so don't use it for posts.

Hemlock, Eastern. Found in the northeastern United States and in Canada; sometimes it is called Canada hemlock and sometimes hemlock spruce. A good wood for frames and other members of play equipment but unsuitable for posts.

Hemlock, Western. Adapted to conditions in the western states. Suitable for most of the same uses as Eastern hemlock, although even less durable in the ground.

Juniper. Found in Texas and some places in other southwestern states. This tree is often mistakenly called cedar. It is a premier post wood and can be put straight into the ground without protective treatment. With its red heartwood and white sapwood, it makes an attractive lining for chests and for window seats.

Lignum Vitae. Imported from Central America. An unusually hard, heavy, waxy—or soapy—feeling wood. Holds up well to water. This wood is likely to be found in tools, like mallet heads and handles, rather than be cut into boards for building purposes.

Hickory. Arkansas, Tennessee, Ohio, Kentucky, where its smoke makes some of the tastiest hams and bacons in the world. Its use for building rather than barbeque interests us here, however, so we must point out that hickory is one of the hardest of hardwoods. It makes good wagons, wagon wheels, and tool handles. You'll have to drill guide holes for nails and screws through this wood, and it is subject to attacks of decay and insects. In spite of its strength and toughness, then, it may take more of your time than you want to spend when making play equipment.

Mahogany. Found in Florida, but other states are not sufficiently tropical. Imported from Mexico, Central America, Honduras, the West Indies, central Africa, and other tropical countries. Most widely known for its use in cabinets and furniture, for it takes a beautiful finish when its open grain is filled. An expensive wood, mahogany will be outside the budget capabilities of most families.

Mahogany, Phillippine. Found in the Philippines. This isn't really a true mahogany, although it can be found in long, wide boards clear of knots. Used in furniture and interior trim, this wood will usually be a bit more expensive than native woods.

Meranti. Found in Indonesia, the Philippines, and neighboring countries. A wood with a very straight grain and almost no knots, it is light and durable for its weight, but not really strong enough for most play equipment applications. It is used mainly for trim and cabinets.

Mesquite. Found from Texas to California. Because of its growing habits, this tree doesn't produce many long, straight boards. It is popular among hunters as a rifle stock material and among backyard cooks as one of the hottest burning barbeque woods. Farmers press it into service for posts, but it is much less durable than juniper.

Oak, Live. Found in the southern Atlantic and Gulf coast states and in Oregon and California. It is extremely hard, tough, and durable, so it is used in wagons, ships, and farm implements. It will bend your nails and blunt your drill bits; however, if you are prepared to drill guide holes for nails and screws, it is sometimes so cheap it is a good buy for play equipment.

Oak, Red. Found in both Virginias, Tennessee, Arkansas, Kentucky, Ohio, Missouri, and Maryland. This is a heavy, tough, strong, coarse-grained wood that doesn't last well when exposed to weather unless its big pores are filled with preservative. When treated with preservative, it makes good railway ties. Limit its use to playhouse interiors unless you treat it to hold up to the weather.

Oak, White. Found in Arkansas, Indiana, Kentucky, Maryland, Missouri, Ohio, Tennessee, and both Virginias. A heavy, hard, strong, tough hardwood that is easier to work than some other oaks. Used for both interior and exterior applications, tool handles, farm implements, furniture, and railway ties, it is a good wood for play equipment.

Pine, Norway. Found in the states bordering the Great Lakes. Light, strong, and about medium hard, it is a good building wood, though no good for sticking in the ground. Protect with paint or stain when used outdoors.

Pine, Ponderosa. A northwestern tree, used for flooring and sheathing of houses. It is also good for fence boards, but not posts, and for shelves because it doesn't warp too much.

Pine, Sugar. Found in California and Oregon. This is a light, soft, easily worked wood that takes nails well (with little splitting). Used for interior trim and other interior uses where strength is not important. This limits its usefulness as a material for play equipment.

Pine, White. Found in the northern tier of states from Maine to Washington and down into California and Idaho. A soft, straight-grained wood that takes nails without excessive splitting. It is durable in the rain and, therefore, makes a good wood to cover the outside of playhouses. It isn't as strong as other woods, however, so it should not be chosen for such things as climbing frames.

Pine, Yellow. Found from Virginia to Texas. A hard, strong, heavy, tough wood that is the most important building lumber in the region where it grows. The heartwood is even durable in the ground. A good choice for play equipment.

Poplar. Found in the Mississippi valley, the Virginias, Tennessee, and Kentucky. Because poplar is soft, cheap, brittle, and weak, you might wonder why it is even cut into boards. The answer is it makes good shelves and boxes, is fine textured, and easy to work with. Confine its use to boxes and shelves and drawers for holding toys and other play gear, and be sure it stays under a roof, well away from rain.

Maple. Found in all states east of Colorado and in southern Canada. Although it makes superbly beautiful furniture, it is also so tough and strong that it can be made into bowling pins, tool handles, and railway ties. If you can afford it, it is a useful lumber for play equipment.

Redwood. California. Although it is not so strong as fir and yellow pine, it is very resistant to decay and makes a good wood to use for posts and for boards that will be exposed to much rain.

Spruce. Found all along the northern tier of states and in central Canada. Although light, soft, and not too strong, if used in big enough pieces it fills the following bills: ship masts, oars, baskets, and railway ties. Use big pieces in your play equipment.

Sycamore. Found in most of the 48 contiguous states. Also known as a plane tree, the sycamore is more widely used for its summer shade than for its wood. It has a reputation for lacking strength and for being brittle. Much of it goes into chipboard.

Teak. Imported from India, Burma, Thailand, and Java. A strong, durable, easily worked wood that holds up well when exposed to moisture. It is used in boat building and for cabinets. It is strong enough for play equipment but too expensive for the average pocketbook.

Walnut. Found in the eastern half of the United States and in Texas, New Mexico, Arizona, and California. It makes such beautiful furniture and cabinets and rifle stocks when its coarse grain is filled and polished and it won't find its way into much play equipment, in spite of its hardness and durability and resistance to warping and cracking.

Western Larch. Found in the northwestern United States. A relative of the pine family, the larch (also called the tamarack) is cut into boards for most building purposes. Some boards will contain pitch pockets, but others will be suitable for many purposes in play equipment. Square posts cut from larch have a medium resistance to rot and insects but can readily be used if treated with a preservative.

Index

Index

OTHER POPULAR TAB BOOKS OF INTEREST